ABOUT THE BOOK

This brief memoir recounts the journey of a man and lessons he accumulated on leadership by observing and questioning the status quo, and asking the penultimate question of why, from his childhood home in the small island of Bahrain, to his formative years as a student and professional in England, to his adulthood as a business leader, philanthropist, influencer and family man.

The book's key observation is that there is an excess of rulership while leadership is almost always in deficit. The book questions how we can move from one to the other, which examples can we rely on in every sphere of our lives and how transformative more leadership would be.

FROM RULERSHIP TO LEADERSHIP IN THE ARAB WORLD

The brief memoir of
a non-conformist

KHALID ABDULLA-JANAHI

Archway Publishing books may be ordered through booksellers or by contacting:

Archway Publishing
1663 Liberty Drive
Bloomington, IN 47403
www.archwaypublishing.com
844-669-3957

ISBN: 978-1-6657-3692-3 (sc)
ISBN: 978-1-6657-3691-6 (hc)
ISBN: 978-1-6657-3690-9 (e)

Library of Congress Control Number: 2023900584

Print information available on the last page.

Archway Publishing rev. date: 02/21/2023

"Stay far and always be safe."

– My grandfather

These words have echoed through my life and have served as a warning, a guide, and a comfort to me at different times. My father's father would repeat them to me in colloquial Farsi when I was young, translating the phrase from an Arabic proverb.

What he did not know is that the original saying was in Arabic: **Go far and come back safely**, *which traditionally applies to family matters.*

In his broken understanding of Arabic, my grandfather's words carried more wisdom than I first imagined: stay far from the center of power and you will be safe.

Every man and woman must choose the level of personal freedom with which they are comfortable. We each choose a path either to conform or go our own way. Some have fewer choices than others and may lose their freedom if they choose a path that is unacceptable to those who rule them. In the future, I hope we can all go far and come back safely, offering options to the next generation.

DEDICATION

This book is dedicated to the best leaders I have ever known, the four women who have shaped my life: my grandmothers, my mother, and my wife.

This book is also for all the young women and men who are trying to make sense of the current state of chaos so they can build dreams of the future. May they use their freedom to choose the life they want for themselves and for the next generation. May they become the leaders the world so desperately needs everywhere.

CONTENTS

Dedication .... **vii**

Prologue .... **xvii**

Introduction .... **xxiii**

Evolution Not Revolution xxiii
The Calculus of Chance xxiv

Structure of this Book .... **xxix**

PART I: A BRIEF MEMOIR **1**

Chapter 1: Nonconformist 3
My Parents 3
Teaching Ways 9
Constant Companion 11
Parting Ways with the Family 12
How Holi Am I? 14
The Gulf of Oil and Gas 15

Chapter 2: Responsible 18
My Grandmother 18
Pearl Divers and Tailors 22

Chapter 3: Meritocratic 25
Boyhood 25
Onion to the Rescue 27
False News 27

A Passion for Movies ... 28
Life on the Move ... 30
Winds of Change ... 32

Chapter 4: Empathetic ... 33
My Mother ... 33
The Reckoning ... 35

Chapter 5: Open-Minded ... 40
Secondary School ... 40
"A good mustache makes a man for many reasons." ... 42
A Teenager in Lebanon – A Utopian Dream Interrupted ... 43
First Day of Intellectual Freedom ... 45
The End of an Era ... 47

Chapter 6: Pragmatic ... 49
A Teenager in Manchester ... 49
Fun at University ... 52
Bombay Interlude ... 58
New Name, New Me? ... 59

Chapter 7: Listener ... 60
Torn Between Two Lovers ... 60
The Souq ... 62
The Brief Return ... 64
Going Backwards ... 64
An Offer I Could Refuse ... 65
The Absence of Merit ... 66

Chapter 8: Driven ... 68
Carrying Hot Coffee Up the Ladder ... 68
Training on the Job ... 71
Compost Corner ... 73
Hierarchy ... 73
The Long Return ... 74
Acceptance of Others ... 75

Chapter 9: Responsive ... 76
On the Job ... 76

Chance and Love 79
Chewing Khat in Yemen 80
Hopes for Peace 82
Paris II 83

Chapter 10: Trusted 85
Kuwait at War 86
Trust Your Instinct, Do What Feels Right 88

Chapter 11: Motivator 96
Leaving Bahrain for Switzerland 96
Tigers, Cubs, and Scouts 98
Critical Thinking 100
Rules and Freedom 101
Home and Away from Home 102
Jahannam Can Wait 103

Chapter 12: Representative 105
Finding an Arab Voice for Change 105
Axis of Evil and Future Presidents 108
Iraq in 2003 109
Arab Business Council 110
Clorox in Cairo 114
ABC in Bahrain 116
Back to India 118
Vote as I say, not as you want 119
Combatting Human Trafficking 123
Meeting Adjourned 124
End of the Arab Business Council 125

Chapter 13: Inclusive 128
Moroccan Soiree in Davos 128
You're Iranian 132
May 26, 2016 134
Insider/Outsider and a Troublemaker, Too 135
Improving the State of the World 140

PART II: OBSERVATIONS 143

Observation 1: Idealism and Pragmatism.......................... 146
Independent Accountability...147
Public Servants... 148

Observation 2: Davos... 150

Observation 3: Arab Voices in Davos............................... 152

Observation 4: The Success of Dubai.............................. 155
Competition.. 156
Dubai – Part of the Real World.................................... 157
Non-bursting Bubble... 157
Copycat... 158
Opportunity Knocks Winner.. 158

Observation 5: Redefining the Social Contract 159
So-called Arab Spring.. 160
New Social Contract – A Must...................................... 160
International Social Contracts...................................... 161

Observation 6: Male Guardianship and Women................ 163

Observation 7: The Shrinking Pie..................................... 166
Meritocracy 167

Observation 8: Global Leadership in the Time of Crisis: The Case of the Pandemic............. 168

Observation 9: Conformity is Unsustainable 173
Time Bomb...174

Observation 10: The Social Contract Emergency 176
Mini Me 177

Observation 11: When Growth is a Myth 180
Education Challenge.. 182
Look in the Mirror... 182

Observation 12: It's High Time to Fight Hypocrisy 185
Politeness vs. Hypocrisy.. 186

Observation 13: Why a Wealth Tax? 188
Shrinking Middle Class 190
VAT Hurts the Poor 191
Next Taxes 192
Wealth via Relationship 193

Observation 14: Trying to Avoid a Crash Landing without Crushing the Middle 195
Immediate Challenge 196
Need for Unpopular Decisions 196
Private Sector 198
Balancing Budgets 199
Future of the Youth 200

Observation 15: Great Visions and Wasted Opportunities .. 204

Observation 16: Leadership through Ethics 207
Evolution vs. Revolution 208
No One Above the Law 209

Observation 17: When Extortion becomes Legal 211
Lucky Common Sense 213
Nonstop Walking the Talk 214

Observation 18: The Clear Need for Transparency in the Gulf Drive for Investment 216
Legal Redress 216
New Driver 218

Observation 19: The Neighbor Who Flew Too Close to the Sun 221
Pay to Play 223

Observation 20: The Middle East Needs Evolution, Not Revolution 224
Deliberate Process of Evolution 225
Cultural Shock 226

Observation 21: Breaking Free from the Vicious Circle 228
True Modernity 230
True Intellect 230

State of Denial 231

Observation 22: Stability Through Sustainability..... 232
Population Growth and Unemployment Dilemma 233
Invest in Infrastructure..... 234

Observation 23: Skewed Middle East Equation 237
Long-term Goals 239

Observation 24: Yes-Men Taking Over as the Middle East Elite..... 240
Tabalas and Lappies..... 240
Parasitic Behavior 241

Observation 25: Nepotism..... 243

Observation 26: Governance Yes … Governance No..... 244
"You Did Not Raise Your Hand."..... 245
Bollywood Saga 246

Observation 27: Freedom of Expression..... 248

Observation 28: Creating Opportunity..... 250

Observation 29: Education and Employment 252
Mismatch..... 253

Observation 30: Protection..... 256
Wasted National Wealth..... 256

Observation 31: Red Herrings..... 259
Palestine 259
Sunni–Shia Divide 262

Observation 32: The Fourth Estate: Wishful Thinking in the Arab World? 266
Notable Exceptions..... 267
The Sword of Damocles..... 267
Dissent..... 267
Mercenary Editors..... 268
Western Media..... 268

Observation 33: Give Peace a Chance 270
Observation 34: Unofficially Exiled 272

PART III: MOVIES 273

Conclusion 309
Jack of All Brands 309
Disruptive 311
Contemporary Perspectives 311
Arab World Today 313
Love Thy Neighbor 314
Born Free 314

Epilogue 317

Acknowledgments 321

APPENDIX 327
Extract 1 .... *329*
Extract 2 .... *370*
Extract 3 .... *376*

About the Author 403

PROLOGUE

THE WHISPER THAT SPARKED A FLAME

Have you heard the one about the movie star and the son of a dictator in a room with a chartered accountant? It's the story of how a spark led me to write this book. An American movie star lit the flame that led to setting this book into motion. More than 18 years passed between that moment in 2005 and when I felt the time was right. From the Arab Spring to the devastation wrought by the COVID-19 pandemic, and even the war in Ukraine, the Arab world has evolved at a slower pace than its geographical neighbors, and one would need to be blind not to see it.

Indeed, the thinking behind this book started in 2005. On a cold starlit night, I drove through the mountains from my home in Geneva and checked into a hotel in Davos. I was not new to Switzerland, nor to the Annual Meeting of the World Economic Forum (WEF), where I was headed, but I was always excited about this rarified global gathering of political and business elites, civil society organizations, and even movie stars. The packed snow made it easy to walk to the dinner gathering in my suede shoes. When I arrived, I spotted Richard Gere at a nearby table and couldn't help but think of his shiny shoes in *An Officer and a Gentleman*. Having watched countless movies as a kid in Bahrain, I had attempted to create my own personal style amidst the conformity of bankers and financiers, but I was known for my vast collection of ties, not for my shoes.

Even I, so often in meetings with people from contrasting cultures, could feel the momentousness of one the young Gamal Mubarak's rare visits to Davos that crispy night in January 2005. Earlier that same year, his father, Hosni Mubarak, the president of Egypt, who had by this time ruled over the country for 24 years, would take measures to change the laws to grease the wheels of Gamal's slippery ascension to the presidency. He was pushing through an amendment to Egypt's constitution prohibiting political parties with fewer than five years in government and less than 5% representation in parliament to nominate a candidate.

I looked neither like the lanky, dark-haired Gamal Mubarak, second son of Egypt's president, nor like the silver fox full-head-of-hair Gere. With my shiny head, full mustache and faint Iraqi accent, I am a Bahraini. Although I was born there, I no longer live there, and yet I am probably more Bahraini than most Bahrainis who live there.

Gamal was already being touted by the foreign press as the ascending ruler of Egypt to assure the power grip that his father, at that point in 2005, held for 24 of the 30 years before his dramatic fall in 2011. Was this appearance of the educated businessman who had become leader of Egypt's National Democratic Party an inkling of what was to come six years down the road? Hosni Mubarak's strong arm and military origins belied his desire to bring peace, as vice president to Anwar Sadat during the Sadat–Begin Camp David Accords.

That night in Davos, I was skeptical of Gamal, seeing him as merely a product of the favoritism of his father, the iron-fisted ruler who held onto power through his tripartite system of civil government that included the control of the military, the intelligence services, and the police.

It was my seventh consecutive visit to the Annual Meeting in Davos and I was one of four speakers in a session. I was there to represent the business voice because I was the elected vice chairman of the WEF's Arab Business Council (ABC). The room was full of public figures from the Arab world and Arab business community. All the chairs were taken and latecomers were standing in the back. Of the four speakers, I was the first to arrive. I greeted the highly respected moderator, Ghassan Salamé,[1] who asked me whether I wanted to be the first speaker. I told him that, since I was the only business voice, I wished to be the last.

The room was packed and buzzing with anticipation, eager to hear the reformist voice of the younger Mubarak. Gamal was the second speaker, after Bassem Awadallah,[2] followed by Salam Fayyad.[3] All conversations focused on reforms in the Arab world. After listening to Gamal for over 15 minutes, the wave of disappointment in the room was palpable. When my turn finally came, I stood up and thanked Salamé for allowing me to speak last, remarking that the last speaker is usually in a bad position

---

[1] Ghassan Salamé is a Lebanese academic based in Paris. He served as the Minister of Culture of Lebanon from 2000 to 2003. He was dean of the Paris School of International Affairs (PSIA) and professor of International Relations at the Paris Institute of Political Studies (Sciences Po). Salamé headed the United Nations Support Mission in Libya from 2017 to 2020.
[2] Bassem Awadallah served as economic secretary to the Jordanian premier from 1992 to 1996. He was appointed head of Jordan's royal court in 2007. Subsequently, Awadallah moved to Dubai and founded the company Tomouh, and was reportedly living between the United Arab Emirates and Saudi Arabia. He was recently imprisoned for alleged "incitement against the ruling system" and "sedition" in Jordan.
[3] Salam Fayyad is a Jordanian-Palestinian politician who was finance minister of the Palestinian Authority from June 2002 to November 2005 and prime minister from June 2007 to June 2013.

because everyone before them has covered the subject so they are forced to improvise. However, I said that was not the case on this occasion.

I said that, like everyone else in the room, I had waited anxiously to hear the future head of the largest Arab country talk about his reformist vision but that, for the first 12 minutes of his 15-minute talk, he had spoken only to defend his father's accomplishments over the prior 24 years. I concluded my address by saying that if the session proved anything, it showed that the Arab world was irrelevant to the rest of the world and would carry on that way as long as it had rulers and not leaders.

"Mr. Mubarak," I asked, as I ended my turn and looked directly at him, "How can we find our way from rulership to leadership in the Middle East? Will you give us a road map for the future?"

After I spoke, Richard Gere stood up from his seat across the room, stopped at my table, leaned over, and whispered in my ear, "Khalid, you really must pursue this important question."

INTRODUCTION

EVOLUTION NOT REVOLUTION

That encouraging whisper led me to 18 years of listening and observing, asking questions, and trying to find answers. This book is part memoir and part observation on why being a nonconformist and vigilant observer has compelled me to ask questions. I want to share my perspective on the great importance of critical thinking, dialogue, conversation, and debate to ultimately create change that enables people the freedom to choose for themselves and determine their own value in society. My goal is to foster conversation, provoke opinions, encourage critical thinking and disruptive actions, but never to breed enmity.

I believe in evolution. When I look back over the past 20 years at the Arab world, I see that we have not experienced any real evolution with a very few exceptions; instead, we have actually experienced devolution. This devolution could mean the next uprising. The leadership must be strong enough to act on their words and implement reforms through an evolutionary process in order to disrupt old patterns and create positive change.

Over time, I have formulated the questions that can create a road map to the future, and the answers that can guide us to change, to evolution. What are the traits of an effective leader? How can a ruler change and evolve into an effective leader? What are the traits of a leader who allows people to have agency, to be citizens and not subjects, to express critical thinking and find the dignity to work hard and feed their families, to thrive and to act as innovators, creating a sustainable and healthy future for the Middle East and for that matter anywhere else in the world?

These questions led me to a search for the answers to myriad questions, providing me the opportunity to meet brilliant thought leaders and agents of change. I want to see change for the Middle East that brings innovation, critical thinking, and agency for each individual, in the manner that only leaders can inspire in their citizens.

THE CALCULUS OF CHANCE

If our lives are the sum of all our choices, I can say without regret that mine have added up to a most interesting, challenging, and beautiful equation. I was never brilliant in math, yet patterns and equations have always led me from one step to the next. I became a partner in an international accounting firm, but then moved into banking. When we are young, we often ask many questions without always waiting for the answers. In fact, I have never claimed to have the answers, but I have always sought them. This book presents far more questions than it can begin to answer, and it is often easier to see the patterns of others and their faults and hypocrisies than to see our own.

Although I was never an outstanding student, I could see from a young age that I didn't want to comply with the pattern of so many of my peers, which required conformity and subservience. I was always critical of myself, and at times was my own worst enemy, but this led me to a kind of freedom that helped me to gain success, kudos, and wealth, all on my own terms and because of my own hard work and choices. My art is the art of closing a deal and connecting people. I am neither a mathematician, nor a writer, nor an artist, but my imagination frees me to travel far and try new things.

I chose to seek out a meritocratic structure in my life, where hard work and ethics count most of all. Perhaps that is why I became an accountant, always asking questions and conducting audits based on international accounting standards and an ethical and legal playbook of equations. I trusted those patterns to be there for me and when I sat down for my required English language entrance exam in order to study in Lebanon, I quickly realized I really wasn't sure of the answers to any of the questions, so I played with the number of potential choices for each question, created a pattern, and proceeded to fill in all my answers in a fraction of the time allotted.

The proctor frowned at me with disappointment when I turned in my test. Much to my surprise, when the final scores were posted, mine were above average. The pattern of answers I had devised sealed my fate and got me a ticket to the next fateful step in my life, my move to Lebanon to continue my educational journey. I thrived in Beirut, thrilled by my cultural awakening to literature, music, and films. Alas, this time in the educational paradise of my youth was cut short in September 1975 by the onslaught of the Lebanese civil war. While many of my Bahraini peers went to study in Texas, I went to England, where I completed university with a double major in computer science and accounting.

Despite my pragmatism and my attraction to logic and patterns, I am not without emotion. I am writing this book because I have tremendous compassion for the millions who have suffered and are still suffering from COVID-19 worldwide, from conflicts and wars, injustice and inequality, and the minimum of 60 million young people under 30 who live in MENA (Middle East and North Africa) and have limited prospects for their future. We are on the precipice of change, with many forces converging to push the regimes of the Arab world to either implement urgently needed reforms or face more disastrous consequences. What does it take to evolve from subject to citizen? What traits and actions are necessary for a real leader in these times of plague, unrest, climate change disaster, food and water shortages, and extreme poverty? The paradigm of subject and ruler must shift, and we must choose to evolve or perish. We must rewrite the social contract, starting with all of the choices we make, in order to find agency, to find our voice, and to create the right patterns around us, or disrupt them and find new answers. My goal is to inspire a younger generation to become leaders and to analyze what changes need to be made and can be made to create more egalitarian societies in MENA and the world.

As a chartered accountant, who by the nature of his profession generally listens more than he speaks, I have had the opportunity to listen, observe, and participate, to converse with leaders and rulers, to dream of what is possible, and to ask the questions about how we can get there.

STRUCTURE OF THIS BOOK

Part memoir and part observation, this book begins with chapters that describe people and events that have shaped who I am. Part I relates memories that, taken together, explain my journey to becoming a nonconformist. Many moments in my life are of course excluded from these pages, but those I've included are relevant to my aims in this book of promoting independent thinking and debate, fostering dialogue, and encouraging disruptive actions in the pursuit of a better world.

Part II is a collection of reflections on the Arab world, gleaned from my own experience. These observations are offered as eye-openers and food for thought.

Movies are a lifelong passion, one that from a young age exposed me to religious, social, cultural and geographic differences, shaping to a certain extent my understanding of life. This book acknowledges that influence with myriad mentions of my favorite films. Part III lists 100 movies that have affected and enthralled me.

The Conclusion recaps why I think it's important to disrupt old patterns and create positive change, why it's important to be a nonconformist and to tell it like it is. To my mind, it's the only way to instigate positive change and elevate people.

The Epilogue briefly introduces the Maryam Forum, created to help build transformational leadership for an uncertain future in the Arab world and beyond. The need for good, accountable leadership is an important theme that runs throughout this volume. The first extract in the appendix relates to it.

The last two extracts in the appendix, although they date from 2002 and 2005, are important in the context of this book. The first UN *Arab Human Development Report*, published in 2002, is cited several times because of its focus on creating opportunities for future generations. *The Arab World Competitiveness Report 2005* outlines the prospects for growth but also the impediments to improving competitiveness in the region. These reports' findings are still relevant despite the passage of time, and the need to address shortcomings in the areas of freedom, empowerment, and knowledge in the Arab world are all the more urgent today.

PART I
A BRIEF MEMOIR

The following pages recount memories of certain events, more or less distant, that most shaped my life. They have affected my take on life, who I have become, and what I stand for. I illustrate each chapter with a trait of leadership, which became evident as I traversed that period of my life.

CHAPTER 1

NONCONFORMIST

"Watch out about choosing your pals. You know what I mean: don't let them choose you."

–Frank Stark, played by Jim Backus

Rebel Without a Cause (1955)

My parents shook off the shackles of conformity to work and raise a family on their own terms.

MY PARENTS

I have always loved maps. And as much as we cannot map or predict our future, I can always ponder the maps of the past and imagine other times. Manama, the Bahraini capital city where I was born, has been a thriving port since around 3300 BCE, when it was part of the ancient civilization of Dilmun. Its ships traded with the Sumerians from the northern tip of the Gulf Sea all the way to the Indus Valley in South Asia. The great Euphrates and Tigris rivers, the life forces of the eastern arm of the Fertile Crescent, discharge into the Gulf Sea at the southern edge of modern-day Iraq and cover what are now Iraq, the Syrian Arab Republic, Lebanon, Jordan, Palestine, Israel, Egypt, and parts of Turkey. In ancient times, the countries comprising this area were known as Egypt, Phoenicia, Assyria, and Mesopotamia—the cradle of civilization.

As a boy, I could understand just from tracing the lines on the map that powerful forces converged in this Gulf region, and that our little island of Bahrain was an entrepôt for the heady mix of people, politics, and culture passing through. The island of Bahrain had long been a power player with trading ships and invaders swarming over the waters to buy and sell pearls, dates, fish, and other goods. Ships sailing through the Gulf had to pass it on their way to Saudi Arabia and the rest of the Arab world. The Greeks, the Portuguese, the Arabs, and the Persians all had staked a claim. Much later, from 1869 to 1971, the British governed Bahrain as its protectorate. It took more than one hundred years for Bahrainis to gain their independence.

Walking through *Bab Al Bahrain*[4] as a boy of seven, I entered

---

[4] *Bab Al Bahrain*, which means "Gateway of Bahrain," is a building located at the entrance of the Manama Souq in Bahrain's capital. Built in 1949, it

the *souq* through a stately whitewashed archway. The Gateway of Bahrain gave me a glimpse of freedom to a world beyond the comforts of my family home. Little did I know that the magnificent archway, which seemed so vast in my childhood, would someday lead me away to a life outside of Bahrain and beyond the confines of the state. The archway shrank for me in later years, its grandeur diminished by changes to the world, to me, and to Bahrain.

When I was growing up, the *souq* was the center of the community: the streets where it all happened, where men negotiated business deals, men and women flirted, and men sat for hours drinking tea and smoking *hookahs* at *ghawa khaneh,* traditional cafés serving tea and coffee and homemade goat milk yogurt, chickpeas, and *bajalah* (broad beans) while discussing the world as they saw it.

My story begins with my parents. My father was born in the time of the British colonial treaties. He witnessed the drive for Bahraini freedom and independence from Britain, and with his own independent spirit, the country's newfound independence encouraged his own passion to live of his own free will, creating his destiny as best he could.

My mother was a girl of just 14 and my father was 17 when

---

once overlooked the sea, housing the government's administrative offices. Located behind *Bab Al Bahrain* is the old Manama Souq.

they married. He had completed only the first six grades of school and was working with his father and older brother when his marriage was arranged. Although my parents were not direct cousins, they were fourth cousins. My mother was the eldest daughter of her family. They considered her marriage to be the best way they could protect her because she had no education and was basically illiterate.

When my mother was just 16, she gave birth to me, her first child, on Christmas Day in 1958. For one week, I was named Issa, a first name meaning Jesus in Arabic, until my grandfather, the head of our household, changed it to Khalid.

My father was restless and rebellious and longed for independence. He remained with his father and brother in the contracting business for a year after my birth. And then, taking what little money he had, he left home to start his own business. He struggled for the first six or seven years, but he refused to ask his father for support, nor would he allow his wife to ask her family, although they were considered upper-middle class. After leaving his father's large house and compound, he had no one to turn to about discussing his problems.

By the time I started school in 1963, my parents and I were living in Riffa, in the southern part of Bahrain, where I attended primary school. My parents soon moved back to Manama. It was not until the 1970s that people in Bahrain began to receive subsidies from the government in the form of housing, land allocations, and jobs. In the 1950s and '60s, my father and most of his generation worked hard for every penny they earned, which was the norm in Bahrain and poor neighboring countries. Even though these were oil-producing countries, the British and Americans took everything. They gave just peanuts to the ruling class, to keep them happy and compliant, but nothing to the average citizen—most of whom had nothing.

When I was a little boy, I worried about my dad and would sit and wait for him to come home. I worried because he had to make his way on foot and by bus, back and forth to Manama every day. I waited for him each afternoon at sunset, with his tea on the table.

In my early years, before my siblings were born, I enjoyed a deep closeness with my mother and father, an understanding borne of my child's intuition, and although I was too young to comprehend the exact nature of the problem, I could see they were struggling. For me, my closeness with my mother and father provided me with great comfort throughout my life. Although these were hard times, I look back knowing I lived in a time of progress, and I learned a great deal from the adversity I experienced.

My father tried to pick up the pieces of his lost business.

I grew to understand that my father was more of a creative salesman and marketer than a manager. My mother, who had no education, was a better manager. By virtue of her mindset, she often had a clearer picture of what was going on than my father did. He was in a partnership with a man who cooked the books and stole a lot of money from him, leaving my father to fight in court. The courts, however, did not favor my father, which is exactly what others told him would happen. They understood that the system did not favor those without the money to pave the way to justice. Fair or unfair, he had to abide by the system and start over.

Because he was a proud man, my father refused to go to his father and tell him he'd made a mistake. His parents had taken care of my father and mother and me, and now that they were on their own, the couple decided not to have any more children for another four years. My father could have returned to his extended family and developed another business with his father, but he was stubborn and determined. He respected his family, but he wanted to prove to himself and others that he could succeed on his own. He felt compelled to carry his own burden and work on his own with only his wife to offer emotional support. For several years, we were forced to change homes every year to three years, moving whenever it was hard to pay the rent.

Over the next five years, and for the rest of my primary years,

I attended Abdul Rahman Al Dakhel Primary Boys' School in an area called Qudaibiya. At first, we lived in a house my father had built. He was busy building and selling houses. I went to school on foot, walking there from home in only three minutes. Then my father struggled with his business, lost the house, and was faced with bankruptcy. We had to move out and rent a place in a different, more affordable neighborhood of Busaiteen, on the second largest island called Muharraq, which is connected by a bridge to Manama. Every morning I took a bus from our home in Muharraq, which dropped me at the base of the bridge, and I walked across into Manama and on to school. I was eight years old and had to leave early to get to school by seven in the morning. At times, when I did not have money for the bus ride, I walked most of the way, there and back. In winter, I left in the dark before sunrise to get there on time, and then walked back home at one in the afternoon.

TEACHING WAYS

School was an interesting experience where I encountered two types of headmasters. In my first three years at Abdul Rahman Al Dakhel School, the headmaster and most of my teachers were Bahrainis. The headmaster (and teachers) did not believe in or use corporal punishment to discipline students. Instead, they used soft power to engage students, even the very young, and to gain respect.

After those initial years, I was thus shocked upon returning from my summer vacation to find that the headmaster and most of the teachers had been replaced. I learned that they had all been sent to Abu Dhabi to teach there on the request of Abu Dhabi's ruler.

The last two years with the new headmaster turned out to be a nightmare. The difference between the two principals was like chalk and cheese. The new headmaster believed in physical punishment, which was evident from the long whip he carried (which measured about his size, 165 cm long) when he walked down the corridors.

As much as the previous headmaster had made me love going to school, the new one had the totally opposite effect on me. I started skipping classes. So being whipped in front of all the students before we started classes became routine.

I recall the first time the headmaster whipped me in front of the students and faculty. He ordered me to open my hand and show my palm. The first hit was extremely painful, but he continued to whip my hand with what felt like all the force he could muster. After 10 whips or so, my palm so swollen that I no longer felt any pain, he finally stopped. Later that day, I was called during a class to the headmaster's office. Standing in front of him, he asked me why I didn't cry. Putting on a brave face, I told him I didn't feel the pain to the extent I should cry. Using a threatening tone, he advised me that, for my sake, he hoped there would be no new incident that would require me to be whipped again. He added that if it were to happen again, he would only stop when I cried. I passed this information on to the other boys who were likely to be punished by the headmaster. I spent the rest of my last two years of elementary school being whipped at least twice a week. The boys cried as soon as he raised his whip. The only one who didn't was bad boy Janahi.

Growing up, I often thought to myself how lucky the students in Abu Dhabi had been to have experienced the excellent group of teachers and our former, exemplary headmaster.

CONSTANT COMPANION

Being a TV addict, I used to do all my homework and comic book reading at night when everyone was asleep. As I shared a bedroom with my siblings up to my last year in school, in order not to wake them, I studied or read under the blanket with a flashlight. I did that whether it was summer, sleeping on the roof in the early days, or winter, sleeping inside with a blanket. I did not have my own room until my final year of school when my father built a new house; even when my family went away to Dubai, I was sharing the room with my uncles. So I will never forget my 11-year companion, my flashlight, and stock of batteries.

PARTING WAYS WITH THE FAMILY

When I was in middle school, my father had an opportunity to work in Dubai. My mother and my siblings went with him. I stayed behind and lived with my maternal grandparents in their big house so I wouldn't miss school. In their houses, my grandparents controlled everyone's lives. Much like my father, I eventually left the family home because I also felt the need to prove myself. I pushed myself to get through school, to be a top student, and to get a scholarship to university. I was the first one in my paternal family to graduate from university.

At one point in the early days of my career, as I started getting more work and job offers, I reached a turning point. I was told I had gotten this far because the system had allowed me to get this far. I was told the system was responsible for my success and had educated me and done everything for me. I was a young man and could not accept this insult. It was an insult that people I knew, childhood acquaintances and some people in my own family, were telling me. It was an affront to me because I knew whatever I had achieved was due to my father and my mother. My mother made sure her eldest child, despite the difficult time growing up, learned to do things for himself.

I understood from a young age the importance of family and the importance of leadership within the structure of the family. The way I looked at it then, and still look at it now, is that any success I achieved was because of my parents, especially my mother, and any mistakes I've made in my life I brought on myself from my surrounding environment. Despite their lack of education, my parents taught me through their own often difficult choices that I, too, could strongly reject conformism and nepotism in my own life.

The kind of leadership that my mother set as an example for me is the kind we must instill in all areas of society: in the family, education, business, and government. We need to teach people independence and critical thinking so they can be self-sufficient and work hard, first for themselves, and then for their communities.

Ultimately, I believe a man or a woman gains self-esteem from hard work and the courage to think for themselves. In retrospect, I was an outlier and defied the odds because my family was exceptional in the midst of a society that was stacked against the individual, a society in which there was implicit cronyism and favoritism between the educational system and the system of governance. My parents shared the cultural and religious values of the large extended family but stood outside the expectations of the ecosystem and fought for the little bit of self-determination they could create for themselves.

HOW HOLI AM I?

The movements of people from Iran and other countries surrounding the Gulf were similar to the migratory patterns of Europeans in the late 18th and 19th centuries. Just as Europeans had left for the United States or other places with modern industry and economic opportunity, my family had moved across the Gulf from Iran to Bahrain in search of a better life for themselves and their families.

I am from Bahrain, but my roots are from Janah in Iran and Basra in Iraq. When I was born, before the oil boom, Bahrain was still a British protectorate and the country was a melting pot of rich and poor. Indigenous populations moved there for its port of commerce, and many nationalities lived side by side in harmony. My family and everyone we knew considered themselves proud Bahrainis. Both sects of Islam, Arab and Persian Sunnis and Arab and Persian Shiites, coexisted without conflict. The migrants who settled over several centuries are called *Holi.* We were *Al-Hawala (Al Hwalah),* people who go away and then come back.

During the British times, in the Gulf, the indigenous people perceived their neighbors as their equals. After the British left, divisions between groups began to harden, separating people by class, geography, or religious sect. Societal hierarchies took shape. People were increasingly regarded as subjects rather than citizens. Slowly, because of these perceived differences, enemies were created and, at the same time, individual freedoms eroded. A notion was introduced that a number of groups of enemies existed against which the population needed to be protected. Bahrain, like its neighbors, became a rentier economy and people relied on the government for protection and subsidies for their livelihood.

THE GULF OF OIL AND GAS

When I went to school, we used Egyptian textbooks that were published under Gamal Abdel Nasser's regime, the iconic voice of Arab nationalism. At that time, the sea near my home was called the "Persian Gulf." In the 1970s, in the Arab world, it became known as the "Arabian Gulf." But whether it's the Arabian or Persian Gulf doesn't make much difference. The world at large only looks at this part of the world for two reasons: oil and gas. It might therefore be fairer to call it the "Gulf of Oil and Gas." To shorten it, I refer to it as "the Gulf" in this book.

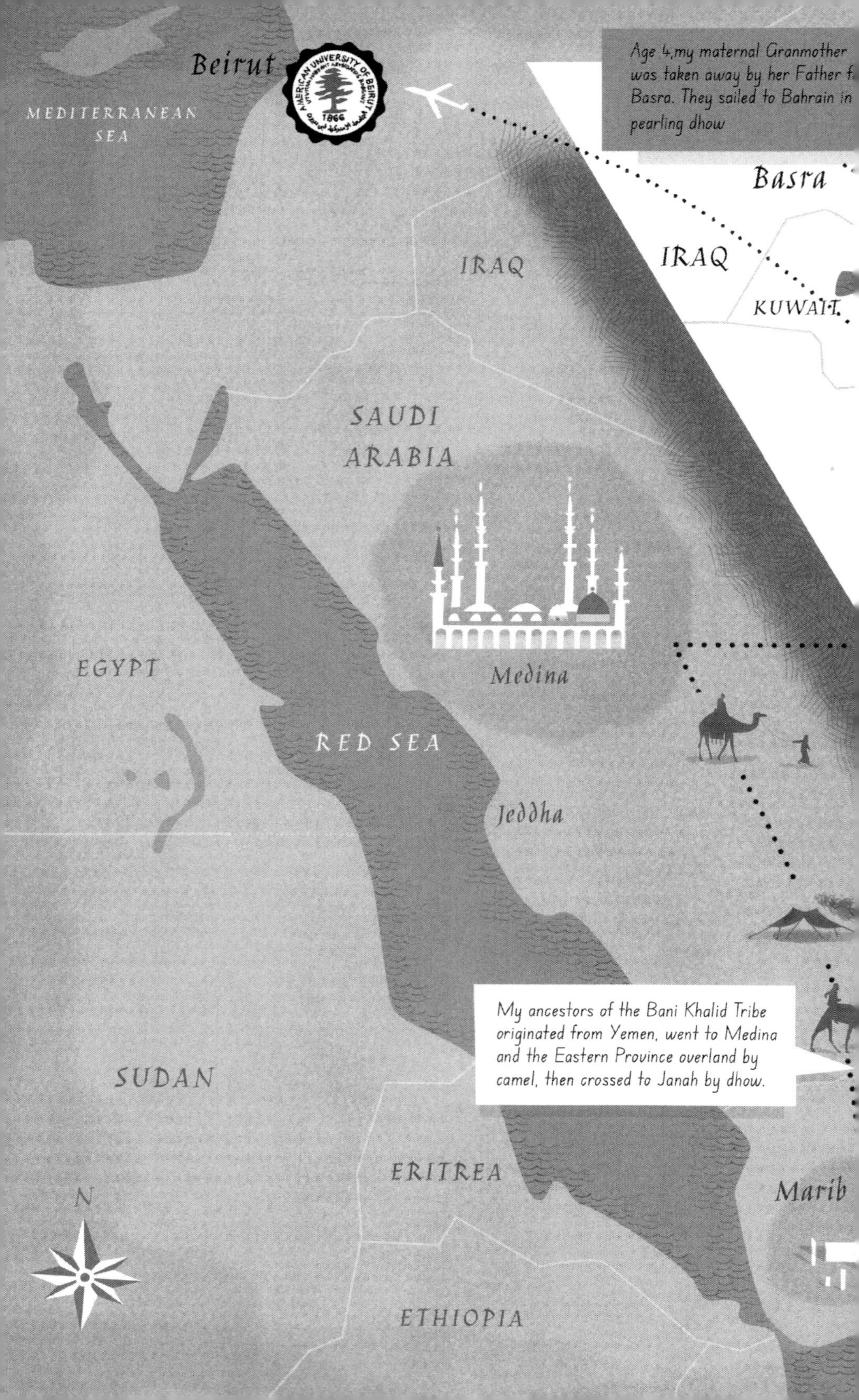
Beirut
AMERICAN UNIVERSITY OF BEIRUT
1866
MEDITERRANEAN
SEA
Age 4,my maternal Granmother
was taken away by her Father
Basra. They sailed to Bahrain in
pearling dhow
Basra
IRAQ
KUWAIT
IRAQ
SAUDI
ARABIA
EGYPT
Medina
RED SEA
Jeddha
My ancestors of the Bani Khalid Tribe
originated from Yemen, went to Medina
and the Eastern Province overland by
camel, then crossed to Janah by dhow.
SUDAN
ERITREA
Marib
N
ETHIOPIA

MY MIDDLE EAST

IRAN

IRAN

Shiraz

My other 3 Grandparents sailed from Janah to Bahrain across the Gulf

Janah

BAHRAIN

GULF of OIL & GAS

QATAR

Dubai

GULF of OMAN

Abu Dhabi

UNITED ARAB EMIRATES

OMAN

YEMEN

EN

ARABIAN SEA

GULF of ADEN

CHAPTER 2

RESPONSIBLE

"I am at a place from where I don't even get any news about me ... ... I used to laugh from my heart, but not anymore"

*- From the Bollywood movie, **Waqt.** The movie title means **Time** in Urdu.*

Carried off by her father at an early age, she didn't see her mother for over 30 years, yet she overcame mistreatment and taught us tolerance.

MY GRANDMOTHER

My maternal grandmother's story was one of great resilience and determination. She was half Iraqi and half Bahraini, born in Iraq, in Basra. I believe my mother's strength came from my grandmother, who quietly endured harsh treatment from an early age.

When my grandmother was four years old, her father divorced her mother without informing her of their divorce. He left his wife in Iraq and took his four-year-old daughter, my grandmother, with him on a dhow to Bahrain, southward through the Gulf.

By the late 19th century, pearling dhows that went from port to port would have taken them from Basra to Manama. By this time, telegraph cables existed on the seabed and steamships made the journey from one side of the Gulf to the other. The pearling dhows were feeding the demands of the European market and were not set up for an express trip by dhow along the coast. The steamship passage would not have been affordable and so my grandmother's first voyage probably took several days.

In the 1920s, this journey, surely fraught with perils, must have been extremely frightening for a small child. Essentially abandoning his wife, divorcing her without her knowledge and taking away their child, my great grandfather set sail to a faraway land. It wasn't illegal at the time; men owned their wives and their children. It would be more than 30 years before my grandmother saw her mother again.

Soon after my great grandfather arrived in Bahrain with his young daughter, he married another woman. From a very early age, as the family grew, my grandmother was poorly treated. She was the only child from her father's first marriage, so she became the babysitter for her half-siblings, shouldering tremendous responsibility to look after them.

It was not until my great grandfather passed away in the 1950s that his eldest son from his second marriage (my grandmother's half-brother) decided to go to Basra to find his half-sister's mother. My grandmother had not seen her mother since she was four and was by now in her 30s.

My grandmother traveled with her half-brother. By then, she had already had four children, three of whom traveled with her: my aunt, my uncle, and my mother. When she was at last reunited with her mother in Basra, she discovered that she had three half-sisters she had not known existed.

As luck would have it, my grandmother's eldest brother was rewarded for finding his half-sister's family and discovering the sisters previously unknown to her. He promptly fell in love with my grandmother's oldest half-sister – if you can follow this puzzle, you will understand that neither of my grandparents had the same mother or father. They were not blood relatives, but their families were certainly intertwined before and after they married.

We are known in Bahrain for these family connections, including this one: my uncle on my mother's side and my aunt on my mother's side were married, and my grandmother was the sister of both the groom and the bride, in the middle between them.

Another shock for my grandmother was when her husband, my grandfather, married his second wife, who must have been 18 or 19 at the time. My grandmother was in her late 20s then. Owing to the fact that my grandfather had two wives, my mother was the eldest of 15 children, nine siblings and six half-siblings, giving me 14 aunts and uncles, seven of whom are younger than I am.

To provide one more example of just how many branches our family tree has, I will tell you about my only sister, and that she is married to the son of my great-auntie and great-uncle, which makes my brother-in-law the son of the half-brother of my grandmother, the man who found her mother and then married her half-sister.

My grandmother spoke little of her childhood, but I did know she was treated badly, more like a servant than a wife from the time she was married at the age of 14. It wasn't until she was pregnant that her stepmother's sister realized just how badly she was being treated and took her away, caring for her during her pregnancy. This step-aunt kept my grandmother in her own home instead of taking her to her father or husband. She returned to them only after her baby – my mother – was born.

My mother was greatly influenced by her mother's resilience and learned to navigate the inequities of a large family as a teenage bride. Nonetheless, she later imposed some of the same hardships on her children.

PEARL DIVERS AND TAILORS

About 400 to 500 years ago, many tribes moved from the Gulf's western shore to the eastern shore, motivated by commerce and war. Just as Europeans had left for America and beyond to discover new worlds, many villagers embarked on voyages that took them to the other side of the Gulf. Because it was long before these countries had their current names, we can say the people moved from the Arabian Peninsula to the Iranian side. It wasn't until the 19th and 20th centuries that they started to come back, due to faster transport and economic opportunity.

My family were Sunnis, who came on the Iranian side from a small village called Janah. Over the years, it grew to be a small, little-known city about one and half hours' drive to the coast in the south of Iran. According to the 2006 census, Janah had a population of 5,636, within 1,322 families. Today, there are over 35,000 thousand Janahis in Bahrain alone, with more Janahis living abroad than in Iran. Nowadays, Janah can be reached by plane – if and when flights are available – by flying from Bahrain to Lar and driving about an hour and half to Janah. In the old days, it was possible to fly to Shiraz and then travel by car up and down the roadless mountains, reaching Janah some 14 hours later.

My maternal grandfather was born in Iran in Janah, the youngest of four brothers. One brother stayed in the village and died there while the other three left for Bahrain. He and his brothers worked together, but eventually each built businesses of their own in Bahrain that served as the family's financial foundations in Manama. The first of the family to go to Manama was my grandfather's eldest brother, who left Janah in 1915 to work as a pearl diver in Bahrain. Around 1920, my grandfather's second brother moved to Bahrain, also initially working in the pearl diving business. He was essentially a businessman and entrepreneur and, with his brother, soon started a tailoring business. Understanding the value of focusing on a niche, the brothers steered their tailoring toward making full Arab dress wear for men. Four years later, my grandfather, the youngest of the brothers, joined his older brothers in the business in Bahrain. The pearl diving days were waning, so my great-uncles and grandfather had adapted to the times. From tailoring they moved on to trading and exporting to Iran. Because Iran did not have the traditional full Arab dress for men at the time, my grandfather worked with his brothers to expand the tailoring operation into a prêt-à-porter business, shifting their focus to mostly Western clothing. Together, the three brothers' tailoring business and shops thrived throughout Bahrain, Doha, and the Eastern Province town of Khobar.

My paternal grandfather was also from Janah. In 1910, he left for Bahrain without his family, traveling back and forth to Janah over the years. Around 1930, he brought his family to Bahrain and established himself as a builder, contributing to the construction of *Bab Al Bahrain*.

My grandfathers and their generation, as a whole, saw Bahrain as a land of great opportunity and a true melting pot. This generation took risks, settling in Bahrain and establishing businesses that served over time as the island's bedrock of commerce for generations to come. My family along with many other families created businesses that played important roles in shaping the country. They embraced the idea of equality among all individuals, and the belief that people could succeed in Bahrain regardless of their origin, religion, or race. For the women, of course, it was a different story, as it would take years before the practice of marrying them off at an extremely young age would end and they would be allowed some of the same opportunities for education or business as men. I took pride in my family and their role in Bahrain and, from an early age, I believed all of us could succeed on our own merits.

CHAPTER 3

MERITOCRATIC

"In all the fights between the whites and the Indians,
it's the whites who've always started the trouble."
– The Lone Ranger, played by Clayton Moore

Growing up, I watched countless American TV shows dubbed in Arabic and snuck out to the cinema on Mondays, Thursdays and Fridays to watch foreign and Arabic movies, allowing my imagination to take flight across religious, social, and geographic boundaries. I learned from TV that you don't have to kill to get justice.

BOYHOOD

When I was born in 1958, Bahrain was a small place with no more than 150,000 people. We lived in my paternal grandfather's house in Al Awadhiya in the eastern part of Manama, where most people lived in little houses close to one another. By contrast, my grandparents lived in a large house where 20 people resided.

Both my grandparents had televisions at the time although, for most people, TV was a luxury. Many members of the family would crowd around and watch shows together. I joined in around the age of four, once I began to understand what I was seeing. The black and white boxes offered us Aramco TV programming from Dharan, Saudi Arabia that began each day around 4:00 pm and continued until 10:30 pm, with the exception of Thursday nights when we could watch until midnight.

There was only one channel, yet it offered me a full cultural education, starting the day with a course in Arabic and a reading from the *Quran*, then moving on to an English lesson. After the lessons came the cartoons, but I was not a cartoon guy.

The great Egyptian diva, Umm Kulthum, was an early influence on me; I sat mesmerized by her soulful, haunting voice that transfixed each generation – my grandparents, my parents, and me. On the first Thursday of each month, she performed live in a theater and the recordings were broadcast live on the radio. She sang with a full orchestra, with over 10 violins, performing her repertoire of powerful songs of lost love, longing, and regret.

ONION TO THE RESCUE

It was the first day of Ramadan in 1966. My mother was giving birth to my third sibling at home. The doctor who attended to her during her first three childbirths was with her, along with my maternal grandmother. I remember her name was Dr. Matthews, but she was known in Bahrain as "Metuse." My father, my two young siblings, and I sat outside the room waiting for the birth of the new member of our family. We could hear my mother's pain. Suddenly, there was silence. My grandmother came out of the room and asked my father to go to the kitchen to get an onion cut into two. My dad followed her instructions, immediately bringing her the cut onion. She went back into the room and, around four minutes later, we heard the baby cry. Apparently, at birth my newborn sibling did not breathe for five minutes, but the smell of the onion helped him gain consciousness and provoked his first cry, marking his healthy start to life.

FALSE NEWS

In 1967, we heard about the Six-Day War on the radio. Everyone was glued to *Sawt al-Arab* (the "Voice of the Arabs"), the pro-Nasser 18-hour-a-day program broadcast by Cairo radio across the Arab world. The voice of the main presenter, Ahmed Said, still resonates in my ears. For six days, everyone believed that the coalition of Arab states – Egypt, Syria, and Jordan – had won the war and Israel had been destroyed. We were therefore very surprised a few days later when Arab nationalist Gamal Abdel Nasser announced the coalition's loss.

A PASSION FOR MOVIES

I loved silent short films and by the age of five, I had seen many of those starring Buster Keaton, Charlie Chaplin, Harold Lloyd, Ben Turpin, Billy Van, and Laurel and Hardy. The shows in English were dubbed in Arabic and it seemed natural to me that the Lone Ranger, Zorro, and the cowboys and Indians all spoke a language I understood. Of course, references to Christianity, pork, or alcohol were edited out.

I often watched TV with my uncle, whom I greatly admired for his rebellious spirit. From him, I came to understand that the Indians in the Westerns were as much the heroes as the others and that nobody was a second-class citizen to anyone else.

By the time I was seven years old and well accustomed to moving houses, I had established my own mischievous independence and self-reliance. Watching movies in nearby cinemas had exposed me to many scenes of human pain and suffering. The Bollywood movies, American films, cowboy westerns, and Arabic dramas had expanded my understanding of life and my imagination, allowing me to witness life far from my tiny island home.

My Cinema World in Bahrain (1964–1974)

At the time, Manama's theatres were clustered in one small area by the sea, just beyond the *souq*. In the early 1940s, the Bahrain Petroleum Company opened a movie theater for its staff, although it closed in 1991. In the 1950s and 1960s, eight new cinemas opened in Bahrain, six of which were located close to where I lived: the Al Hamra, Al Nasr, Awal, Al Zayani, Zubara and Bahrain. This was extremely convenient for me as a little boy. Most of them were on or just adjacent to Zubara Avenue, a cluster of magic palaces that transported me to other worlds. The Al Hamra opened in the 1970s, attached to the Al Nasr, the first to be air-conditioned. The Awal, once demolished and rebuilt, was the main cinema, featuring all kinds of movies. Just 500 yards away, the Al Zayani, named after the Zayani family, offered Arabic movies. I also loved the Al Gosseibi Cinema, just a bit farther away. From the 70s onward, I would sometimes see two movies in a day, paid for by my father's mother who would secretly supply the money for my tickets.

LIFE ON THE MOVE

From the day I was born on December 25, 1958 until I left for Beirut in August 1974, I lived in 13 different places. My family moved our household from one house to another until I was 16 years old.

Today, Bahrain covers 780 square kilometers. When I was born, before land was reclaimed from the sea, the land area of Bahrain was less than 700 square kilometers, much of it desert.

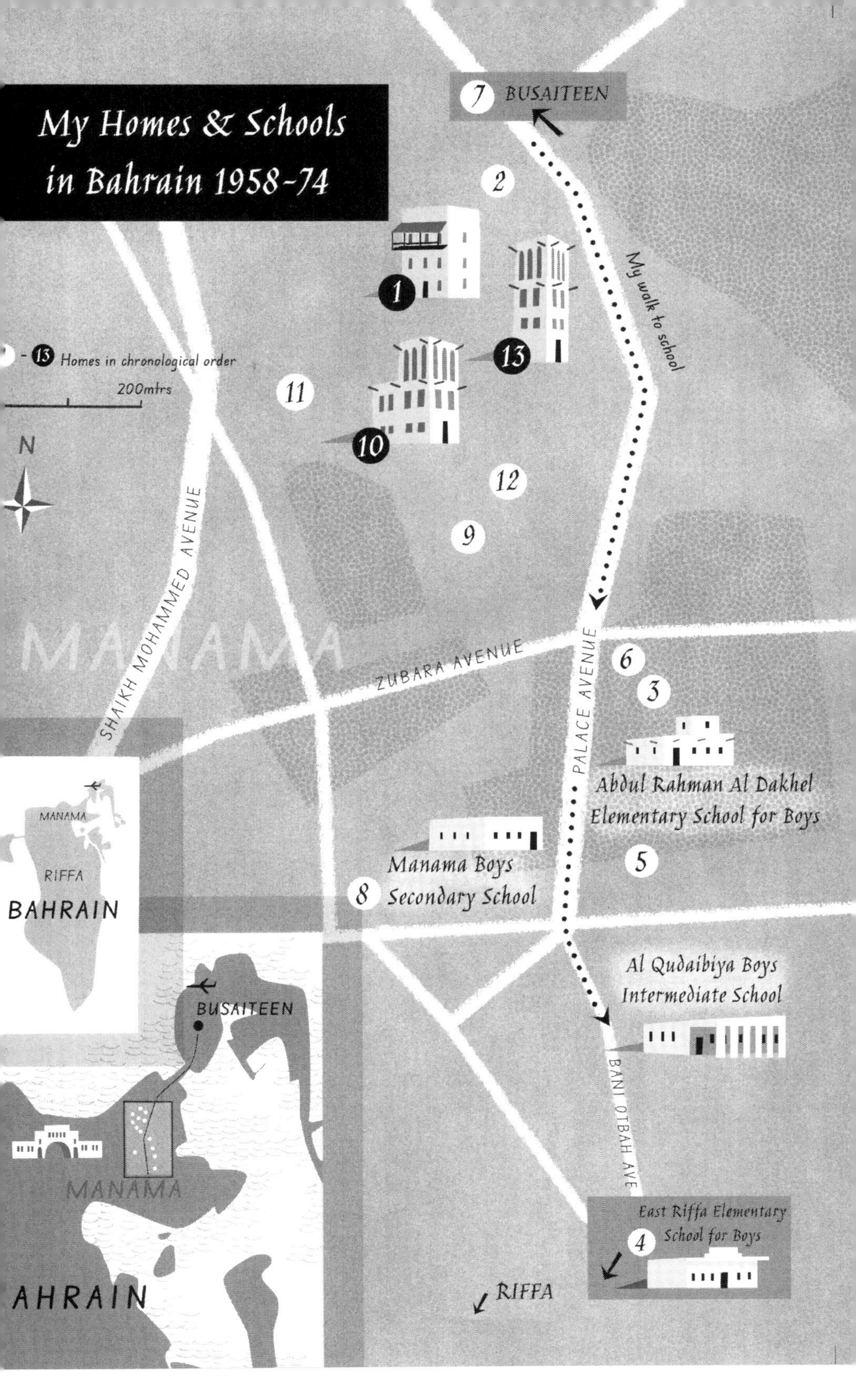
My Homes & Schools in Bahrain 1958-74
BUSAITEEN
My walk to school
- 13 Homes in chronological order
200mtrs
N
MANAMA
SHAIKH MOHAMMED AVENUE
ZUBARA AVENUE
PALACE AVENUE
Abdul Rahman Al Dakhel Elementary School for Boys
Manama Boys Secondary School
Al Qudaibiya Boys Intermediate School
BANI OTBAH AVE
East Riffa Elementary School for Boys
RIFFA
MANAMA
RIFFA
BAHRAIN
BUSAITEEN
MANAMA
AHRAIN

Moving from house to house within the confines of a relatively small city gave me a feeling of real instability. For many reasons, I developed the feeling of having to be ready to move at any moment. But every move, every new place, was a new adventure, and this attitude has made me adaptable, able to be packed and ready in 15 minutes and on my way to catch a plane. I learned to cope with whatever was thrown at me. Well, almost anything.

WINDS OF CHANGE

The late 1960s were a restless time for Bahrain and I could smell the winds of change. Protesters from the Popular Front for the Liberation of Bahrain and others took to the streets and were tear gassed by the British as they chanted for independence for their small island state. By the age of 10, I tasted the tears of protest while running with others. Strikes and riots took place and workers were laid off not far from the protected streets of my family compound. I understood from an early age that voices of dissent could indeed bring positive change and I felt great pride when, because of the will of the people, a United Nations referendum declared Bahrain an independent state in 1971.

My earliest concept of justice and the rule of law came from watching *The Lone Ranger*, featuring the masked hero who fought for the underdog and took justice into his own hands along with his Native American friend, Tonto. The Lone Ranger never took revenge or killed any of the bad guys he captured. He turned them in to the sheriff to receive their judgment and believed in due process and the rule of law to find justice.

CHAPTER 4

EMPATHETIC

"Dry your eyes, baby; it's out of character."

– T.R. Devlin, played by Cary Grant

Notorious (1946)

I first watched Hitchcock's Notorious dubbed in Arabic with my parents. My mother loved Ingrid Bergman. Years later in Geneva, when my mother visited, I translated the entire movie as we watched in English. She passed away six months later.

We experience moments that align our priorities forever.

MY MOTHER

One day when my mother was 14 years old and playing outside with her friends, she was called inside and found all her belongings packed in bags so she could be taken to marry a man she had never met. Women had no options to work outside the home or to get further education. Their only education was to learn extracts from the *Quran* by heart.

Against all odds, my paternal grandmother and my mother were very good at arithmetic. They were faster and better at numbers than their husbands, which I think explains why I was always better at numbers than words. My grandmother and my mother taught me how to add, subtract, multiply, divide, calculate squares – in essence, to do basic arithmetic. My mother would sit with me for hours, teaching me to add and subtract until I was fluent with numbers.

The women of my young life shaped me. I believe I became a fighter and a person who stands up for himself because of my mother. She was different from my maternal grandmother, who was passive and kept quiet when others were speaking. She had borne trauma and mistreatment most of her life, yet she was kind and loving. She never stood up to a fight and instead took the brunt of whatever the men in her life dished out or told her to do. My mother, on the other hand, was someone who, if slapped once, would slap back twice. If she did not agree with someone or felt an injustice had occurred, she would speak up and fight for her opinion or way of doing things. If she believed in something she would go for it. She was a passionate person who fought with my father and her family if she felt she needed to be heard. It is therefore in my DNA to fight for what I believe and to speak up.

I am grateful for the fighter in my mother. When she was only 30, health problems took over her life and she was forced to manage diabetes and all the heart problems and paralysis that came with her ailments. Her strong will and passion served her well during the 37 years she suffered from the poor health that led to her death at the early age of 67.

I was greatly affected when my father left Bahrain to work in Dubai in 1969. Dubai was one of the seven Emirates that formed the United Arab Emirates (UAE) in 1971 and 1972. Those six Emirates – Abu Dhabi, Sharjah, Ajman, Umm Al Quwain, Fujairah, and Ras Al Khaimah – in addition to Dubai, were part of the British protectorates, as were Oman, Qatar, and Bahrain. "British protectorate" was a nonsensical term, as the British protected us from nothing but our own freedoms. As I already mentioned, when my father left for Dubai in 1969, my mother and the four siblings my parents had after me followed him later that year, while I stayed in Bahrain with my maternal grandparents.

THE RECKONING

When I was 13, my parents unexpectedly returned from Dubai. It was August 1971, and my mother returned because she was pregnant and intended to give birth in Bahrain and then return to Dubai with my father for his work. On September 9th, the obstetrician we knew as Doctor Metuse came to our house to deliver the baby.

When my mother's bleeding became intense, the doctor rushed her to the hospital. She was not yet 30 and about to have her sixth child. I and my father, maternal grandparents, and my mother's paternal uncle went to the hospital with her where the German doctor (his name was Dr. Departau, if I remember correctly) announced that he needed to operate to stop the bleeding. We all waited, sitting just outside the operating room. This was a terrible, frightening situation for a young boy. My mother was suffering, and my immediate family was standing by, the first time any of them had ever been to a hospital for an operation. My mother was in surgery for four hours. The family was very scared, remembering that her cousin had died from the same bleeding during childbirth several years earlier. I huddled next to my father and grandfather. My grandmother sat by the door, hysterical that the operation was lasting for what seemed like ages. I was overwhelmed, blaming myself for all the mistakes I had made in my life and filled with self-recrimination. My grandmother was feeling her own waves of guilt, regretting that she had forced her daughter to marry at the age of 14. She wailed at my grandfather, telling him that he was also responsible for many of their other bad decisions. This was the first time I saw my grandfather cry.

Suddenly, blood poured from under the door to the operating room. There was much blood, a shocking sight I have never forgotten. Most of us at the time had never been brought up to see these things, but I had seen things like this in the many movies and television shows I had seen by that time. I was an expert on script thinking and storytelling and watching. I'd seen this kind of tragedy before, perhaps in a Bollywood movie, or an Arab movie, or an American movie, and now I made the connection between those scenes and what I saw now and realized the inevitable outcome of the story. It suddenly hit me that my mother was gone.

This was a huge moment for me, and it significantly shaped my character as I saw the blood rushing out into the waiting room, and the nurses running in with more blood to replace the blood she was losing. Those four hours were an impossible experience, and I am certain everyone in Bahrain's main hospital could hear my grandmother's sobbing. My grandfather also cried, wracked by the guilt my grandmother was heaping on him. I felt great sympathy for my father, sitting there dazed, wondering how to cope with his wife as she struggled between life and death.

The only person who seemed sane was my great-uncle, who

attempted to calm the others. As a Sufi would do, he took this all in stride, as he believed in accepting whatever God wanted, wishing for the best no matter what God does. Now that I'm getting older, I tend to forget things, but this is one experience I will never forget, blood flowing from under the door before our eyes. Neither will I forget the faces of my grandmother and grandfather as they wept.

After four tortuous hours, the German doctor came out and, like a movie script with a happy ending, said, "It was tough, but a healthy son is born. She has lost a lot of blood and must stay under observation in the intensive care unit for the next 72 hours. We will go from there, but she can never give birth again."

The doctor's words, that she was okay, were wonderful to hear, but the true music to my ears was knowing she would never give birth again. She had suffered so much, and I did not want to see her face the same fate as her cousin who had died during the birth of her sixth child. In 1971, in our part of the world, the health system, especially for women, was very different from the system we have currently. Today, doctors can spot pregnancy complications several months in advance and avoid many catastrophes. My parents were lucky to have come back to Bahrain for this last birth.

I did not see my mother again for 72 hours. Then four days

after the birth, the first thing she said to me was that she wanted toothpaste and a toothbrush. I was very relieved that she was herself again and did not leave her side for many days. I was also very happy at that point that they decided to stay in Bahrain. This event changed the course of my own life in many ways. I placed myself in the role of my mother's caregiver because I saw that my siblings were too young to take this on. I see my youngest sibling as more of a son than a brother because of the 13-year difference between us.

The experience with my mother has informed the way I have dealt with people throughout my life. I have tried to keep in mind that everyone has a story of loss or pain.

CHAPTER 5

OPEN-MINDED

"May God bless you with a deep heart, Beirut."

– Oum Walid, played by Leila Karam

West Beirut (1998)

The movie, West Beirut, brings back sad memories, but also gives hope. My idealism bloomed in Beirut until the war started and I had to leave.

SECONDARY SCHOOL

When I was growing up in Bahrain, we did not have the distinction that exists in Britain between grammar and comprehensive schools. Everyone went to secondary school. When I was in secondary school, top students were put in a separate class where they had access to the best teachers and advanced lessons. I excelled at mathematics and sciences and was therefore among those top students.

The class was comprised mostly of Bahraini students, with a few Egyptians (including the sons of an Egyptian ambassador) and Palestinians. During the first year, two teachers made a lasting impression on me. The first was the calculus teacher, a Coptic Egyptian called Morries. He was good at recognizing a student's potential, building on it, and encouraging them to love the subject. I certainly excelled in the course due to the way he conducted his classes.

In contrast, the second teacher was the Arabic language and literature teacher, named Wajih, who was Palestinian. He took an instant dislike to me (perhaps because I spoke *Holi* Farsi with other students outside the class). He used corporal punishment, slapping students with a heavy hand. I was his prime target. The second time he slapped me, I complained to the school supervisor (a well-known Bahraini sculptor). He said the teacher was wrong, and that I had two choices. I could slap him back and be expelled from school, or I could accept being slapped and take it on the chin until the end of the year. He nodded his head as if to say, "There's no way out." The next time the teacher slapped me, I gave him my usual smile, which enraged him further and I received two additional slaps.

I assume he then realized that I was playing with him, as that was the last time he hit me. I suppose this conflict resolution technique – putting yourself in the shoes of the person you have a conflict with – came to me by natural instinct. Nevertheless, this teacher must take a lot of blame for my hatred of beautiful Arabic literature.

"A GOOD MUSTACHE MAKES A MAN FOR MANY REASONS."[5]

As I grew up, my language skills left much to be desired, be it in Arabic or English. During my final year of secondary school, my English teacher, who was Scottish, gave up on me. We had an informal pact: I could do whatever I wished during his class time provided I did not attend his lessons. That year, however, my Arabic teacher, who came from Egypt, would get angry with me instead. One day, his exasperation reached a peak and he declared, "I swear, if you pass the final exam, I will shave my mustache." Mustaches were a big deal back then and a matter of pride for many Arab men.

I passed the English exam, obtaining the minimum passing grade – I suspect the examination board did me a favor on

---

[5] A quote attributed to singer John Oates, an American musician best known as half of the rock and soul duo Hall & Oates, with Daryl Hall.

that one; it would have been difficult to fail me with such high marks in other topics. That was not surprising. What came as a shock, however, was my Arabic grade. I ranked among the top five Bahraini students nationwide in the subject. I was very surprised, but nonetheless decided to act so my Arabic teacher would follow through on his pledge.

Because I performed so well, my dad gave me a small allowance to congratulate me. For my first purchase, I went to a small convenience store and bought shaving cream and blades and then went to the teachers' room. He was sitting with the other teachers and asked me what I was doing. I answered that I did not want to waste his money and gave him the cream and blades.

On the next day, I happened to see him. He had shaved his mustache. He had kept his word.

A TEENAGER IN LEBANON – A UTOPIAN DREAM INTERRUPTED

I saw multiple-choice exam questions and computer punch cards for the first time when I took my English language college entrance exam. I had three hours to complete 200 questions. It took me 10 minutes to figure out the first two answers. I moved to a more efficient system – or so it seemed at that time. I analyzed the number of possible answers, flipped a coin I had in my pocket to see if it would show heads or tails when it landed, and filled in the answers accordingly; the hand of fate was on my side, as if all my luck was meant to be. To guess the correct answers, I had created patterns and applied them to choosing my responses. I completed the test on that basis without ever expecting to score so high that I would be accepted to the American University in Beirut (AUB) in Lebanon.

Three days after receiving the test results, I got a call to meet the Director of Scholarships at the Ministry of Education of Bahrain. A family friend, he congratulated me on passing the entrance exam. I thought he was joking. He insisted, saying that I received one of the highest marks. It would only take a few weeks before my surprisingly high performance would be revealed as pure coincidence, when I actually moved to Beirut.

A few days later, the top candidates from Bahrain, about 15 of us, were called to the office of the minister of education. We crowded into his office where he congratulated us on our paid scholarships to the top university in the region. Bahrain had no university at the time, so we had to travel outside the country to attend higher education, which was paid for by the ministry of education. The minister wished us well and then cautioned, “Remember, you are going there to study. You will be exposed to many ideas and influences that will deter you from studying and push you to think outside the box, so only think about studying."

His words were a turning point for me. I was incredulous. This was the first thing he told us, and I immediately felt myself irrevocably adjusting my outlook on life as I processed his words. Here was a guy telling us to go outside to simply study, without being deterred by political ideas or outside influences. Of course, we were bound to embrace the chance for free expression and would naturally return home with changed ideas. But we were being told not to be open to other points of view and not to think freely or get distracted.

For my finally-free, 16-year-old spirit, this was too much; I wanted to learn as much as possible about dissenting and opposing points of view and to soak up as much knowledge and culture as I could that was "outside the box." The idea of studying only to return home to fit in and conform was not on my horizon.

FIRST DAY OF INTELLECTUAL FREEDOM

I landed in Lebanon during Ramadan. I missed my mother's cooking, her *Iftar* meals with *harees,*[6] Bahraini rangeena,

---

[6] Not to be confused with the spicy Tunisian harissa. *Harees* is a dish made of cracked wheat and meat.

a special date dessert, and the best crème caramel I have tasted to date, uniquely flavored with saffron, cardamom, and pistachios. However, the Lebanese cuisine helped me overcome my homesickness. I remember breaking fast on my first day with *shorbat adas*, a lentil soup, and Tabasco, which I tasted for the first time and have loved ever since.

On the next day, like all other incoming students, I attended orientation week. Unlike other students, my English was so poor that I barely understood anything. The staff at AUB quickly discovered that my high test score was just luck. Mr. Abood, who oversaw orientation, even asked me if I was truly the person who had sat down to take the entrance exam. He laughed when he learned it was all about patterns and probability.

He put me in a special English program where I spent more hours than the others learning the language. At the time, AUB used a relatively innovative language technique, in a music lab, where students were immersed in songs. I would spend three hours a day listening to music with English lyrics and singing along. My favorite songs were Don McLean's *American Pie*, John Denver's *Take Me Home, Country Roads*, Cat Stevens' *Morning Has Broken*, Demis Roussos' *Goodbye, My Love, Goodbye*, and Lobo's *Me and You and a Dog Named Boo*.

In the 1970s, the Bahraini student movement was very

well-known, and the members of the Bahraini Students Union's Beirut branch were known for their revolutionary ideas; leftist and socialist, the mindset at the time was to believe that there must always be room for freedom of expression, debate, and discussion. About 100 students from AUB and Beirut Arab University (BAU) were part of the student union. They rented a cheap apartment off campus where they could gather to talk, play ping-pong, eat hot dogs, and relax. It was an eye-opening introduction to life outside of Bahrain. The apartment had a big living room and five rooms, with plenty of space for students to gather for lively, thought-provoking talks and discussions.

Many of those who had presented themselves as revolutionary at that time later became ministers and high-ranking officials, and totally forgot their revolutionary mindset. Many fell back into the self-preserving mentality of conformity when they returned to Bahrain and were more concerned with finding and keeping their place in the hierarchy than with looking at the good for all. I don't fault them for that and was grateful for their examination of justice and the concept of all for one and one for all.

THE END OF AN ERA

I fell in love with Lebanon and am forever grateful for the chance I had to experience a cultural and intellectual awakening in my short time at AUB. I was immersed in movies and music. The Lebanese diva Nouhad Wadie' Haddad, better known as Fairuz, then appeared in a musical, *Mais El Reem*, which I saw six times.

Everything changed in September 1975 with the beginning of the civil war. Many of my Bahraini peers went to the United States to study in Texas. My mother, who rarely interfered with my choices, strictly forbade me from going to Texas. She felt in her heart that if I left for the US, I would not return, and I think she was right. I went back home to Bahrain to plot my next move and apply to colleges in England. I was 17 and thought of those next six months as a mini vacation despite the entrance exams and applications ahead of me.

CHAPTER 6

PRAGMATIC

"You just cannot believe, Ben, how loveable the whole damn thing was. All summer long, we were together."
– Staff Sergeant Raymond Shaw, played by Laurence Harvey

The Manchurian Candidate (1962) – (well, actually in my case, the Mancunian Candidate)

My pragmatism introduced itself to me when I arrived in Manchester.

A TEENAGER IN MANCHESTER

I landed in Manchester and was profoundly shocked. The weather, the food, the architecture were all dull and so different from what I had loved in Beirut. It took me a little while to change my mind.

I loved Beirut so much that I tweaked the expression "Paris

of the East" and called Paris, where I stopped on my way to Manchester, the "Beirut of the West." My aunt accompanied me to Manchester to take an English language course. Upon arrival, we were greeted by my uncle, who was also studying at the University of Manchester and learning classical music.

He informed us that his music teacher, whose husband was Mexican, had invited us for dinner. He warned us not to eat before dinner because he expected our hostess to have prepared a Mexican feast. They served a beautiful, spicy soup, and then the main course arrived in a huge foil-covered dish. When they unveiled it, it was a pig's head. I felt sorry for our hosts. At the time, no 24/7 food delivery service existed. So they went to the closest Chinese restaurant to get takeout.

Some of the luck that got me into university in Lebanon stayed with me and got me into the University of Manchester. I was just about to turn 17 and was eligible until I turned 18 for free tuition as well as room and board. I could even ride the bus in Manchester or get healthcare free of charge. Everything was paid for by the local council. I was amazed by the level of public service, although I could not help but think that they were probably this rich because of the money they had taken from so many countries over the years. It was a sort of payback to provide so much in return.

I had to take the A-level exams and compete for a place in the program after the first year. The Greater Manchester County Council was clearly labor dominated at the time, and it was easier to get my tuition and expenses covered. That all changed under Margaret Thatcher in the 80s and I had to find a way to pay for my second year of university. The University of Manchester was my fifth and last choice of schools. I didn't much like the place when I arrived but found it interesting to see the impact of the social fabric on politics and vice versa. As much as I did not appreciate leaving Beirut and moving to Manchester, I did see how lucky I was and reminded myself that this was in fact where the Industrial Revolution had started.

I had planned to study electrical engineering and noticed that Manchester was the first to offer double majors at the time. This was a new option in the United Kingdom in the 70s. The choices were computer science and mathematics, computer science and economics, computer science and accounting. I knew I didn't like the word "economics" and I knew I loved math. I knew nothing about computers but I thought I might as well try something different. Some of my top choices required more A-level scores. Manchester happened to be the first university in the UK in the 1950s to offer computer science as a course of study. I did not have great insight into what my interests were or what computer science was about; I was going to the University of Manchester because it was easier to get in with one A-level exam. It was my luck. And I was prepared to hang on to that luck and see where it would take me.

FUN AT UNIVERSITY

I was also lucky to have fun roommates to spend time with when we weren't studying. We had plenty of time for being young and stupid. One of my buddies at that time was Ben Elton, who later became a well-known comedian, actor, author, playwright, lyricist, and director. He was a part of the London alternative comedy movement of the 1980s, became a writer of the sitcoms *The Young Ones* and *Blackadder*, and was a stand-up comedian on stage and television. We appreciated each other's sarcasm and wit. He was studying drama and I went to see the plays that he directed, wrote, or produced while we were in school.

Ben and I were part of a group of 10 who shared a corridor on the same floor in the Grosvenor House dorm. We also shared the kitchen, bathroom, and toilets in our hallway. It was a mixed dorm with young women occupying the adjacent hall, and Ben was my next-door neighbor. We went clubbing every night and had fun late-night escapades. We regularly had lunch at "On the 8th Day", a vegetarian restaurant. I still remember its whole wheat apple crumble, served with a cashew nut sauce. For my birthday, Ben gave me a copy of the great comedy writer Spike Milligan's very sarcastic book, *Adolf Hitler: My Part in His Downfall*, published in 1971. Spike Milligan was known to all at the time as the brilliant stand-up comedian, TV personality, and writer of *The Goon Show* on the BBC. Ben told me he saw me as more of a comedian than himself and, although I knew this was far from the truth, it gave me the confidence to express humor in English and across different cultures.

Ben and my buddies at the time were an important part of my education, whether I was learning to express myself through sarcastic, subversive humor or gaining the confidence to speak with girls. I got a part-time job as a bartender, which I also credit as being a key part of my education. Even though I was the server, I gained the confidence to converse and entertain with my sarcasm and knowledge. I made sure to follow the TV series *Coronation Street*, which took place in Manchester, and *Crossroads*, which was based in the Midlands. That gave me endless conversation material to chat up girls at the bar and make their husbands and boyfriends happy, as they all had a good time. This helped me raise money from tips, which I desperately needed. I also used my sarcasm and humor to connect with others that made me feel less of an outsider, even though I was clearly a foreign student.

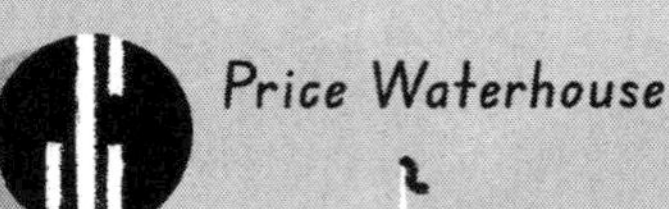

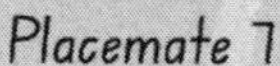

MY UNIVERSITY & EARLY PRICE WATERHOUSE DAYS IN MANCHESTER (1975-1986)

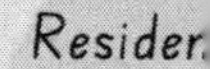

Plaza

svenor House
udent Halls

urn Building

University of Manchester

FALLOWFIELD

Residence 1

BODDINGTONS
on Pub

ALLEY
ANGE
WITHINGTON

Residence 4
Old Landsdowne Rd
Residence 5

Broughton Park F.C.
(Rugby Union)

Residence 6

Didsbury Lawn
Tennis Club

ON-
RDY

I enjoyed the freedom of staying out until dawn with my buddies, drinking beer and listening to bands at dark basement parties. We were regulars at the *Auto Club* and the *Continental Club*, then called the *New Conti*. This was a kind of hanging-out that I had not experienced in Bahrain or Lebanon. I remember one night at around 3:00 am, we came upon a loose parking meter, which, in our youthful foolishness, we somehow yanked out of the ground. In our drunkenness, we took it to our dormitory. Had we been caught, we would have gone to jail. We managed to cover it with our coats and took it back to our dorm where we were greatly amused by our treasure. It ended up in the room of a guy named Jason, who was a splendid guitarist. Another time, as we didn't want the meter to be lonely, we took a traffic light – in fact the red, green and yellow lights within it. We were young and free and allowed ourselves to do stupid things.

We were late-night regulars, or should I say early-morning customers, at the Plaza Café, a legendary Somali restaurant that remained open until 4:00 am, run by a man named Charlie Ali. The chicken biryani with chili was a life-or-death proposition that we somehow managed to survive despite our drunken foolishness and bravado. We competed to see who could finish the chicken and rice with red chili-infused oil that was served in a big pile on an oval platter. I was a regular from 1976 to 1980, always there with my buddies at 2:00 am and we were the last ones out at closing time.

While in Manchester, I had stayed in touch with the Bahraini student Union and went to London to attend the meetings. In the 1970s, it was usually a joint meeting with other groups, including the Kuwaiti students. The long-weekend gatherings were fun, with singers brought in from the Gulf as well as food and other treats from home. It wasn't always in London, as events took place in Maidenhead and Bristol as well. I attended these joint events for three years in addition to participating in our own Bahraini student meetings. At one point, I was elected to the planning committee.

I went back and forth to London for these committee meetings and enjoyed the train ride from Piccadilly Station in Manchester to Euston Station in London, two stations that are very close to my heart. I had a personal ritual of stopping at Foyles bookstore. I would get out at Euston Station and go into the underground, on the Northern Line going to Tottenham Court Road, which was only one or two stops away. I loved sitting in Foyles for hours and reading the books on cinema. I was always surprised that they let me sit there for hours, browsing the books. I felt I knew something about movies because I had seen so many, but the more I read about cinematography, scriptwriting, and production, the more I realized how little I really knew. I made it my mission to sit and absorb as much knowledge as I could in this sacred spot far from campus and far from math or computers; it was a world of magic to me.

Later, I would perch in my bed late at night studying actuarial math, statistics, and accounting standards, wearing my *dishdasha* like pajamas for comfort. As I burned the proverbial midnight oil, I put rose water on my palms and splashed it in my hair, and kept some in the kitchen to put on my fruit salad along with orange water; these cultural habits were a connection to my roots. Eventually I left the dormitory and stayed in an apartment by myself before graduating.

BOMBAY INTERLUDE

I went back to Bahrain for the summer holiday in 1976. My father was unwell and, in those days, people who needed to see a medical specialist would travel to Egypt or India. My father scheduled an appointment in Bombay (now Mumbai) and asked me to go with him, promising to make it worthwhile. Our trip was due to last two weeks. Unlike me, my father had a gift for languages and, in addition to Arabic, spoke Urdu and Persian fluently. He had many Indian friends who facilitated our trip.

Although, by then, my father had never been to the movies, he knew how much I loved them, especially Bollywood movies. In Bombay, I took him to the cinema for the first time. We saw *Sholay*, which I had already seen in Bahrain. We also saw *Amar Akbar Anthony*, a tale of three brothers.

While we were there, my father organized a surprise excursion through one of his friends. We drove to a beautiful house on the outskirts of town to a party organized by another friend. There, I met Ashok Kumar, the iconic Bollywood star. We engaged in a long and passionate conversation. I enjoyed myself very much and received a full education in Bollywood culture. Ashok was an entertainer. He told us that he had always wanted to be a singer while his brother, Kishore, had wanted to be an actor. Fate is curious, because Ashok became the famous actor, and Kishore, the famous singer. We left the party after five hours, as my father thought we had overstayed our welcome. I could have stayed much longer.

NEW NAME, NEW ME?

It was also around this time in the late 70s that I changed my name from Khalid Yusuf Abdullah Janahi to Khalid Yusuf Abdulla-Janahi. I dropped the letter "h" in Abdullah and added a hyphen. My father was not pleased that I changed my last name. But I feel honored to carry his name, Yusuf, as my middle name. I changed my name because a number of people were named Khalid Janahi, one of whom was also in Manchester. The name change was quickly used in publications and became my official name going forward.

CHAPTER 7

LISTENER

"It's like I was playing some kind of game, but the rules don't make any sense to me. They're being made up by all the wrong people. I mean no one makes them up. They seem to make themselves up."
– Ben Braddock, played by Dustin Hoffman

The Graduate (1967 version)

My return to Manama was a turning point: from then on, I accepted that my choices would always keep me outside of any inner circle.

TORN BETWEEN TWO LOVERS

A lot had shifted for my generation in 1979 around the time of the revolution in Iran. There was enthusiasm to fight for the causes of our time, including the Palestinian cause. Hopes were quashed, first in Bahrain, where there had been hope of reforms and change, since we were no longer a British protectorate, but it became clear that not being a colony was not going to change things for the better for the younger generation. The Iranian Revolution created an excuse for the regimes in the Arab world to deviate from readily reforming.

I had felt great hope for the revolution in Iran. I had visited the country many times and seen its beautiful city, Shiraz, and the beauty of the landscape, but I had also observed that this was a rich country with very poor people. In my youthful idealism, I had hoped the revolution would improve the Iranians' quality of life. Students like me wanted to see some inequality pushed out. Iranian students pushing for change, whether inside or outside, were not communists, but they did look to the ideals of socialism, communism, and equality for all as the basis for all change. Some people were calling these young people communists simply because the regime in Iran was protected by the Americans and the CIA that had kept the Shah in power. This mistrust of the British and the Americans is still felt all over the Middle East today.

I was hopeful that the revolution would bring equality to the people and would pull people from the bottom upwards, allowing them to enjoy equal opportunity with everybody else. That was very much the hope of many but, in 1979, things quickly changed when Iran became a theocracy, the repressive form of government still in place there today. It was a great disappointment to people in the region, the place where the Sunni–Shia divide took hold to separate the masses. Sunnis and Shiites had been living peacefully side by side in Lebanon and other places for years, but this political and theocratic divide changed everything.

From the start of the Iran–Iraq war in September 1980, when people asked my opinion about the opponents and the war, I told them the war was emotional for me and made me think of the Mary MacGregor song from 1976, *Torn Between Two Lovers.* I believed the situation should not be framed as a conflict between Ruhollah Khomeini and Saddam Hussein but instead should be a people-to-people, country-to-country situation. I have blood in me from both sides. I was torn between two lovers, between Iraq and Iran, because it was a useless war. It was a war for which we are still paying the price today.

THE SOUQ

When my maternal grandfather followed his brothers to Bahrain, they settled in Manama, in the neighborhood where the British Embassy and old palace had been.

After three or four years, my grandfather and his two brothers started a business to import shirts, shoes, and jeans to Bahrain and export clothing to Iran and Iraq. Manama was at that time a kind of modern free zone and my grandfather and great-uncles not only built their import and export business but opened three tailor shops, with one branch for each brother.

The first of these shops was in the *souq*. The *souq* was then about four times bigger than a midsize shopping mall. People lived near the *souq,* and it was an integral part of our lives. Our families and friends lived within walking distance of each other. My grandfather never liked cars and from the age of 10 upwards, when we all lived in the same area, we walked about half an hour to the *souq*. My grandfather would walk four times a day, going to prayer in the morning, coming back at lunchtime, returning at 3:00 pm and coming home again by 7:00 pm. He prayed five times a day, going early on Friday mornings to the mosque. That was the norm at the time, and all three brothers lived in the same big house. I think my grandfather wore *thobes* for comfort when praying five times a day. It's possible to always wear the same color, and have 10 of them washed – easy, simple, and ready to go.

I was certainly influenced by my uncle's offerings of Western clothing, and my mother, for someone with very little education, was very westernized and insisted that we wear Western clothes. I seldom wore a *thobe*, putting one on only when I went to the mosque with my grandfather for Friday prayers. As a boy, the only reason I went was because I needed the money to pay for my cinema forays. I felt I had to make him happy, and I also wanted to get spending money from my grandmother. They were not aware of my sneaking out to the movies until later, when my grandfather discovered this fact and laughed, saying, "So now I understand; I am a sinner and have taken responsibility for your sins!" I replied, with my own dose of sarcasm, "Well, at least you've gotten it off your chest and may God forgive you for that."

THE BRIEF RETURN

After graduating from the University of Manchester, I finally returned to Manama for a quick visit in 1980. Life had changed. My family and friends were familiar to me but it was a shock to see how much Bahrain as a whole had changed. There were more "haves" and "have-nots". In addition, the distinction between Sunnis and Shiites became mainstream in the public discourse.

GOING BACKWARDS

I noticed other changes that were a culture shock for me. When I left in 1974 there were more girls without hijabs than with them and by 1980 there were many more girls wearing them. Even our three most important Muslim holidays had shifted. Growing up in the 1960s I looked forward to Eid al-Fitr, marking the end of Ramadan, Eid al-Aldah, The Feast of the Sacrifice and the

Prophet's birthday, Mawlid al-Nabi. But when I returned there had been a backlash, and the hymns that men sang in the mosque, hymns of joy for the birth of their prophet, were now considered a heretical act. I had been moved by the men singing these hymns of praise and appreciation and was sad to learn that was now a ritual of the past.

AN OFFER I COULD REFUSE

When I finished university, Bahrain was a booming banking center, having replaced war-torn Beirut as the financial capital of the Middle East. I had two options: working in banking, or working for the government or a government agency. At the time, only one qualified Bahraini chartered accountant from England and Wales existed there. I could have accepted one of the several phenomenally large salaries I was offered and launch myself on the road to enormous wealth. Instead, I chose not to try to fit into that system.

I had seen peers jump at one of those two choices, many with less education and training than I had, and they had found it hard to move anywhere else. Like my father before me, I decided at a young age that having less wealth while keeping my dignity and being my own boss was the right choice for me. What I earned was from my own hard work. After returning from

Manchester and walking through the *souq*, I could feel a crack in the old ways. I returned to the UK at the end of 1980 and did not return to Bahrain until 1987 when my father came to get me in London.

THE ABSENCE OF MERIT

Upon my return to Bahrain in 1980 and later in Jeddah in 1982, I was offered comfortable jobs and financial security. But it seemed to me that surely a guy with an international degree from a prestigious university should be able to land the same job as a guy without the intellectual capacity of his well-educated peers but who was favored by the system. The latter had no room for the ambition to learn more and move up with experience and accomplishment.

Many young people, once offered this comfortable alternative, are then unwilling to rise up the hierarchy normally; in the region and in the Arab world as a whole (perhaps with exceptions in certain places), they are not born into a meritocracy. They do not accept to go through the process because they see that their peers and others who do not have the brainpower are suddenly running the show. They see that often others move ahead due to nepotism, meaning they've climbed up the ladder simply because they are a son or daughter of someone in the hierarchy. They see that someone from the "haves" is clearly showing them that they are from the "have-nots." So they ask themselves, "Wait a second, why am I wasting my time? I can go and work in the government and I'll be paid twice as much. And I won't have to do anything; I can just sit back because I will never be a boss and they will never allow me to be a boss."

I saw many young people who did not want to take the harder option in a meritocracy. If I had stayed in Bahrain, I could have reached the top position in a bank much faster and would soon have earned $2 million a year. I could have started at an annual salary of $250,000 or $300,000. I chose not to. One of my peers who did not have a college education worked in a bank; by the time I returned in 1987, this guy was top management and was secure in his position as a well-paid "yes-man" for the bank.

Many years later, I even saw that many of my peers were now on the Shura Council and held other prestigious positions requiring a lifetime commitment to this conformist system. They had to stay satisfied and toe the line. Many of my peers accepted this conformity and it worked for them. They settled into a life where they were accepted and agreed to the terms of this one-sided social contract.

Instead, I decided to train with Price Waterhouse in Manchester as a chartered accountant.

CHAPTER 8

DRIVEN

"When a man's got money in his pocket,

he begins to appreciate peace."

– The Man with No Name, played by Clint Eastwood

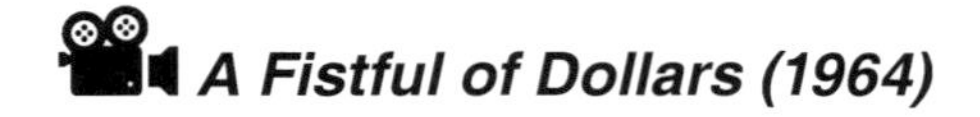

A Fistful of Dollars (1964)

Life changes when one gets their first job and their first real salary.

CARRYING HOT COFFEE UP THE LADDER

I was the only non-white person in the Manchester office during my first two years at Price Waterhouse. Other brown people worked in the London office, but not in Manchester until my third year there. Margaret Thatcher had come into power, and a recession had led to many liquidations. The economy was restructuring, and the many liquidations kept us working at all hours to serve clients.

The first three years of a chartered accountant's life in any firm is very challenging. When I started out in the UK at Price Waterhouse, I had to train and study at the same time. At that point, I was also the guy making coffee, not because people looked down on me, but because I was the cheapest in terms of charging the client. My time was less valuable, so I did the grunt work. When the team was assembled in a room, whether four or 10 individuals, I was the guy running around and doing the printing or copying, because from a client service perspective, I was the cheapest. The employee either understands this at the outset and then works their way up the ladder, or rejects this, in which case they will not survive.

I believed that, in this business, I would get only one chance to climb the ladder. Whether someone is a consultant, an accountant, or a lawyer, things don't happen by saying, "I am who I am and so I should be at the top." It's only possible to get to the top by proving you deserve to be there. Around my second or third year at Price Waterhouse, a partner and an investment banker both advised me to go into investment banking because I seemed like a deal maker and connector. Another partner told me he would retire at age 52. I kept this in my mind as an aspiration. I wanted to become a partner as soon as possible and aim for this early retirement. In reality, I moved into deal making 15 years later and did not stop working until I was 58, six years behind schedule.

Despite my place as a junior accountant, I learned from the senior partners how to act with grace and humility. One evening during a particularly stressful project, I was asked to go to the lobby to get Charles Godwin, a senior partner in the Manchester firm, and bring him to the audit room. Eight of us up on the fifth floor were crunching toward a very big client's final audit. The senior partner was in charge of that audit and would be the final sign-off to clear the audit.

I went to the lobby and watched as people exited the lift, expecting the senior partner to flag me down. Several women came out of the elevator as well as a smallish older man with a briefcase. I told myself that this man could not be the senior partner Charles Godwin, although I had never met him and didn't know what he looked like. I waited for the lift to return several times, but nobody else came out, so I walked to him and asked him, "Excuse me, are you Mr. Charles Godwin?" He replied, "Yes, I am," and I said, "I'm sorry, my name is Khalid Abdulla-Janahi." He looked at me with kind eyes and said, "Yes, I know." It was an interesting moment for me; I learned how this man, although he knew me by name, had stood quietly and patiently until I addressed him. I didn't know his face, but since he knew my name and that it was an Arab name, it was easy for him to assume, since I was the only brown person there, that I was Khalid. But he didn't wish to act on such an assumption. He was kind and gracious and did not wish to make me feel bad in any way. I learned a lot from that moment of the importance of being gracious.

TRAINING ON THE JOB

Although I did not return to Bahrain for seven years, two years into my training, I did return to the Middle East in 1982 for a two-month Price Waterhouse assignment in Jeddah, Saudi Arabia. I was brought in as a junior auditor because I was the only Arabic-speaking one in the UK at the time. Our client was a bank and they needed somebody who spoke the language. That trip turned out to be one of the best things that happened to me in terms of being recognized for my skills and knowledge going forward.

The streets of Al Balad, the 7th-century part of Jeddah with its narrow lanes, tucked away but close to the sea, reminded me of home. In Jeddah, I expected life in the *souq* to be much the way it had been in Manama before I had left home. But I could feel, as I walked through the Jeddah *souq*, that the carefree and relaxed atmosphere I had experienced in the *souq* of my boyhood had shifted to a more commercial and businesslike activity. People were rushing here and there, not stopping like in the old days to chat and say hello. The young men were now wearing suits and serious faces as they met to hustle and sell their wares.

Everyone at the Jeddah bank assumed I was an Iraqi. I was dressed in Western clothes and my slight Iraqi accent was like a red flag – it was clear that people were generally not fond of Iraqis then. Everyone was negative and nobody was helpful. By the second week, when everyone at the bank where I was working learned I was a Bahraini, they became supportive. Some of them asked me why I didn't wear the local *dishdasha* like they did. For them, it was an important symbol and it seemed like a slight insult to them that I was not wearing it. For me, what I wear is an individual choice; it can be a political choice, an outward symbol of individuality and freedom of expression.

On that occasion, I met young people from the Gulf who were looking to return to Bahrain for a high-ranking job with limited to no accountability. Many who studied abroad just wanted to go back to the Gulf to be a boss. They wanted to sit at the table and tell others what to do. They didn't want to be bothered with the challenges of working hard and competing to rise up the ladder.

COMPOST CORNER

Two others were in training with me at the time, and we were studying and working simultaneously. We sat together in one corner of the room and called ourselves the "Compost Corner." We probably didn't make up the name, but we adopted it. What we all three had in common was that we were not very successful with our studies but we were good at the work. Ultimately, two of us became partners in the firm, many years later, and the third had a very successful career in the United States. We still have reunions for the people who joined our cohort and still call ourselves the "Compost Corner and friends." We just had our 40th reunion, although it was delayed for two years because of COVID-19.

HIERARCHY

I had to deal with a hierarchy at Price Waterhouse to achieve the level I reached, but at least I could see that hierarchy. I saw in black and white how things were arranged for us, and I could see that we had all started out as equals. The hierarchy at Price Waterhouse in the UK was fairly transparent, and we understood that we had to compete. Our success depended on how hard we worked and our level of excellence as we climbed the ladder and competed with each other.

As I worked hard and made my way up the ladder to become a partner at the firm, I looked at how I might change the mindset of the young people where I came from so they could accept that they, too, had to go through the same process to get ahead.

THE LONG RETURN

The first phase of my career ended suddenly when my father came to London on a cold evening in January 1987. Always elegant and dashing, dressed in an overcoat over Western clothing, he spoke to me quietly and firmly, “There is a reason you must come home now: your mother is not well.” It was time to return.

About four months later, after making arrangements at my job, I returned to Bahrain to care for my mother as her health declined. I returned for ten and a half years and took the first good opportunity that presented itself to leave again. What saved me from the inability to fit in was that I took the plane often; the saving grace of those long ten years was that I traveled all over the region, to Yemen, Dubai, Saudi Arabia, Egypt, Jordan, Iraq, and more. My chartered accountant role covered clients in these countries, and I traveled all the time.

ACCEPTANCE OF OTHERS

I learned from my mother that one may enjoy success, but not the success that is built on the strength of others. Nor should one enjoy success that's built on appeasing others, but instead one that is for the good of others and the benefit of all. As a boy, my father was my hero and I looked up to him, waiting every day for him to come home from work. As I grew up, my mother was my greatest influence. Yet she never pushed me or pressured me. She made me choose for myself whether to come or go. She never interfered and she never asked me to return.

Occasionally, she did have her say and was influential in my decision to study in England. She told me not to go to the US to Houston or Austin with my peers but to Manchester, where my uncle was staying at the time. She pushed me without pushing me, and I give her credit for any and all of my success.

Despite the long hours and hard work, I greatly appreciated my freedom in Manchester and London in those years. I liked earning money and only spoke with my parents every few months, which was the norm in those days. I felt independent and that I finally belonged.

CHAPTER 9

RESPONSIVE

"You are the most mysterious, beautiful, angry person
I have ever met ... ... I am falling in l ... ... Sarah.
Sarah! I am falling into the pool with you!"
– James Leeds, played by William Hurt

Children of a Lesser God (1986)

My destiny to love movies was my destiny to find love.

ON THE JOB

When I returned to Bahrain in 1987, I'd come back to be close to my mother. In Bahrain, I had begun a new role still at Price Waterhouse as a Manager. The transition was very hastily prepared and the manager I was replacing only had a brief time to meet me before heading to London. I was introduced to only a few clients in Manama and the region in a formal handover, and had to introduce myself to the rest.

On my first day on the job back in Bahrain, I once again changed my mind about whether to wear Western or Arab dress. On my first day at work, I wore my freshly washed and pressed *thobe*, also known as a *dishdasha*, and my *keffiyah* head scarf, also known as a *ghutra,* and made every attempt to fit in and feel comfortable among my peers. By the end of the day, however, I was so uncomfortable that I longed for a suit and jacket. From the second day onward, I wore my UK uniform in navy and gray consisting of striped suits with ties.

At this point in my career with Price Waterhouse, I'd gone from a medium-sized office in Manchester to a very large office in London, and now found myself in a very small office in Manama that served clients in Bahrain and the Gulf as a whole. Although it was smaller, there was more face-to-face time with clients, which I enjoyed as I preferred to meet people in person.

I introduced myself by telephone to various clients and set up times to meet them for lunch. One of the clients I spoke to, a British managing director from a large brokerage firm, agreed to meet for lunch at Chicos, a famous Italian restaurant. Many bankers and finance professionals went there for lunch but he and I had never met before.

When he sat down with me, the first thing he said was, "When you spoke to me on the phone, I thought I was talking to a white man from Manchester, because of your strong Mancunian accent, and I am surprised that you are Khalid Janahi. I thought you were a white man with an Arab name!"

That first lunch was very memorable for me because of his comments. It was my first time in that restaurant because he had invited me there. Over the years it became a very familiar place where I ate often with clients and family members. I remember very well my arrival in that office and my reentry into Bahrain where I was mistaken on the phone for a white man with an Arab name.

Bahrain was a hotspot for banking at the time, with over 400 licensees in different aspects of financial services at the time, which were then served by the "Big Six" accounting firms, of which Price Waterhouse was a leader.

A sense of hope permeated the region at the time, a hope for peace and a better life. With the end of the Iran–Iraq war on August 20, 1988, a great feeling of happiness pervaded the air. My business dealings also improved as both Iran and Iraq were in my portfolio of clients from then on.

CHANCE AND LOVE

One night in London in early 1987, I went to the movies, as I often did, to see *Children of a Lesser God* starring Marlee Matlin and William Hurt. It was a romantic movie about a teacher for the deaf and a deaf janitor who fall in love. As I was leaving the Empire Cinema at Leicester Square, I saw two women exit the theatre after the film ended. One of them seemed like an apparition. She was a stunning young woman, and in that fleeting moment I felt butterflies in my stomach and a quickening of my heart. I knew nothing about the woman I admired but thought maybe she was Persian or Indian. In another moment, she was gone.

A year later in 1988 in Bahrain, I was visiting one of my aunties, one of my mother's younger sisters, at the College of Health Sciences where she worked. She had some photos of herself with a group of colleagues traveling to Egypt and Oman and other places. In one of the pictures, I saw her. I saw the woman who in my mind was the same girl I had seen that night at the cinema. I asked my auntie about her and, yes, she had been in London to complete a master's degree.

I then found a way to visit the campus to look for her, at first without talking to her. Luckily, the head of the section was someone I knew from AUB and I went to see him on the pretense of chatting about old times in Beirut. I asked my aunt for a formal introduction and, at last, I was able to talk to her. We started dating and enjoyed many long conversations and dinners together. I courted her for six months before we were married in 1989. I felt ready to embrace responsibility for more than just myself.

Getting married was the first element of responsibility, but the big moment of realization for me came when my first son was born in 1993. That is when I felt the real risk. And I felt how much my parents had done for me at that time, because having a child and being a father means sleepless nights when they are sick or have a temperature. Having my own children revealed to me the enormity of what my parents had gone through and what they had done for me.

Marrying me may not have been the best option for my wife considering the sacrifices she made but, for me, it was the luckiest event of my life that has brought me joy ever since.

CHEWING KHAT IN YEMEN

I had clients in Yemen and was drawn to this country of very proud people. The real, indigenous population were to my mind true Arabs in how they embraced their history and culture. I saw mostly foreigners when I traveled in other Gulf countries, but in Yemen and Oman I had more authentic conversations with actual citizens. I traveled there on a regular basis to meet with clients, and each time I grew both personally and professionally.

I had two *khat* experiences when I was there with clients. Seven or eight people and I were invited for lunch on a Thursday, which was the last day of the work week at that time. We were offered a heavy lunch and as guests were expected to eat what was offered as a sign of honor and respect to the hosts. After lunch, we went to the top floor of the very large rectangular house. Many comfortable seats were available in which to smoke one of the many hubbly-bubblies, known also as hookahs or shishas, the tobacco pipes with a long flexible tube connected to a container in which the smoke is cooled by passing through water. Tea, whiskey, and Coca-Cola were set alongside each shisha, as was a pile of green leaves. Each person had their own pile of leaves, and we were told it was the finest *khat* available and that it came from Ethiopia.

I had never chewed it before. I followed the example, doing what the others were doing, chewing and keeping the leaves on one side of my mouth and letting it drip. The idea is to store the chewed ball in the cheek and release the active components in the juice while continuing to chew and drink.

The effects of the *khat* on the client were very mild, but those of us drinking whisky and Coke along with it found ourselves very high, very quickly. The immediate effects of *khat* can include rises in heart and breathing rates, elevated body temperature and blood pressure, and increased alertness, excitement, energy, and talkativeness that can last between 90 minutes and three hours. The aftereffects can include lack of concentration, numbness, and insomnia. I suffered a very sore and damaged jaw and an upset stomach afterwards. Yemenis are addicted to *khat* and spend as much as 10% to 30% of their income to buy it.

The second and last time I chewed *khat*, I purposely asked for it. Early in 1989, a team and I had to finish a job under great pressure, needing to report to London with a finished project in a matter of hours. We had to stay alert. Crunching the numbers in our hotel room, we stayed up for 36 hours straight and got the report completed on time. Unfortunately, we paid the price the following day because it really knocked us out. That was the last time I had *khat*.

HOPES FOR PEACE

The Taif Agreement in October 1989, known as the National Agreement Accord, negotiated in Taif, Saudi Arabia, was implemented to end the decades-long war in Lebanon. Lebanon had been a Garden of Eden; it was now shattered. There was optimism about the future, but there was also a pervasive fear that it could slide back to the chaos experienced during the long war.

PARIS II

Years later, in 2002, I was indirectly involved in Paris II, a negotiation led by the late Rafik Hariri, a business tycoon and politician who served as the prime minister of Lebanon from 1992 to 1998, to secure a $4 billion loan to Lebanon for reconstruction. I was asked to help raise money to rebuild the country after the war. I received a call from the Bahraini finance minister asking me to meet the prime minister to discuss how Bahrain could rally the support of regional Islamic banks to help support Lebanon. Bahrain could not supply the support on its own but, in its role as a banking center, it could rally Islamic banks and financial institutions to contribute to the loan for Lebanon.

I started working with the finance minister of Lebanon, Fouad Siniora, who would later become prime minister. Our goal was to bring the Islamic banks together for financing to the tune of $2 billion. I had to take initiative and bring everybody together, which I did. But, unfortunately, in Islamic finance, bonds, which are called *sukuk*, must be based on the purchase of an asset that is sold back later. The *sukuk* is a financial certificate which, according to Islamic law, cannot bear or pay interest and thus is strikingly different from a Western bond. The issuer must make a contractual promise to buy back the bond at a future date. For our purposes, we would need the parliament of Lebanon to approve the assets attached to the *sukuk*, which was extremely unlikely. Nevertheless, we tried hard to make it work and, finally of course, it didn't. The parliament would not approve the assets needed to secure the *sukuk* and the country didn't fully recover. Sadly, Lebanon has taken a tragic turn for the worse in recent years and its economy is in shambles.

CHAPTER 10

TRUSTED

"Do not speak to me of rules. This is war!

This is not a game of cricket!"

– Colonel Saito, played by Sessue Hayakawa

The enemy knew my accent.

When I found myself unexpectedly back in Bahrain in the late 1980s, I felt purposeful, productive, and of service to others. I was serving clients in the Gulf, building the business for Price Waterhouse, learning to manage clients, and leading a team. It was a time of joy and hope for me personally and for the region. I was hopeful that the Arab leadership in the region was changing and was in the process of taking responsibility for the people. All that would change overnight on August 1, 1990.

KUWAIT AT WAR

At about 2:00 am on August 2, 1990, Iraq invaded Kuwait. One might imagine that when a country is invaded, the skies might darken and the distant rumblings of artillery might cause much panic. There was none of that. I was awakened in the night, and I knew something was wrong.

What we did not know then was that this was the start of a seven-month occupation that would eventually lead to the devastation of Iraq. Ultimately, the country would not recover from its rogue attempt to take control of Kuwait's oil. The enemy of the day, the Iraqis, would soon become their own worst enemy.

I was working then at Price Waterhouse with a client who was based in Cincinnati, Ohio. The client wanted to acquire a business in the Gulf, where they had already had a presence, and to expand and add businesses in Saudi, the Emirates and Kuwait. We had finished our due diligence work and the evaluation, and everything was set to go. Three guys were arriving from Cincinnati, and it was the first trip to the Middle East for all three. Everything was ready for their arrival on July 28, 1990 in Dubai and then their onward journey to Kuwait on August 1st. They would leave to go back to the United States on August 3rd. That was the plan.

Two weeks before their arrival, suddenly a buzz started to

circulate that Iraqi troops were on the border of Kuwait. I received a call from them asking, “By the way, is it safe to come, you know, with what’s going on?” My answer was simple: “Listen, I cannot give you any sort of an answer. You are closer to the CIA than I am, so I’m sure you guys can check and see if you’d be given the green light.” They were given the green light by the State Department, and everybody was ready to travel. It was agreed that when they got to Kuwait, they would immediately register with the US Embassy. We met and when we finished our work in Dubai, the three Americans and I got on a plane to Kuwait.

We boarded the plane at 6:00 am and by 8:00 am we had arrived, gotten a car, and headed to the embassy to register. We proceeded to the hotel from the embassy. The Americans wanted to stay in the city center but, at my suggestion, they agreed to go to a hotel farther away – a lucky decision for us. We soon got to work and had a full day of meetings with the clients to whom they were pitching their business. We were entertained and, although this was Kuwait where alcohol was forbidden in theory, we were invited out for dinner, during which we drank lots of whiskey. We returned to our rooms, all of us a bit tipsy. I got into bed with the lights and TV on, and promptly fell asleep from booze and exhaustion. I was awakened by a strong knock on my door. When I opened the door, one of the Americans was standing in front of me. I remember his name was Scott, and I’ll never forget the look on his face. In a pinched voice, trying to cover his concern, he said, “Saddam has invaded Kuwait. What should we do?”

TRUST YOUR INSTINCT, DO WHAT FEELS RIGHT

“Well, let me just wash my face and brush my teeth,” I responded. He sat down and I called the other two, who came to my room. The four of us discussed what to do. I said, “There’s a car outside. Just get in the car and I will drive you out to the south at once because we’re on the south side. We’ll just drive to the south toward Bahrain and first into Saudi Arabia.” Michael, the guy in charge of the group from the US, answered, “Well, no, we have to call the embassy.” The embassy told them to just stay put and not go, insisting that they remain where they were. I was getting annoyed and trying not to show my agitation.

I took the phone handset and said, “Listen, they cannot stay put, because the Iraqis will be here and they’ll be taken hostage immediately. So, they cannot stay.” The person at the embassy responded, “They are not leaving the country. That’s the protocol. They’re not leaving the country! They are staying.” And I said, “Okay, but then they have to get out of here, because this is bad here. A friend of ours has an apartment here and they are going to go and stay there." After half an hour of discussion, they finally agreed and asked for the address.

A Lebanese man I knew, Hassan, arrived at the hotel in his car to pick them up and take them to his apartment on the outskirts of the city. As if on cue, half an hour after he left with them, Iraqi troops arrived at the hotel.

I went down to the lobby to tell the concierge that I would stay one extra night. The young Iraqi soldier in charge approached me, seemingly unused to his newfound authority and his role as aggressor. As soon as I greeted him and he heard my distinctly Iraqi accent, his body language changed. Perhaps my Iraqi ancestors were there to protect me. I explained where I was from and he said, "You shouldn't stay here, you should just leave. You can get a car and go back to Bahrain now and nobody will stop you."

Of course, I did what I felt compelled to do. I left for the apartment to make sure the Americans were okay, knowing it was not right to leave them. One of them was an Orthodox Jew and another, Scott, I would soon find out, was a diabetic. I could not in good conscience leave them and run away.

My Lebanese friend and I both knew we were in more danger than the Americans if we were caught helping them. We knew they would be taken hostage, but we would be shot on site. It was as simple as that. It was a problem to leave and a problem to stay. We set about procuring insulin for Scott, who had only brought a five-day supply with him to Kuwait. My friend and I drove his car from one pharmacy to another, now all controlled by the Iraqi soldiers, in search of insulin. My Lebanese friend negotiated a deal with one of the soldiers and paid him $1,000 for 90 days' worth of insulin for the American. I told Scott that I couldn't reassure him of anything but at least he had enough insulin for 90 days.

The five of us stayed in the apartment for two weeks. Then, on the 14th day, I received a phone call from the Bahraini ambassador, who told us, "You've got to get out now. Now is your chance to come to the embassy and leave from here, because we have access. We've negotiated with Iraq; we can go but, if you don't go now, you will be stuck here for good. So, it's up to you." I knew I had to leave because there was no phone service and fewer and fewer options for communicating, so I left. I went to the embassy.

To my astonishment, the ambassador greeting me said, "Go now and get on that empty bus." I got on the bus and, half an hour later, it filled up with people I knew I should not be on a bus with. Everything had quickly gone from bad to worse. First, I was with Americans for 14 days and suddenly I was on a bus with the ruling family of Kuwait who had been given temporary Bahraini identities. I told the Ambassador, perhaps sounding as though I was pleading, "I've just been with Americans for 14 days and I could not sleep at night. Now you're putting me in a bus with these guys. I mean, come on. What's going on?" Firmly, he looked me in the eye and said, "Just go and don't say anything and don't talk to anyone. You have to be on this bus." So, I did.

There were actually three buses, and I was in the one with all the royal family members. It took three hours to get from the embassy to the border. Those were the longest three hours I've ever lived through. Iraqi soldiers were everywhere as we went from checkpoint to checkpoint. After I crossed the border and then arrived in Bahrain, I immediately contacted the Americans' head office. They had already set up a 24-hour situation room. I admired the way the Americans took ownership of their staff and the fact that they had already put risk analysts in place to strategize an extraction.

I explained to them in great detail where the apartment was located and everything that had happened before I'd left for the Bahraini Embassy. From what I understood, ex-marines and special forces went in and got one of the men out. I only discovered this because they came to my office in Bahrain to tell me. The other two men were captured and taken to Baghdad. Many people worked behind the scenes to get them out of Iraq, which finally happened in September, more than three months later.

We would learn later that Saddam Hussein allowed many expatriate women and children to leave, but the men had been forced to stay. Many had hidden in apartments, stairwells and even in the US Embassy, but some were found and sent to various locations to be used as "human shields" to deter the amassing foreign forces from bombing his much-needed sites. On Saddam Hussein's orders, men were relocated to vital Iraqi installations, such as airports, power plants, weapons factories and communications centers, where they were detained without medical care and basic provisions, and with very little food.

Reverend Jesse L. Jackson, Sr., the American politician, political activist, and Baptist minister, was instrumental in getting the hostages out of Baghdad. Some felt he was interfering with the traditional lines of diplomacy and was using the hostage situation for his own political capital but, to me, he was taking action, following moral duty, and not listening to bureaucracy. He had been known to jump in and work around the bureaucracy in efforts to free hostages in the past. This time, he obtained an invitation from the Iraqi Embassy but was restricted from making contact by the US State Department. He then got involved by using the fact that he was planning a TV show and had a new role as a journalist to make direct contact. He claimed this was a legitimate approach, especially under the circumstances as it seemed that nobody else was contacting the Iraqis on behalf of the American hostages.

I understood later that Scott's company had helped fund the flight that took the hostages out of Bagdad. Years would go by before we fully understood the repercussions of leaving the hostages behind. Another American, whom I did not know personally, who had not been allowed to leave and was detained in the US Embassy, was also a diabetic. His American employer, a global company, had not managed to get him out or help him with the long-term, permanent, and devastating medical conditions brought on by not having insulin while he was detained in Kuwait. I had at least, I thought to myself, trusted my instincts and insisted on getting the men to the apartment, which gave us time to procure the insulin. We were indebted to Hassan for making this possible before the soldiers arrived at the hotel.

Just over a year later, my wife and I were invited to the United States as guests of Scott's company. They graciously hosted us for a wonderful week in Cincinnati, Ohio. I was asked to speak at a luncheon they hosted with their top management, the chief executive of the group and many others who I imagined had been in the situation room at the time of the hostage crisis. I said I felt horrible thinking about the agony that these Americans had gone through. I knew that the minute it happened we should have gotten in the car and left; we would never have been in the position that we were in because at that time everything was open. I recounted how we were already in the south, so we could have driven about 35 minutes to Saudi Arabia and then on to Bahrain, and everybody would have been okay.

My point was that we had followed the bureaucracy's instructions not to leave. But sometimes choices must be made based on one's own decision-making process and on doing what is morally right. At times it's a gut feeling and at times it's based on an assessment that takes into consideration different aspects, but at that moment it had been very clear to me that we should have left immediately. We had had to face grim realities by not leaving. The moral of it all for me was to never listen to bureaucracy, to listen instead to your heart, even if it tells you something totally different from what others are telling you. You will know what to do when you listen to your heart.

I said the true hero was my Lebanese friend who had kept us all in his apartment for two weeks and had put his life in danger to procure the insulin for Scott. I reiterated to this group of Americans thousands of miles away in a sunlit luncheon in Cincinnati that if the Iraqis had found the Americans in his apartment, my Lebanese friend and I would have been shot and the Americans taken as hostages. I told the executives what I had learned: "You know, you ask yourself the question, if I could go back again and do it differently, what would I do? The only thing I would do differently is to put my foot down and say, 'let's get into the car and I'll just drive you,' and I would just drive them out."

CHAPTER 11

MOTIVATOR

"The world is full of nice, ordinary little people who live in nice, ordinary little houses on the ground."

– Father Robinson, played by Sir John Mills

Swiss Family Robinson (1960)

We became a Swiss family, settling in a new country and building new habits.

LEAVING BAHRAIN FOR SWITZERLAND

By July 1991, I had become a partner at Price Waterhouse. The longer I stayed in Bahrain, the more I understood that one had to conform to some degree in order to get things done. The divide between being a conformist and getting what you want in business became all too clear to me in a small place like Bahrain. I felt it was time to give back to society and decided to join the Rotary Club, a voluntary charitable organization of professionals who want to give back to the community.

Bahrain had two Rotary Clubs at the time: the Rotary Club of Salmaniya, established in 1971, of which I was a member, and an older one, the Manama Rotary Club. Both clubs included big players, who were top chief executives, and indigenous Bahrainis, who were professionals or merchants from diverse businesses and banks, as well as foreigners, who were white, Indian, German, American and other nationalities and who were professionals working in Bahrain as bankers. The club played an important part in networking and was a key to business development. It was a place to meet and develop relationships with decision-makers in Bahrain.

An ironic and interesting course of events that began when I joined the Rotary Club would also be part of the reason why I left Bahrain. The year of the club's presidency starts on July 1st. Soon after I joined, I became president-elect for 1997 and was slated to start as president on July 1, 1998. By that time, I had left Price Waterhouse and had accepted a job involving Islamic finance and Islamic banking. Although I never actually took on the role of president, I was at this point associated with the club. In fact, the president-elect from 1998, a founding members of the club who never wanted to be president, had to serve for two years until a replacement for me was elected.

A lot of rumors over the years have suggested that Rotarians are Freemasons. The myth is that every Rotarian is a Freemason. When I announced that I was leaving the firm and would take a job in an Islamic bank, many people were upset that I was leaving my team and the firm, and were envious. Suddenly, rumors circulated that I was a Freemason, although a Freemason and Islam do not go hand in hand. How could I be a Freemason doing Islamic finance and Islamic banking? It all started here, with a great deal of talk and a big propaganda campaign against me. Pressure was also put on me to take a role in the Bahraini government, but I did not want to. I found myself neither close nor far away so, heeding the words of my grandfather, I decided to go far and, maybe later, come back safely.

TIGERS, CUBS, AND SCOUTS

Soon afterwards, my wife and I found ourselves in a winter wonderland in Geneva, Switzerland with our two little boys. The snow, the lake, and the mountains around us seemed to quiet the chatter and gossip we had left behind in Bahrain but, all of a sudden, we were parenting far from home and our families, and I was working for a bank for the first time in my life.

I was already a world traveler, but it was not only the landscape and language that were different; I felt a culture shock in my first three months in Geneva. I lost count of how many speeding tickets I received in those first few months. Once, unknowingly, I dropped my son off at a Tiger Cubs meeting (this was the pre-scout phase, which is followed by Tigers, then Scouts) at a house in Chêne-Bougeries by a cemetery. Two months later, in 1999, I received a traffic ticket by post from the authorities for 120 Swiss francs because I stopped my car in front of a cemetery. I had the right to question it but, of course, I paid all my tickets. Someone, an upright Swiss citizen, had seen me park my car for 10 minutes illegally and had proceeded to denounce me. This incident told me everything about how the Swiss mindset works: rules are for everyone, and rules take precedence over everything.

The more one stays in Switzerland, the more it grows on you. Every person has rights and responsibilities, and everyone exercises their rights. Even though I lived in the same house for 23 years and didn't know my neighbors, I felt comfortable there and that I had a right to live there peacefully with my family. I felt that high taxes were a small price to pay for a sense of peace, freedom of expression, and the rule of law.

My years in Switzerland with my wife and sons, and my work in the bank, offered me great learning and growth. I saw my sons grow up and, most of all, I witnessed my wife's sacrifice for our family and her courage. She was successful in Bahrain and had left a career behind to devote herself to motherhood. She had worked during her childbearing years and had given up a hard-fought career when she moved to Switzerland.

To me she was the finest example of leadership, and I learned from her how to be a good parent. In raising our sons and putting their interests before her own, to me she embodied the best traits of a leader. She instilled a strong sense of Swiss identity and belonging into them. Unlike my own mother, for whom the role of wife and mother had been imposed upon her from a young age, my wife was educated and privileged and had made the conscious sacrifice to devote herself to her family. When one of our sons became an Eagle Scout at the age of 16, he delivered a speech in which he said his mentor had always been his mother. I was brimming with pride and overjoyed when I heard this because that's how I felt about my mother.

CRITICAL THINKING

What is the one attribute of successful entrepreneurship that all entrepreneurs have in common? It is critical thinking. A look at successful entrepreneurs in the US shows that many of the best known, if not all, are antiestablishment. Even Bill Gates of Microsoft and Mark Zuckerberg of Facebook are antiestablishment. They are outliers: they think outside the box and place no limitations on their thinking. They have no issue with saying, "This is wrong and we will do it the way we think is right. We don't care." Innovation happens when people who are antiestablishment decide to do things differently. It does not happen when people are within the establishment.

RULES AND FREEDOM

Watching the Lone Ranger and Zorro on TV when I was a boy, seeing them do good for everyone in the village and in surrounding towns against the army and bad guys, must have influenced my way of thinking and dealing with people. Some might call me antiestablishment. I believe it depends on which establishment one is talking about and on where one is located. In Switzerland, I would not say that I'm antiestablishment. I am very reserved, and I am happier to observe the rules in the Swiss police state than in an Arab state for the following reason. In Switzerland, what are we getting in return for following the state? For one, I can think outside the box as much as I want. With freedom of expression, I know I am valued for who I am and not for what I have. Also, I like that, in Switzerland, the driver or house cleaner and the CEO of a bank or the head of state are equal before the law. I not only respect that but appreciate it, and I am happy to have paid into the social welfare system and conformed to this establishment over the years knowing we in Switzerland can express ourselves freely, are equal under the law, and are rewarded for our hard work.

HOME AND AWAY FROM HOME

From Geneva, I was still very connected to Bahrain and Islamic finance, straddling both worlds. I reported to the chairman of the board, son of a king, someone more princely than most princes I have met. HRH Prince Mohammed Al Faisal Al Saud was a great mentor to me. I was young and he saw the nonconformist in me, which he appreciated. Most people thought we were friends. He was a true politician at heart, who thrived in business. I traveled to the Gulf from my base in Switzerland; I was still from Bahrain and went there often but, as my sons grew, I began to realize I might never move back.

HRH Prince Khalifa bin Salman Al-Khalifa, the late prime minister of Bahrain, had also been supportive, though he knew that I was not a conformist and had opinions that differed from most others'. He realized that although I sometimes had an opposing viewpoint, it was for the greater good.

I will never forget his encouragement and guidance when I was offered the opportunity to move to Geneva in 1997. He was firm about backing my nomination for the position and insisted on providing a personal reference. For that, and that alone, I will always be indebted to him.

Even when I left Bahrain, I knew that His Royal Highness was supportive. In late 2000, I was contacted by one of his ministers who told me he wished for me to visit him in Bahrain. Three days later, I was in his personal office.

He told me that he had nominated me to be a member of the newly formed Higher Council of Economic Development, which he chaired. This was an honor for any Bahraini, let alone for a Bahraini based abroad.

JAHANNAM CAN WAIT

Summers in Geneva are beautiful. Surrounded by mountains, with a view of Europe's highest peak, the Mont Blanc, which keeps its snowcap during the hottest months, the place seems like it's been blessed by the Gods. Daylight lasts until 10:00 pm, and sunsets can go on for hours. Each summer evening I spend in Geneva feels like watching a painting.

My father first came to visit me in my new hometown in the summer of 2002. He spent three weeks enjoying the beauty of the country. We went up the mountains, visited charming villages in neighboring France, and enjoyed strolling along the lake or sitting in the garden with the view of Lake Léman. While he was curious to know the place his son, daughter-in-law and grandsons were now calling home, he also hoped this visit would convince us to move back closer to him.

By then, we were very attached to our adopted home. He did not convince us to return with him and I drove him back to the airport. When we arrived there, as we were parting, he looked at me and said, "Son, we do not know what will happen in the next life." My father has remained very religious throughout his life and he could not help but judge the more secular lifestyle I was living. He continued, "It seems to me that your chances of going to heaven are low. This is heaven on earth. Enjoy it during this life."

In Arabic, *Jahannam* means "hell." Ever since, I have felt that leaving heaven on earth would be a mistake, and that Jahannam can wait.

CHAPTER 12

REPRESENTATIVE

"All for one, one for all!"

– Motto of the Musketeers Porthos, Athos, and Aramis, and D'Artagnan, played by Gene Kelly

The Three Musketeers (1948)

When 9/11 shook the world, it was about time for the Arab world to build a reform agenda. Unfortunately, the wind was taken out of the sails.

FINDING AN ARAB VOICE FOR CHANGE

My first trip to the WEF Annual Meeting took place in January 1998. I was part of a delegation arranged by my employer at the time, a company serving as an official Davos partner that year. The rarified world of Davos fascinated me immediately. Where else could I meet world leaders, movie stars, and government dignitaries in the same room? These meetings gather a diverse group of thought leaders and invite them to exchange questions and ideas about how to change the world for the better.

I was afforded many opportunities to ask questions and express my thoughts at my first WEF Annual Meeting in Davos. I also spent a great deal of time listening to the pan-Arabist voices on hand, absorbing their perspectives and possible solutions to problems in the Middle East. I often feel an immense surge of idealism at Davos. It is a fascinating forum and I believe the WEF makes a difference in the world. The more I have learned at the meeting, the more questions have come to mind. Always at the top of my list of questions are those that ask how we can reform education and encourage critical thinking in the Arab world.

I admire the WEF's commitment to improving the state of the world and I value its mission:

> The World Economic Forum is the International Organization for Public-Private Cooperation. The Forum engages the foremost political, business, cultural and other leaders of society to shape global, regional and industry agendas.

I believe we must all work to improve the state of the world, not to improve the state of ourselves. It must always be "all for one and one for all," and we must embrace the need to give something in order to get something. Above all, we must take action.

After the September 11 attacks changed the world in 2001, people's and institutions' priorities shifted. The destruction of New York City's World Trade Towers and the deaths of more than 3,000 people led to harsh repercussions throughout the Muslim world and the Arab region in particular. Even in Switzerland, I sensed an us-versus-them mentality and a newfound Arabophobia. I understood then that a unified Arab voice was more important than ever. I felt a growing urgency to find my own voice, mentor a younger generation, and take a leadership role in my community. I was eager to start an honest discussion about the mistrust and resentment we were all noticing. At Davos in 2002, I heard the familiar sound of what I call the "dialogue of the deaf." I had heard it endlessly between Palestinians and Israelis, and I heard it now as people pretended to chat with one another when the only thing they really wished to hear was their own voice, delivering private messages to their minds instead of engaging in actual conversations with others.

At around that time, Arab thought leaders released a compelling publication entitled the *Arab Human Development Report (AHDR)* by the United Nations Development Programme

(UNDP). The report urged governments in the Arab world to commit to fundamental change and move beyond the status quo. According to the UNDP, the report was "prepared and owned by Arabs as an advocacy tool designed to appeal to a wide audience, spur public debates and mobilize support for action and change through processes of consultation, research and report writing. The AHDR articulates the perceptions and priorities in the region and serves as a source of alternate policy opinion for development planning across varied themes." The AHDR report on the state of the Arab world was extremely negative.

Soon after the release of the AHDR, the WEF issued *The Arab World Competitiveness Report* that discussed the ways in which the Arab world lagged behind other global regions in the areas of innovation and competitiveness. The authors wrote that they were appalled by the inequities in the Arab world they read about in the AHDR report. To give credit, King Abdullah of Jordan was one of those who really believed Arabs could close the gaps in their systems and reform their society.

AXIS OF EVIL AND FUTURE PRESIDENTS

The WEF exceptionally moved the 2002 Annual Meeting to New York. I was part of a private symposium of 25 people at the Waldorf Astoria, where the discussion centered on what

US President George W. Bush had referred to as the “axis of evil.” Then Senator Joseph Biden made a very valid point: he understood why North Korea was part of the axis but couldn’t grasp why Iran and Iraq were listed as part of it.

Later, in January 2004 in Davos, where the WEF Annual Meeting returned from 2003 onwards, Joe Biden took part in a panel discussing American foreign policy. I asked a question about invading and occupying Iraq. He lost his temper and went into a tantrum, pointed at me and said, “You guys deserved Saddam Hussein.” In moments like that, there’s only one thing to do: smile to aggravate the tantrum. I was nonetheless surprised by the 180-degree shift in less than two years.

IRAQ IN 2003

In 2003, US propaganda against Iraq was mounting, and I felt it was an unjustifiable escalation. There were clearly no weapons of mass destructions in Iraq, and I felt sorry as I watched US Secretary of State Colin Powell try to prove the contrary to the United Nations and the world. In March when the US invaded Iraq, I was at home in Geneva watching TV, glued to CNN and the BBC, puzzled and saddened by the news.

Unlike during the Six-Day War, where our access to the information had been delayed, we would see the invasion live.

We even saw the Iraqi minister of defense in a propaganda exercise as American troops marched on Bagdad.

I had never been a fan of Saddam Hussein, a known tyrant. But invading a country on false pretenses, knowing it would destabilize an entire region and cause immense suffering among its people felt like a terrible injustice. How can one justify invading a country which is 6,900 miles away to defend and advance some business interests, and which does not pose any existential threat to the invader's security, and then give lessons on morality to the world? I was angry at Tony Blair for going along with George W. Bush. I don't think this war would have been possible had the British not immediately supported the US invasion.

A few days after the so-called "Mission Accomplished" speech by George W. Bush on May 1, 2003, celebrating the US victory, a dinner took place in Washington. It was overheard at the dinner that Richard Perle, an adviser to the Pentagon, anticipated that, a year from then, US tanks would be in Tehran, with Iranian people waving American flags.

ARAB BUSINESS COUNCIL

In 2004, on the heels of these negative reports about the Arab world and the profound disruption it was facing, the WEF established a new committee called the Arab Business Council

(ABC), which would draw its members from all over the Arab world and within its business community. Most of these individuals were already affiliated with the WEF and attended the Davos meetings.

Members of the new ABC quickly established their determination to act as an independent agency. This provided them with the freedom to engage with any of the region's business leaders they chose to consult. The council's goal was to collaborate with a broad range of individuals and organizations to devise concrete ways to promote change. Many of the council's members worked outside their countries' governments, others were part of their governments, and still others were leaders in the business community. The ABC's agenda was to find ways of improving the state of the Arab world by articulating specific recommendations for systemic reforms. I believed the ABC could be a positive, meaningful vehicle for change.

Although the independent ABC existed for just four and a half years, it launched conversations that deepened its members' and guests' understanding about how to improve institutions and implement reforms. Once its executive committee was established, members of the ABC voted against creating additional committees, stating that the executive committee alone would elect new committee members. The executive team then began arranging meetings with decision-makers from the Arab world.

Because I was based in Geneva at the time, I was asked to serve as an executive committee member. I was the only person council members knew who lived near the WEF's headquarters, also located in Geneva. Once I was elected vice chair of the executive committee, the work took off energetically.

We examined the UNDP and *Arab World Competitiveness* reports and initiated important discussions with their authors. Before long, the ABC was hailed as the amazing brainchild of the WEF.

To my mind, the ABC was established as a group that would participate fully in all the steps involved in creating change. We worked at paving a road to positive evolution, independent of Arab world governments. We met with Tunisians, Moroccans, Egyptians, Syrians, Lebanese, Bahrainis, and Emiratis. We met decision-makers at the highest levels of government and introduced what I called "soft reforms" or small, nearly invisible changes within the evolutionary process that could make a difference without upsetting the status quo. In this way, we succeeded in landing modest reforms when truly bold initiatives would have landed hard, resulting in no reform at all.

The ABC understood that change needed to start at the top in each country. We aimed for evolution not revolution. Revolution, by definition, erupts from the bottom up. The ABC started by examining competitiveness within the business community. Basics such as access to capital, the status of labor laws, and the overall rule of law were scrutinized along with the ways in which these policies affected competitiveness throughout the region. We asked insiders about their country's best practices, how they could be translated to other cities and states, and how they could be improved.

We came to the table with a positive mindset and generated great momentum. We received invitations to participate in many other meetings. We were invited to meet with Colin Powell, the US secretary of state at the time. We received another invitation to join the Organisation for Economic Co-operation and Development (OECD). Both invitations came from the Forum for the Future, a group representing developing countries whose headquarters were located in France. ABC members were also invited to join the Council on Foreign Relations, the American think tank, to introduce our ideas for reform to that highly connected group of thought leaders.

Along with ABC chairperson, Shafik Gabr, I was involved in all these meetings and was proud we were widely viewed by attendees as an effective platform for discussing the building blocks of change.

The ABC held its first annual meeting in Morocco in 2004.

The next year, we met in Bahrain, followed by Egypt in the third year, and Abu Dhabi in the fourth and final year. Along the way, we also held meetings in Tunisia. Many of these brought me into contact with heads of state and resulted in some exhilarating discussions and strong connections.

CLOROX IN CAIRO

In Cairo, in 2006, the ABC met with Ahmed Nazif, the last prime minister of Egypt to serve under Hosni Mubarak. He brought three of his ministers and all four Egyptians seemed eager to listen and learn. Chairperson Shafik Gabr was the first to address the meeting. In his beautiful, Americanized English, he welcomed our attendees while I held back. Mr. Gabr and I balanced each other out; my style was always to speak in a very direct and concise manner. I would say something like, "That is wrong, you should change that," while Shafik Gabr approached things differently. "Never tell someone their idea or system is wrong," he advised. "Instead, show them how to change it, they already know it's wrong."

I soon realized I was the only attendee at this meeting with the Egyptians who had not spoken. When Mr. Gabr realized this, he pointed to me and said, "You must say hello!" He was sitting to the right of the Egyptian prime minister while I was sitting to his left. I rose, having decided to address the prime minister directly. "Mr. Prime Minister," I said in Arabic, "You must act by using your name."

The prime minister looked at me quizzically, and I continued, "You've got to be like Clorox, cleaning up everything and getting things going in the right direction." After a moment, the prime minister had grasped my cheeky pun; "Nazif" means "clean" in Arabic, so I was jokingly playing off his name's other meaning. Looking directly at me, the prime minister smiled broadly.

It would be another four years or so before the Egyptian government collapsed and our guest with the Clorox-like last name was deposed. At the time, our interaction had been a hopeful one, affirming that we could work together in a positive way, each landing small soft reforms and promoting evolution – not revolution. I was pleased that he took my humorous remark on the chin and with a smile. My many encounters with state officials had taught me that other Arab world ministers might not have found me so amusing.

The ABC introduced ideas of reform without creating major hassles for anybody. Nazif understood this and, despite the corruption and cronyism surrounding the Egyptian government, he was actually working on reforms. Of course, the power play surrounding the question of who would name Egypt's next president was interfering with the progress toward change that the government was making. The Arab Spring and the dramatic end to Mubarak's 30-year presidency in 2011 had consequences we are still dealing with today.

ABC IN BAHRAIN

Another memorable meeting prior to that time was the 2005 ABC annual meeting held in Bahrain. Because I am from there, I organized the meeting. I approached those in Bahrain's government responsible for handling such events and explained that we planned to invite officials from a number of countries in the Arab world. When I asked for an official letter from Bahrain that would support the ABC's letters of invitation, I quickly realized I was getting the runaround, so I decided to take no notice of the difficulty. Since the officials weren't taking me seriously, we decided to create the invitations ourselves, and the ABC chairperson and I would sign them.

The ABC invited members of the Bahrain business community and officials from across the Arab world to our two-day conference. Among the invitees who accepted our invitation were many government officials. I believe we had three ministers from Egypt, one from Morocco, two or three from Jordan, another from Lebanon, and another from Kuwait, as well as the deputy prime minister of Iraq and the deputy prime minister of the Syrian Arab Republic. Official delegations from a number of countries informed us of their intentions to attend.

The ABC took care of all the logistics concerning the attendees from the moment they landed. We took them to their hotels and made all their other arrangements. The government did not help us but the meetings went beautifully. We invited James Zogby, the founder and president of the Arab American Institute, to introduce a poll of the Arab world; his poll was highly successful. Interestingly, the four Bahrain ministers who appeared at the meeting had assumed they would be the only ministers from any country attending. Once they saw all the ministers from outside Bahrain, the office of Bahrain's prime minister called me. One of his cabinet ministers asked, "What's happening here? All these ministers must visit with our prime minister," to which I replied, "Listen, I'm busy with this thing so you can arrange for a meeting tomorrow morning, although there are actually too many foreign ministers, so I suggest you meet with just two, the deputy prime minister of Iraq and the deputy prime minister of Syria." The next day, both these high-ranking officials met with the prime minister of Bahrain on an official basis. The meeting was arranged through diplomatic channels and I was not involved.

BACK TO INDIA

I went back to India in 2005. By then, the ABC was in full swing, and I was invited as its vice chair to the annual meeting of the Confederation of Indian Industry in collaboration with the WEF. The conversations bore mainly on the Indian potential and prospects for growth, and India's outlook as a future superpower. A few social entrepreneurs were given the spotlight, featuring how their business solutions could solve some of India's social challenges.

At that time, India was opening up to the world, particularly to the West, and reinforcing its ties with the United States and its ally in the Middle East, Israel. Historically, trade ties with the Gulf countries had always been deep. Mumbai is around three hours away from Dubai by plane and so is about the same distance from Dubai as Beirut.

One of the sessions focused on India's relations with the Arab world. I participated in this session with four other panelists. In his introductory speech, one of the Indian officials on the panel stated that Israel's security would be the red line to ensure prosperous relationships with the Arab world. I found this statement to be provocative, given the country's own geopolitical struggle, and historically unfounded. I was also surprised that none of the

Gulf Cooperation Council (GCC) country ministers on the panel reacted to it.

I felt compelled to be provocative in return and, speaking for the Arab countries, said, "I don't think that we're going to have a sustainable relationship without peace between India and Pakistan." Some people in the audience seated at a table clapped. They were all Pakistani.

VOTE AS I SAY, NOT AS YOU WANT

In the fall of 2005, I was invited by a prominent leading British global business publication to a meeting in London to discuss the business opportunities in the occupied Palestinian territory in anticipation of the Palestinian legislative election of January 2006. As it turned out, the meeting had been prompted by a British Jewish business tycoon born in Egypt, as a way of helping the expected new era of coexistence between Israelis and Palestinians.

The invitees to the meeting included the daughter of a Saudi tycoon, two Emirati tycoons, two Egyptian tycoons, an ex-prime minister of Jordan, two Israeli industrialist, and the British Jewish tycoon. The meeting started with an introduction by the host and then we were taken to 10 Downing Street where Tony Blair met us. He encouraged us to invest in and ignite a new era to generate new jobs for Palestinian youth. In the afternoon, we met Chancellor of the Exchequer Gordon Brown, the position he occupied when Britain chaired the European Union, G7, and the Forum for the Future. He reiterated Tony Blair's words of support by investing in and creating jobs in the Palestinian territory. I raised with Mr. Brown the fact that the issue was not about the unwillingness of businesspeople to invest and create jobs, but about the hurdles and challenges that must be overcome before money could be raised to invest. I reminded him that, apart from the two Egyptian tycoons and the Jordanian ex-prime minister sitting in the same room, the rest of us from the GCC were in a state of war with Israel and, by default, could not travel to Israel without the approval and permission of our respective governments. In addition, when raising the money to invest, the burden of risk for the business would be borne by investors. However, the business community could not accept the burden of the political risk, including accusations and implications of "links to terrorism" by the Israelis if operations were taking place in the Palestinian territory. In fairness to Mr. Brown, he agreed that these issues were important to deal with and promised that he would come back to us with proposed solutions. Giving credit where credit is due, Mr. Brown's office cleared most of the issues by the end of November 2005.

Fast forward to January 26, 2006: we were at the WEF in

Davos and everyone was eagerly anticipating the results of the Palestinian legislative elections of the previous day. These were one of only two totally free elections in the Arab world during my lifetime to date. The first one took place in Algeria in 1991, with the Islamic Salvation Front winning the elections freely. However, the deep state, comprised of the army and Western powers, would not allow the freely elected members to govern. The army's coup d'état was supported by most Arab regimes and Western powers.

Disappointment was clearly written all over everybody's face as the initial result showed that the Change and Reform (Hamas) party had won the free elections. Coincidentally, a session had already been planned that evening to discuss the positive future of Israeli–Palestinian coexistence. I was one of the speakers, alongside Israeli and Palestinian representatives and an American congressman. I vividly remember walking to the venue with my friend André Azoulay, the adviser to the King of Morocco and a Moroccan Jew. Like the rest of the people I met that day, he was disappointed with the results of the elections. However, he was worried about the reaction of the Israelis and Americans and, consequently, of the world, and how it might overtake the positive development of the past five years and turn us back to square one. I asked him to share his thoughts at the meeting since he could provide important input.

I remember the sadness on the faces of the people at the venue. I was really shocked when the American congressman expressed his disappointment with the Palestinian people's election of Hamas and warned that businesses that supported the newly elected government and investing in the occupied territory would be blacklisted.

As my turn came, I requested the moderator allow André Azoulay to say a few words. Mr. Azoulay spoke eloquently in his beautiful English with a French accent. The audience listened carefully to his words and his warnings of a backlash if the elected people were not allowed to govern freely. (Years later, unfortunately, his warnings came true.) I spoke after Mr. Azoulay. I first congratulated the Israelis and Americans for allowing the most free elections, not just for the Palestinians but for the whole Arab world, since those in Algeria in 1991. With the wonderful turnout of 75% of eligible voters casting their votes, the election could be considered a success. Although the result left everyone disappointed, including myself, the voice of the people should not be discounted. I reminded them that, if they had not wanted Hamas to win, why had they allowed Hamas to nominate themselves for the elections? I further briefed the people in the room on the meeting we had had in London a few months earlier and how positive the vibes had been at the time about a bright future for Israelis and Palestinians alike. Yet, this was a clear message from the West that you have a vote only if you vote the way we say, not as you want.

COMBATTING HUMAN TRAFFICKING

Dr. Aleya Hammad, a scholar and humanitarian from Egypt, was among the first to bring the issue of human trafficking to the world's attention and to stress the responsibility and role of the private sector in addressing it. In the early 2000s, she resided in Geneva, after a long tenure at the World Health Organization (WHO). We met for the first time in 2005. We both shared similar views on the importance of human dignity, and she briefed me on an initiative she aimed to launch to combat human trafficking in the next few months, asking me to join its inaugural meeting and be involved.

In January 2006, I therefore attended the launch of the Suzanne Mubarak Women's International Peace Movement initiative End Human Trafficking Now. To gain traction, her initiative needed an influential ally and, at the time, Suzanne Mubarak was one. To give her credit, I do believe that she genuinely believed in the cause and did not exclusively seek positive publicity. The initiative was successful at placing human trafficking high up on the list of global priorities to be addressed by global organizations.

At Mubarak's invitation, business leaders first gathered in

Greece at a meeting hosted by the Greek Ministry of Foreign Affairs, co-sponsored by the International Organization for Migration, the UN Development Fund for Women, the UN Office on Drugs and Crime, the World Bank, the Geneva Centre for the Democratic Control of Armed Forces, and the Foundation for the Child and the Family.

I became involved in this initiative with other business community members, including prominent Egyptian businesspeople, and signed a few pledges. One thing that puzzled me was that the initiative aimed to support Interpol in creating and maintaining a dedicated team. Funds were raised; I do not recall the exact amount but it was not a great deal considering the need to enforce such important standards.

Despite recent improvements, we remain behind on this issue, particularly in the Gulf countries. Many reports on domestic and worker abuses in this part of the world exist. I fear the conflict in Ukraine will only exacerbate this worrisome trend, unless the world at large, including Arab countries, act.

MEETING ADJOURNED

The ABC received much attention from the international press and online media, including CNN and CNBC. Journalists and on-air commentators contacted us to get information about our work. I believe it was about this time that the management of the WEF began to feel we were taking our independence too far.

END OF THE ARAB BUSINESS COUNCIL

From my perspective, the ABC was one of the WEF's most successful initiatives, with its members all working vigorously to take solid action to promote soft reforms. It was not always easy, but we succeeded in convincing people to accept the notion of reform and get it started in their own regions.

We achieved this end by acting in increasingly independent ways. We looked at all aspects of Arab economies. We studied all elements of trade apart from the oil industry, which accounts for an altogether separate revenue stream. Compared to the oil industry, all other trade sectors contribute just a fraction of revenue to Arab countries' overall economies. Thought leaders and the media approached us for comments concerning our research. This interest was directed at just the ABC rather than the WEF. It soon became clear that the independent nature of the ABC could not continue in perpetuity. The ABC was an offshoot of the WEF, part and parcel of it. Some WEF managers routinely sat with ABC members during executive committee meetings and even participated in some of the decision-making. But it was clear that our activity was increasing our own unique visibility across the Arab world, where we were known as one of the few groups actually effecting reforms.

In 2008, the ABC was given two choices: we could either go our own way or return to the fold and allow the WEF to take charge, in which case ABC's internal elections would be abolished and the WEF would decide the way forward. I could see that the ABC was becoming a problem from the WEF's perspective because the council's activity wasn't always in harmony with the WEF.

I believed that the ABC should go its own way, registering as a separate entity and moving forward as a fully independent organization. But in the end, the ABC did not go its own way. Instead, it was taken over by the WEF and eventually died away. By 2008, the spirit of the original ABC was completely gone. The WEF appointed people with big names and important connections for the sake of appearances, but those big names and connections from the Arab business community took no action whatsoever; the WEF did everything. Before long, the group's staff consisted mainly of faces either directly involved or closely associated with governments. No real concepts of reform were even established.

Although our ABC eventually vanished, it was an exciting four years of close-knit collaboration among a dedicated team committed to pursuing a common goal. I'd like to think that our challenging questions and discussions may have contributed an infinitesimal strand of DNA to the evolution of the organism that is the Arab world. I would also like to think that pushing for reforms is the right way to go; it is a means to reconnect governments to their people. Personally, I learned a great deal about how people can lead and how they can learn to think critically outside the confines of the cronyism of Arab governments. All too often, people must conform simply to survive, without any opportunities to speak out or engage in critical thinking.

I always challenge the boundaries of communication that constrain people from stepping outside their comfort zone. My ABC cohorts came to expect that, at any time, I might raise eyebrows by saying something provocative, but I believe my comments stretched people's boundaries and created nearly invisible yet meaningful movement in the evolution of our region.

CHAPTER 13

INCLUSIVE

"He's a terrible man. Please stay at the party.
Let's have a wonderful time."
– Hrundi V. Bakshi, played by Peter Sellers

My experiences in life might have made me less of an idealist and more of a pragmatist. Yet, I still pursue change, trying to build on the lessons learned, and hope for a better future.

MOROCCAN SOIREE IN DAVOS

In the past, on the last night of the WEF meetings in Davos, a soiree sponsored by two participating countries often occurred. These were wonderful evenings of entertainment, food, and social interaction. On the last Saturday night of the conference, this “country soiree” took place in two rooms, in the grand hall and in another, smaller hall adjacent to it. Preparing two rooms provided each of the host countries with an opportunity to reign over their own parties, one known as the Big Congress and the other as the Swimming Pool. During the soiree, people cruised from one space to the other as if attending one big party.

Everyone looked forward to the soiree and the chance to network. People were not seated at tables and instead walked around, grazing at long tables of food and drink. Culturally specific entertainment, in addition to music, dancing, and conversation, was usually introduced by the host countries.

In 2009, I suggested to one of the managing directors responsible for the event that I try to get a group of countries from the Gulf region to be the hosts. Many participating countries were trying to get the allocation, but he liked the idea and asked me to provide more information on the possibility as soon as possible. My plan was promising, even though it diverged from the long-standing hosting arrangements of soirees, such as the soiree thrown by Egypt in 2005, when Gamal Mubarak attended the Annual Meeting. That soiree was a fantastic success.

In 2009, I immediately approached the man from Bahrain and the man from the Emirates who would arrange this Arab-world-hosted event. Both agreed to my plan, but two weeks later they refused to commit. I didn't want to lose this opportunity to showcase an Arab country, so I thought about finding other Arab countries interested in making this happen. As I was about to go to Morocco on a business trip, I decided to meet with one of the Moroccan king's right-hand men. When I saw him, I suggested that two Arab countries share hosting duties at the next WEF soiree and told him we would help with sponsorship. To this, the right-hand man replied, "I don't think His Majesty will like this, but I will talk to him."

Within a week, I received a phone call from that same gentleman who said, "We will do it, but only under certain conditions." He proceeded to name his terms: that Morocco would be the only country hosting the soiree, that people would not stand but would instead be served food seated at tables, that a chef would be sent to prepare the food, that everything would come from the Moroccans, and that they would also produce a big show directed by a Moroccan director based in France.

This right-hand gentleman happened to be the governor of Tangier at the time, who would later become the minister of the interior. He explained that he would act as coordinator on behalf of Morocco and that Morocco would not pay for the event. I listened to his terms and thought this turn of events would prove most interesting.

I got back in contact with the managing director at the WEF and told him the situation. We wanted to bring Morocco into the fold. I told him I believed this was an opportunity not to be missed. He reiterated that we needed two host countries and asked who would pay for the event. I proposed that my brothers and I would cover most of the costs. He said he would return a final decision, which he did, saying, “Let’s go with Morocco!”

Despite the global economic crisis – or perhaps because of it – the number and the quality of participants at the 2009 Annual Meeting was unprecedented. Forty heads of state or government, the leaders of all the major international organizations, and over 100 ministers made the journey to Davos.

The Moroccans put on an incredible soiree. The movie director displayed a high standard of excellence, with the evening showcasing the multicultural facets of Morocco through dancers and a mock wedding ceremony demonstrating how the event is performed in Morocco. Every detail was attended to in a professional way, with creativity and flair. The food was magnificent and the wine came from a top winery in Morocco. The prime minister and 10 of his ministers arrived in Davos to attend the soiree. The festivities began at 8:00 pm and lasted until the early hours of the morning. The Moroccan evening is one that everyone still talks about. It was the first time that just one country hosted the event, setting a new precedent and becoming the model for the next one-country hosted soirees.

South Africa was the next nation to host a one-country soiree the following year, and later India. Eventually, the country soirees stopped, as the momentum was hard to maintain. The King of Morocco was happy with the outcome of the event, which strengthened the relationship between the WEF and Morocco. The WEF had wanted to have a meeting there for all of the Middle East and, finally in 2010, it reached its goal, holding a conference in Marrakesh. Previously the Middle East meetings had exclusively been held in Sharm El Sheikh and in Jordan.

We wanted to showcase the Arab world, to show its people could be part of the movement to improve the state of the world. Morocco's participation as host revealed its culture while our sponsorship had a positive impact on the relationship between Morocco and the WEF for years to come.

YOU'RE IRANIAN

In early October 2013, at home in Geneva, I received a call from an American acquaintance who had worked with my brother on two projects. He intended to travel from California to Europe on a business trip and wanted to meet me in Geneva.

I took him to a Chinese restaurant that I was sure he would like in Geneva's La Réserve hotel. As the evening progressed, however, I noticed my guest was becoming increasingly uncomfortable.

I asked him what was happening. His story, to this date, puzzles me: the previous summer, he had been contacted by someone from a Gulf state visiting the United States. He had been asked to cancel his agreement with my brother, which would not be possible since the agreement had been formalized. He was promised by the caller that this could be made possible.

My American acquaintance had refused until the caller made it clear to him that he could not work with my brother because "these people are Iranians." The caller leveraged fears of sanctions to create a reaction. That is why he was so concerned.

I was surprised, but answered, "I am Bahraini and this is my passport," taking my passport out of my pocket. "I am sure that if I were Iranian, I would be a proud Iranian, too." It felt like a personal and unfounded vendetta had been launched against us by some part of the establishment.

MAY 26, 2016

This day was one of the most difficult I have experienced since the day of my mother's operation in 1971. I spent the day, from 6:00 am until 10:00 pm, at Geneva's Cantonal Hospital. It was the day my youngest brother, the one born in September 1971, donated a kidney to my middle brother. Complexities having to do with both the donor's and the donee's organs and their diabetes made it a very difficult operation. I recall that the doctor who performed the surgery, who had successfully conducted it in the past, said it was the most difficult he had done. I waited patiently for my two brothers to come out of the operating room. My youngest brother, the donor, came out at around 4:00 pm, after complications arising from removing the kidney. The operation on my other brother ended only at 8:30 pm.

Prior to the procedure, both had asked me to promise not to tell anyone about the operations until they had both come out safely. I thanked my lucky stars that my mother had not had to witness this unbearable situation. At 9:00 pm, I called my family members, beginning with my father and siblings, then phoned my nephews and nieces and the rest of the family. It was only at that point that some of the weight was taken off my shoulders. What this situation showed me was the level of sacrifice that my youngest brother had made as a person with diabetes who can lose his remaining kidney at any time. At the hospital before the operation, his doctor had suggested he think twice before giving away a kidney, but my brother said, "I will never forgive myself if I don't do it because this is for my mother; this would have been my mother's wish."

INSIDER/OUTSIDER AND A TROUBLEMAKER, TOO

Over the years, at international events, symposiums, and conferences, I acquired a bit of a reputation as a troublemaker. I participated in many panels and sessions as a panelist, moderator, and debater. I engaged in many debates, both on the record and off the record. Then came the Arab Spring and, at the beginning of 2012, heated discussions about elections, especially in Morocco, Tunis, and Egypt.

In one memorable session in Davos moderated by Fareed Zakaria, four prime ministers were in attendance: from Lebanon, Najib Mikati, who is currently again the prime minister; from Libya, Ali Zeidan; from the Palestinian National Authority, Salam Fayyad; and from Egypt, Hesham Qandil, who was from the Muslim Brotherhood movement. They were talking about the new wave of change and its many aspects.

When it came time for the questions and answers, I raised my hand and Fareed Zakaria gave me the floor. "I just have one question for all of you, especially the new wave of elected members. One of the reasons the Arab Spring happened is because people were fed up with corruption. So how will you manage the corruption side? From the perspective of an outsider, I see that the old guard has gone and the new guard is coming in, so how do you ensure that power does not corrupt?"

As soon as I asked the question, the prime minister of Egypt, a short man, stood up and started shouting, "You should apologize to me and to the Egyptian people because what you said is dishonorable to the Egyptian people." I was expecting Fareed Zakaria, as the moderator, to ask the prime minister to be silent and sit down because he was talking out of line as well as rude and hysterical. But I realized he was losing ground and there was no point in responding, so I smiled and waited for him to finish his tirade.

Fast forward to Davos in January 2015: Abdel Fattah El-Sisi had been sworn in as president of Egypt in June 2014 and in January flew to Davos, making his attendance the first presidential participation from Egypt in 11 years. The Egyptian contingent at the WEF held an evening function in his honor, to which I was invited. Around the table were high-level officials from Egypt and a lot of influential people in the business world. The head of WPP was there, as well as the heads of Siemens and Shell Oil, who were, I assume, interested in new business prospects.

President Sisi spoke in Arabic with simultaneous translation into English. I had been asked beforehand by the organizers to ask a question and agreed to be the last one. Each of the people who were asking a question would stand up at the table and ask a question into the microphone.

As my turn approached and I took the microphone to speak, the man sitting next to me, a well-known and well-respected politician from Egypt who knows me well, whispered to me, "Don't say anything, just don't," while gently pulling my arm. He knew I was not inclined to sing praise and glory to Sisi while asking my question.

Sitting near me were some Egyptians with whom I was acquainted. They put their heads down the minute I began to speak because they were expecting me to say something controversial. I saw their necks tuck into their shoulders like turtles retreating into their shells. They didn't want Sisi to see that they were sitting near me. I was enjoying the moment and began to speak in Arabic. Referring to how the previous speakers had pumped him up so that his chest was swelling with pride, I said, "I hope your chest can take the weight of what I am going to say." By saying this in Arabic, I was implying that I was about to say something negative.

The ministers looked nervous, no doubt wondering who I

was and whether I was about to say something like I hoped he would not yell at me like the prime minister a couple of years earlier who had told me to go to hell and who had since been banished from Egypt.[7]

As I stood to address the president in my own Egyptian dialect, which I had picked up over the years from movies and music,[8] I could see my Egyptian friends bowing their heads so low that it seemed like they were doing yoga. "Your Excellency, Mr. President," I said, "In your speech, you said that you represent 90 million people, but, I'm sorry, you represent 450 million people, because all Arabs are Egyptians."

As soon as I said this, I saw his chest expand and I thought his shirt might not be big enough and rip. You could almost hear a whoosh of air as heads bobbed up and everybody wanted to be seen. I continued, "You represent 450 million, so what you do is not just for 90 but for 450 million." Of course, he loved it. On our way out after dinner, everybody was shaking his hand, and he held my hand and said, "Thank you very much." He said a conference would take place in Sharm El Sheikh in April to

---

[7] The former prime minister who had shouted at me had in fact been deposed and banished.

[8] Most Arabic-speaking people actually understand and can often speak the Egyptian dialect because of Egyptian prominence in Arabic pop culture (movies, songs, etc.).

support Egypt and he hoped I would come. I answered that even if I didn't receive an invitation I would be there, and he laughed approvingly. In fact, I already had an invitation to attend as one of the speakers.

For me, that was an interesting moment, an example of seeing intelligent people put themselves on hold and kowtow to power, or rather, bow low to hide themselves from possible embarrassment. This is the type of weakness in people that prevents them from thinking for themselves and from allowing critical thinking. They hide their intellect so as not to upset their ruler or their cronies, driven by anxiety or fear, all in the name of survival or personal gain.

The group of Egyptians who had ducked their heads at the start of my speech are people I know, socialize with, and dine and drink coffee with, whenever we're at Davos or other meetings. I was enjoying myself that night with Sisi while also taking pride in my reputation as a troublemaker who asked tough questions during meetings. I consider myself a representative of the Arab world but not a part of its systems. I was a rare voice in the Arab world, and sometimes a bother, often standing up to ask tough but logical questions.

Many businesspeople, chief executives of large multinational companies, only offer praise to power because they hope to advance their own business interests. I don't blame them. At Davos, I ask questions because the meeting only lasts three or four days and I wish to improve the state of the world, not the state of the individual sitting in front of me. To my mind, there's no point in gathering 3,000 people from various important segments of society, all working hard to make a difference, if they decline to ask the tough questions. I come to learn, to question, to collaborate with others on ways we can improve the state of the world.

IMPROVING THE STATE OF THE WORLD

At the May 2022 WEF Annual Meeting in Davos, to my surprise no Russian company or government officials were represented. It's not that I condone the Russia–Ukraine War – I remain horrified at the unjust loss of life – but I believe neutral platforms and dialogue are essential to pursue peace. When I raised the question with a WEF official, I was told Russia had invaded a sovereign country – an unacceptable fact in international law. I answered that in 2003, Iraq, a sovereign country, had been unlawfully invaded by the United States and United Kingdom. Yet American and British officials and companies were nevertheless invited to the 2004 Annual Meeting. His answer was simple: "The Arabs did not make any noise then."

This was a compelling statement. His answer revealed the different standards applied to the world. That conception poses a problem for me: the state of which world are we trying to improve?

As time passed and I participated in a greater number of similar gatherings and in many initiatives, I lost some of my initial idealism, which had probably been naïve in the earlier years of my global engagement. I have become more pragmatic: I still believe, and I am committed to a better world. But I am not sure reforms pushed from the outside, even by other Arabs, can take effect in the Arab world. A transformation of not only our leadership is needed but of the individuals who compose this leadership so they can advocate effectively on behalf of the people and put the common good first, before individual interests.

PART II
OBSERVATIONS

Over the years, I have published articles, shared opinions on panels, and participated in many events devoted to the future of the Arab world and the Middle East. My observations have led me to delve into intriguing concepts essential to good governance and good leadership.

The following pages are a compilation of selected articles and transcriptions of my comments and conversations on panels and in debates.

PAST
TODAY
FUTURE

OBSERVATION 1

IDEALISM AND PRAGMATISM

A major problem in the Middle East concerns accountability. Ideally, all public servants should be accountable to the people. Without this scrutiny, the lines will undoubtedly blur to the point where it will be difficult to see who is the servant and who is the one being served.

Because of the nature of most of the ruling governments in our region, however, many people in public office, from the most senior down, have become too comfortable in their positions, as if they see their jobs as entitlements.

I cannot think of many examples of public servants in the Arab world who resigned from their position for failing to achieve their goals. Are they all so brilliant in our part of the world that not a single one has failed at any task over these many years?

Even the casual observer can see that many are not qualified for their jobs, let alone capable of delivering true excellence. Despite that, few have ever had the courage and strength of character to apologize and declare that they failed to perform and therefore resign from their position. Instead, they have simply been removed or reassigned to other jobs by the same commander who put them there in the first place.

Regulators are generally a good example of this problem. Let me be clear that I am not against regulation. I welcome high-quality regulation, which is beneficial to any industry, but the people in those positions must be unstained by corruption, and saintlier than saints.

Unfortunately, and it hurts me to acknowledge this, many regulators in the Middle East were not at the level they should have been and, as a result, we have all suffered. This not only affects specific industries but the economy as a whole, including the wealth that trickles down to the average person on the street.

Those in public office should realize that there is no shame in resigning from a position to allow someone else an opportunity to try a different approach. The shame is actually in clutching at those positions in the way a child clutches a comfort blanket. These are important positions, and the general public good should always come first, not the whims of bureaucrats or their bosses.

INDEPENDENT ACCOUNTABILITY

Since the Middle East seems to be taking its time in terms of developing a true, lasting solution to this issue, one in which public servants are directly accountable to the people, as a medium-term fix perhaps we should consider establishing an independent accountability body to audit the activities of all government departments.

It is crucial, though, no matter how limited its powers, that this body be accountable to the people and not to another government entity. In this way, public servants would have some fear of losing their jobs or, at the very least, of their scandals being publicly aired.

PUBLIC SERVANTS

The fact remains that many of the problems we face are simply the result of not having the right people in the right positions. The longer we carry on this way, the longer our region will lag behind the rest of the world. Government jobs should never be seen as a right for anyone. They are a duty to the public, not to the masters in power, and no one in any position of authority should forget that. That is why it is called "public service;" it is about serving the public, and the emphasis should always be on the word "service." There are no masters who need serving in this relationship, just the public.

OBSERVATION 2

DAVOS

For more than five decades, the WEF has been "committed to improving the state of the world." This is a bold statement, but having attended the Annual Meeting in Davos for almost half of these last five decades, I can comfortably confirm that the WEF is seriously committed to its mission, one that goes beyond pretty words and the limitations of diplomacy to engage people in sincere conversation and debate that move beyond individual comfort zones in order to create something new.

Traditionally held in January, the Annual Meeting has become "the foremost creative force for engaging the world's top leaders in collaborative activities to shape global, regional, and industry agendas at the start of each year."

Despite the recent criticisms that the Davos meeting is a networking party for the wealthy who pretend to be changing the world when all they want is to curry favor with powerful players and help promote their own agendas, I have found it greatly edifying over my 23 years in attendance. Interacting with an international group of people, including businesspeople, civil society representatives, politicians, and others, was very compelling. The many different perspectives have broadened my horizons.

At Davos, I had my first interactions with people from the US Congress and members of the US administration's cabinet, including the secretary of state and the secretary of labor. Davos is very effective to meet people in governments from all over the world.

What attracted me from the very first day is the same thing that continues to attract me today: the WEF motto of improving the state of the world is a lofty and challenging goal bound to provoke detractors yet, over the course of just a few days, the WEF Annual Meeting is often a very productive gathering. Despite criticisms about its increasingly commercial bent, I get satisfaction from almost every meeting. At times, meeting content weakens, but it always revives at the next one or two Davos gatherings.

While some of the world's greatest minds and most powerful leaders and changemakers actively participate in the WEF's flagship Annual Meeting in Davos to share insights and experiences and discuss challenges and opportunities, I can't help but wonder how, in addition to excellent discussions, the real, implementable solutions will be found, the kind that will truly benefit the world.

OBSERVATION 3

ARAB VOICES IN DAVOS

An Arab thought leader once noted that if we were to erase the Arab region from the world, nothing in the rest of the world would change, because we are basically irrelevant. In fact, life in other places would continue exactly as it is today, because we are not producers, only consumers, and poor ones at that. We make no material cultural, social, economic, industrial, or intellectual contributions to the world at large. If we disappeared overnight, the world might not even notice. Of course, I disagree wholeheartedly with this assessment. The nations of the Arab world represent a variety of complex cultures and contributions that have influenced humanity for thousands of years. Despite the fact that these ideas about our irrelevant nature are false, they are dangerous sentiments that can cause real harm.

To navigate current waves of Arabophobia and Islamophobia, we must engage with our detractors rather than ignore them, and

Davos is one place where we can continue to fight for relevant, essential progress.

The WEF Annual Meeting is a brilliant event that attracts some of the world's greatest minds, yet I often notice that the majority of Arab delegates at Davos seem preoccupied with rubbing shoulders with the big names and consuming rather than sharing knowledge. Unfortunately, I can barely remember the last time an Arab voice shook Davos.

Before 2000, more Arabs attended the meeting than Indians or Chinese but, since then, Indian and Chinese participation has almost tripled. From what I've observed, Arab delegations over the past two decades have consisted mainly of senior government officials and members of the ruling families. Arab business leaders and private-sector executives have almost always stayed close to the rulers, and even representatives from nongovernmental organizations are usually government-friendly if not government-sponsored.

This creates enormous uniformity among Arab attendees, robbing countries of the diversity and depth that makes for honest, in-depth discussions. Arab delegations to Davos do not include innovators, independent thinkers, opposition figures, or critics of the Arab world. Arab delegations are usually different shades of bland, pro-government gray, year after year.

During the months of the Arab Spring, new light was shed on the issues of diversity and inclusion. The bias against diverse representation at Davos is just one example of how things work in our part of the world.

When I first attended the WEF Annual Meeting, it was a much smaller gathering, with representatives of Arab countries drawn mostly from government or the business community, but only the sort sitting in the laps of the regimes they represented. While these individuals would not have wanted to characterize themselves this way, they were mostly conformists for the sake of receiving personal benefits and gaining either wealth in business or status in the government. This conformity has not changed much since those first Arab representatives attended the WEF.

OBSERVATION 4

THE SUCCESS OF DUBAI

It is a modern-day take on the classic Aesop's fable of sour grapes, but Dubai-bashing remains a disturbingly popular pastime, particularly among members of the GCC who are known in Arabic as *Khaleejis*. I understand why this is, but perhaps we should look past jealousy and envy and attempt to understand how or, more importantly, why Dubai has proved the single exception to otherwise standard GCC norms.

As a child, I first visited Dubai in 1969, when there was nothing but the creek to see. There were very few people, and only a small *souq*. When I visited Dubai a year later, it was pretty much the same but, when I returned after university in the 1980s, it had begun its transformation into a world capital. Today, the Dubai skyline competes with the best in the world and, every time I visit, there is something new to see.

Interestingly, Dubai's dramatic success has depended on

the use of the only three natural resources it has: the sun, the sea, and the desert. These assets, coupled with leadership and vision, are the reason it is such a thriving place today.

At the time Dubai was growing at a breakneck pace, armies of pessimists were developing in other states in the UAE and across the oil-rich nations of the GCC. The naysayers insisted that Dubai was just a bubble on the verge of collapse. I have listened to these cynics and their doomsday prophesies since the 1980s and, to be honest, I am surprised they are still singing the same lame tune.

COMPETITION

The ruler of Dubai, Sheikh Mohammed bin Rashid Al Maktoum, deserves much of the credit for what his city is today. He surrounded himself with a team of trusted lieutenants and empowered them to deliver on his vision. What it created, instead of a yes-man system, was competition, which at times led to unfortunate decisions. But the overall result was emulation, forcing each of them to reinvent their strategies on an ongoing basis. The leadership also allowed and facilitated the development of an indigenous private sector.

DUBAI – PART OF THE REAL WORLD

One would have thought that the 2008 global financial crisis and its impact on Dubai would have forever silenced the city's loudest critics, but it did not. The global financial crisis caused tremendous damage to the UAE's largest city but, soon enough, Dubai experienced a dramatic recovery and continued as the only part of the Arab world that was also a part of the real world. During the first days of the financial crisis, an "I-told-you-so" sentiment spread like wildfire, and many predicted Dubai's imminent collapse. That collapse never occurred and, in just a few years, Dubai was once again in full swing, its critics' disdain mostly dismissed. By the time Dubai won the privilege of hosting Expo 2020, it was bursting with energy and back with a vengeance.

NON-BURSTING BUBBLE

Today, the so-called elite across the GCC continue their petty Dubai-bashing, with some complaining that it is run like a corporate entity rather than a country, and others still insisting that it is just a bubble waiting to burst. Some even dismiss Dubai's dramatic achievements because they are man-made and therefore not real.

COPYCAT

Despite all the Dubai-bashing, many places in the GCC, including other states in the UAE, have tried to imitate, even replicate, Dubai's success story. So far, these other places have met with little or no luck.

OPPORTUNITY KNOCKS WINNER

Dubai even thrived during the COVID-19 pandemic. Unlike the rest of the world, Dubai stayed open. Tourism from Israel increased once the Abraham Accords transformed the city. Similarly, Dubai has served as a benefactor during the Russia–Ukraine War, welcoming thousands of Russians and Ukrainians who have moved to the UAE in the last year, creating a boom in the real estate.

Perhaps the Dubai critics should stop trying to play copycat and focus instead on trying to understand how a place with such limited resources could write such an impressive success story. Rather than spending untold millions attempting to imitate Dubai, perhaps we should begin thinking strategically, for a change.

The accusation that Dubai's success is just a bubble is a myth, and we should peek past that massive green monster and take an objective look at *why* it is so successful.

OBSERVATION 5

REDEFINING THE SOCIAL CONTRACT

After independence, most of the MENA governments established a specific kind of social contract with its citizens, based mainly on the redistribution of the flow of money from natural resources, development aid, and other forms of external transfers known as rents. The MENA governments provide its citizens with subsidized food and energy, free public education, and government jobs in compensation for those citizens' tacit recognition of the legitimacy of the political regimes. This means that citizens are barred from any real political participation. However, with growing populations and declining state revenue, some governments have lost their ability to provide all these subsidies and have focused spending instead on social groups strategically important to them, increasingly tying resource provision to complete abstention from political participation.

SO-CALLED ARAB SPRING

The Arab uprisings in 2011 can be seen as an expression of deep dissatisfaction with the social contracts that no longer provided either political participation or substantial social benefits, at least for large parts of the population.

After the uprisings, the MENA countries developed in their own separate ways. While Tunisia went a fair way toward more inclusive development and political participation, some of that change has now eroded. Morocco and Jordan are working to restore portions of their former social contracts that provide some paternalistic distribution. In Egypt's emerging social contract, the government promises little more than individual and collective security, but only on the condition that its subjects will take no part in political matters. Libya, Yemen, and the Syrian Arab Republic have fallen into civil wars with no new countrywide contracts in sight, and Iraq has been struggling since 2003 to establish its social contract, while flight and migration also affect the social contracts of neighboring countries Jordan, Turkey, and Lebanon.

NEW SOCIAL CONTRACT – A MUST

Most MENA countries will need to design new social contracts to reduce current instability and enable physical reconstruction.

To shape a new social contract, we might create a "Competition Policy," a level playing field strongly enforced.

Subsidies should be replaced with targeted cash transfers, giving poor citizens a choice of goods to consume. The public sector should be rationalized to perform the functions appropriate to a thriving government. The state should never function as the employer of first or even last resort. Oppression is not a solution.

Institutions should work together to build independence and professionalism to serve the public good rather than political aims. A new kind of social contract will allow us to tackle our most crucial and difficult issues, including climate change and the refugee crisis. Like the EU, the more developed regions have the responsibility to support less developed regions and to care for citizens from other countries.

INTERNATIONAL SOCIAL CONTRACTS

Ultimately, domestic contracts are insufficient in today's world. An international social contract is what we require. The global availability of common goods means it is insufficient for countries to care only about their own needs and business. The flow of external rent, together with internal rent-seeking, has perpetuated the wealth and power of the political and economic elites in the Middle East and limited the economic opportunities of the wider population. To facilitate cooperation, minimize unhealthy competition, and solve international conflicts, we should strive for greater responsibility along international and regional lines.

OBSERVATION 6

MALE GUARDIANSHIP AND WOMEN

How can regimes in the Arab world reduce gender inequalities and actively practice tolerance of gender differences and preferences? How can the individual nations and their rulers break down gender stereotypes and examine why and how countries outside MENA view the rights and status of women inside MENA? How can a new generation move beyond the master–slave mentality? In which countries is this paradigm a vestige of British colonialism and in which is it entrenched ideology from ancient times? When men in the Middle East accept that women should enjoy freedom of choice, are they not freeing themselves from the shackles of a master–slave mentality for all?

Women suffer from domestic violence, inequality in divorce, and tremendous struggles from the fact that equal rights in child custody battles and inheritance rights are denied to them. The negative social impact of social inequality and gender discrimination has resulted in low rates of employment and education among women. Gender disparities have prevented women from full participation in the workforce; they could be making immense contributions in the form of productivity and innovation, thus strengthening entire economies and uplifting numerous lives. In most of the Arab world, women cannot pass their citizenship rights to their children. Does this mean that their citizenship is less valuable than men's?

There is no longer any social or cultural justification for male guardianship. This policy restricts women from educational and employment opportunities. Despite announcements to the contrary across the Arab world, women are largely unable to achieve or even strive for economic independence. Instead, they must rely on male guardians for their entire economic and social survival.

Islamic rules should not be considered responsible for social discrimination against women. Sexism is a global problem, not a regional or religious issue. Concerted efforts are required for societies to reject the unfounded justifications for male guardianship.

All countries should publicly denounce male guardianship policies and practices, particularly those encouraged and enshrined in government law. Overall, regulations and laws must compel societies to reject the kind of gender discrimination that extends to all aspects of women's lives, including their income and their right to marry or divorce. Sadly, patriarchal systems around the world control their people through subsidies and punishment that force individuals to conform to the status quo. When rulers deny their subjects meaningful incentives to reject gender discrimination, the entire society stagnates and suffers. Compulsory primary and secondary education for all girls would go a long way toward ending gender discrimination in the Middle East.

Today, one positive type of community outlet to which some MENA women can adhere is a peer support system that can help soften the harsh prohibitions of gender discrimination. Through such support systems, women share experiences, help solve one another's personal, family, and financial problems, exchange information, and receive emotional assistance. The members of these support groups also share essential healthcare and nursery facilities and the burdens of housekeeping.

OBSERVATION 7

THE SHRINKING PIE

For decades, some of the Arab governments have hoarded oil riches while passing out favors, jobs, and land in order to tighten control over their subjects' lives. The elite are generally satisfied with the status quo, particularly when GDP per capita is high. But economic dilemmas have grown more tangled over the past two years. The double slam of low oil prices and COVID-19 lockdowns created serious difficulties for the welfare of the economies and individuals in the Middle East. Today, the region's oil-rich countries enjoy extremely high oil prices that have greatly increased their wealth. Even Saudi Arabia, Iraq, the UAE, Iran, and Kuwait are benefiting from the boom in oil prices brought on mainly by the Russia–Ukraine War, yet some of these countries also face enormous long-term economic and social problems, including high unemployment and, in certain countries, their people's dissatisfaction with various government policies. People in MENA are crying out for greater representation in government and more say in their futures. For years, the public sector has been the main employer in the Middle East, but most governments no longer provide the number of jobs people need to feed their families, and government-controlled industries have been slow to privatize and diversify.

MERITOCRACY

Meritocracy must be the way forward. There is little point in educating the public if meritocracy cannot prevail. Governments, rife with corruption, have prevented people from becoming entrepreneurs and innovators. The nature of many Arab societies denies people the right to question authorities. Egypt's recent struggles with a bleak short-term economic outlook led to a serious depletion of capital reserves. Decades of high-level favoritism robbed the country and its people of the benefits of economic and personal growth. There is hope that investment and cooperation among Arab neighbors will begin to help all our countries overcome their financial difficulties and that, in the not-too-distant future, a merit-based economic system will promote entrepreneurship. The Egyptian people are facing intense challenges due to rapid population growth, deep and increasing poverty, widespread youth unemployment, a looming Nile water shortage, and threats to food security caused by climate change.

OBSERVATION 8

GLOBAL LEADERSHIP IN THE TIME OF CRISIS: THE CASE OF THE PANDEMIC

Has there ever been a bigger missed opportunity for leadership than that associated with the COVID-19 pandemic?

Like every major crisis, COVID-19 challenged leaders at every level. We have yet to see the end of the pandemic or fully understand this invisible virus that has wreaked such havoc on societies everywhere, gutting economies and leaving millions of people dead and healthcare systems in tatters. Wave after wave of COVID variants have hit humanity, the rich and the poor, the old and the young. Despite lockdowns, the disease persists today, suggesting the possibility that COVID-19 will become endemic, much like its more benign corona relative the common cold but with much higher costs.

The COVID-19 virus struck at a time when many countries'

immune systems had already been weakened by authoritarian leaders with empty slogans and yes-men-filled bureaucracies. Authoritarian populists gained ground in countries worldwide, undermining constitutional checks and balances and evidence-based policymaking. In the Middle East, political polarization increased the misery of the pandemic. There was little time for ideologies and politics when lives were at stake; we needed solid science, delivered by the world's true experts in the field, to show us the way. Unfortunately, even the scientific and medical communities were blindsided by the virus and scrambled to comprehend, explore, and deliver effective and accurate healthcare information. Mistakes associated with COVID-19 prevention and treatment protocols have produced far-reaching, long-lasting implications. Not a single country in the world was prepared for the destructive power of the pandemic.

This does not mean that people should hand all power to any so-called experts; rather, it is essential that they employ critical thinking and research-based evidence when making healthcare or most other decisions.

Greed and bureaucracy, power grabbing, and a lack of transparency cost the world millions of lives. Responses to the pandemic have been numerous and extraordinary, and they continue to increase exponentially with the arrival of new variants and research. In addition to critically analyzed scientific and intellectual information, the COVID-19 crisis requires a wide range of tangible goods and services, with some commodities doubling in value as the use of others diminishes. The world today is dependent on goods produced both locally and globally.

Thorough, evidence-based research is also essential to an understanding of the realistic scale and speed of commodity and service production and delivery. The steep learning curves associated with new and ever-burgeoning economic and social disasters beg for a larger and better educated workforce. The race to develop a COVID-19 vaccine ushered in a speedy exchange of scientific knowledge, the swiftest collaboration and dissemination of scientific information in human history. On the other hand, actual vaccine distribution has been a global joke played on the world's most vulnerable populations.

Addressing a pandemic should be about fighting the weakest links, whether individual hospitals, political leaders, or particular countries. Leadership is about protecting the citizens who depend on you, but it is also about protecting the most vulnerable.

An effective pandemic response would have benefited from multiple, internationally gathered sources of credible information. The medical journal *Lancet,* the WHO, and many other information outlets blame many of today's problems, especially those related to healthcare, on what they term an "Infodemic," a rapid and far-reaching spread of both accurate and inaccurate information about disease and other issues.

At first, populist leaders around the world belittled the COVID-19 threats to society and suppressed information about it. Later, they weaponized the situation by accusing political opponents of circulating dangerous rumors about causes and treatments. Over time, some acknowledged the science, but the end result was a concerted drop in overall respect and faith in public institutions.

Despite the speed with which they inoculated their people, the US and other wealthy nations dealt for months with the deaths of millions of individuals infected with the virus, many of whom died because they refused to be vaccinated. The lack of a unified mask and vaccine mandate deteriorated into a political debacle, splitting political parties on the right from those on the left and engendering a deep distrust of government overall. This bickering transpired while the deplorably insufficient amount of vaccine allotted to poorer nations led to much misery and death. Vaccine was often commandeered by elites, and many countries lacked adequate funding to purchase more. Many countries were left helpless, unable to protect their populations. Yet the pandemic was a rare opportunity for leaders to make needed improvements to the healthcare sector because people were so focused on their own health.

In times of crisis, leaders should never be afraid of planning for the worst-case scenario. Proper catastrophic planning requires a thorough analysis of a situation, and examining the worst-case scenario focuses minds and creates systems that can reduce anxiety.

Leaders must also cooperate to ensure that global institutions work together in a coherent and cost-effective way. During the COVID-19 pandemic, the WHO came under heavy fire for some of the earliest information it released about the virus, but it had already established its credibility with its handling of the West African Ebola epidemic. The WHO was the only institution that could provide global leadership and inspire the kind of widespread trust essential to the success of countries' interventions in their people's health and healthcare systems. We undermine the WHO at our own peril.

Taken together, these measures provide a sense of the complexity and magnitude of the response that the pandemic required. But the costs of inaction are great in financial and social terms. A successful response can launch the rebuilding of inclusive, meritocratic, and accountable leadership at the national and international levels. The world must heed these difficult lessons as waves of COVID-19 variants continue to strike. We can use every brief moment of respite to rebuild in a more inclusive way, as a time to do good, to heal, and to repair.

OBSERVATION 9

CONFORMITY IS UNSUSTAINABLE

Do not question the powers that be and you shall have a home and a job. Your connections and education will contribute to your status and comfort level within the confines of your conformity. But how long can you stay in place and play your role if your country is going nowhere?

In the Middle East, the chasm between rich and poor is deep. When the pieces of the oil-industry pie are doled out, the youth are usually left with crumbs. Without an aspirational middle class and jobs to encourage ambition, entrepreneurship, or innovation, how can we push the economy forward? Where do we go from here?

The MENA region is particularly vulnerable to trade shocks because of its high food import dependence. Egypt, Sudan, and Yemen, three of the poorest countries in the region, rely heavily on cereal imports from Russia and Ukraine.

Between 2020 and 2021, the international demand for oil increased as COVID-19 restrictions eased. This pushed prices up and, as a result, Middle East OPEC states experienced a massive increase in oil export revenues, from $244 billion to $446 billion per year. Oil prices have continued to rise sharply in 2022 because of the Russia–Ukraine War. On the other hand, Lebanon has seen per capita income and the quality of life plummet since 2019 amidst a severe economic crisis.

Yemen and the Syrian Arab Republic, among the poorest and most conflict-impacted countries, are already feeling the effects of higher prices. In May 2022, the UN World Food Programme warned that, "the war will incur potentially significant consequences on certain food crises in the Middle East." Higher prices, burgeoning humanitarian needs around the world, food shortages, energy issues, and supply strains will all constrain the Middle East's ability to deliver emergency assistance.

TIME BOMB

With a majority of the Middle East's population under the age of 25 and the 30% jobless rate still rising, Arab regimes must guard their newfound revenue and apply themselves to the development of meritocracy, entrepreneurship, and critical thinking. They cannot sustain a culture of conformity and obedience if they want to stay in power. How can we move from a culture of nepotism and conformity to a culture of meritocracy and independent thinking? Meritocracy has to be the way forward. There is no point to education if meritocracy does not exist. Autocratic leadership and corruption have not allowed people to be entrepreneurs and innovators, except those who are conformist.

OBSERVATION 10

THE SOCIAL CONTRACT EMERGENCY

I believe we are on the cusp of a sudden social explosion. People rebel when everything is taken away from them, and the rebellion will come sooner than expected. The people in leadership positions must start changing the social contract they have with the people and share the agony with them, rather than taking and taking. Their old way is to put all the agony on the people and try to stay in power, lengthening their shelf life in musty old cabinets. The rulers and their codependents must implement reforms or they will lose their place on the shelf. COVID-19 and global inflation are accelerating the process, which may prove good for the people from a long-term perspective.

Eventually, the people in leadership positions have to give more to the people in terms of sharing power, not like in a democracy, but power in terms of freedom and of expression,

associated with meritocracy and the possibility to n
successfully within the system, throwing nepotism out.

MINI ME

It cannot be that my child can choose from all the jobs available because I am part of a regime and have ties to it, while someone else's child, born in the same country but without those ties, does not have that choice although that child is 10 times more qualified for the job than mine. It cannot be better for the economy for young, educated people to have nowhere to turn and to have to accept being a part of the system in order to receive the benefits they need.

Voices of discontent are emerging from under the surface and creating rifts that may never be repaired. Many longtime UAE residents have expressed their desire to see their system return to its old ways. The newly relaxed laws may permanently reshape the underlying tenets of the social contract. These societal shifts are changing the relationship between sovereign powers and their subjects. They are forcing changes imposed by the governments and driving many subjects to scramble to find a way forward.

Both Saudi Arabia and the UAE are experiencing an uneasy compromise that indicates the deterioration of the existing social contract. Cracks are beginning to widen and fray the social fabric, from the imposition of value added tax in the kingdom and the enforced reduction of loudspeakers in mosques, to allowing women to drive.

Loyal and obedient Emiratis were at first jubilant about the normalized relations with Israel, but their happiness soon diminished when laws were changed to accommodate the influx of foreigners and foreign investors, and included cohabitation by unmarried couples and alcohol consumption without a license, coupled with anger about the attacks by Israeli soldiers on Palestinians and citizenship for foreigners. The big leap from the old restrictive rules to the acceptance of permissive cohabitation and alcohol indicated just how muddled and confused the social contract became.

OBSERVATION 11

WHEN GROWTH IS A MYTH

We need to carefully analyze the numbers that suggest some of the GCC countries have grown 6%, 7%, or even 10% per annum. The central banks as well as some of the new banks are perpetuating a myth floating around the Gulf today. These banks are basically conduits for somebody with government connections or they are run by a highly influential person in the government.

Take the real estate markets, for example. How can we measure intrinsic value or gauge asset appreciation or growth when the starting point is land, which has zero cost and was parceled out for free and then developed before going to market?

The stock market has been rising in the Gulf, and in North Africa, Egypt, and Jordan. Some of this increase may be the result of initial lower prices. Today, the prices are much higher: the price-to-earnings ratios and the price-to-book are high. Real estate and the stock market are popular again, but we must be incredibly careful in determining the reality of their growth.

Indeed, money has grown, oil prices have increased, natural gas prices and demand look good, but our middle class is badly shaken. I think the middle class has basically been destroyed in the Middle East. It's been destroyed because the gap between the rich and poor has widened. Members of the middle class have either gotten richer or they have hit rock bottom. Today, some people in the Arab world cannot even afford to eat. It is hard for people to make $20, $10, or even $2 a day.

The hard fact that people cannot eat means we must be careful about asserting growth. We must look at the facts on the ground and acknowledge that the majority of people are suffering.

Before talking about growth and about money shifting from the Gulf, first we should look at the necessity of everyday stability and security. People want their neighbor to be as stable as they are, even if they don't share the same language or religion. In each of the six Gulf states, some people live in a much lower economic class than others.

EDUCATION CHALLENGE

Education is the biggest challenge. We must talk about it and take action. We must invest in human capital and start training people at the top. Part of addressing the education issue involves the demand to reform, to become reform-minded and teach leaders how to reform. Reform is not easy to achieve because everyone, including every leader, has to pay a price to achieve it.

I find it difficult to believe that education will be reformed in the Arab world, although I know it's a necessity. The states have been unveiling subsidies and believe they are keeping the people happy, when in fact they are looking down on the people, who have been educated – even indoctrinated – to believe in this codependence.

Oil and gas are exported, but everything else is imported. Relying on all these imports means we must reevaluate how the Arab economies can become sustainable. We cannot rely on the international community and must instead rely on ourselves.

LOOK IN THE MIRROR

We cannot just talk about other governments and about the international community because we in the GCC need to talk about ourselves. We can take social responsibility as an example and look at financial statements. We can examine what is being spent and determine what percentage of our spending goes to research. We should invest in the future, in education, and should not put most of our money in a sovereign fund or in a Citibank or UBS or any such place. We should invest it in our own people. The business community must also take on this burden.

We will not be resilient in the future if we do not recreate our middle class. I'm talking about my great-grandchildren and their children's future. We must create a community that can ward off disaster or that can recover from disaster together. In the event of a catastrophe, we will have no option but to act as one bloc in the GCC. We need champions across the borders to mentor the talented young people and inspire them to raise themselves up and build a thriving and caring economy.

OBSERVATION 12

IT'S HIGH TIME TO FIGHT HYPOCRISY

In the past generation or two, our region has witnessed a rising trend in forced "political correctness." Tempering confrontation with diplomacy is indeed a responsible approach, because it makes living and working with one another – regardless of our backgrounds, opinions, or belief systems – easier and more comfortable. It makes conflicting positions less abrasive. This makes sense in theory but, in practical terms, it can get messy. As with any real-world application of a theoretical concept, a wide range of practical approaches exist but, in the modern-day Middle East, we seem to have chosen the worst approach possible. Theoretically, being politically correct or diplomatic translates into being sensitive to other views and tactful in presenting conflicting opinions. Practically, however, it often translates into one of two extreme approaches. At best, it translates into excessive politeness, such as being too sensitive to too many things, or constantly worrying about offending anyone with the smallest gesture or remark, or diluting language to a string of clichéd euphemisms. At worse, it translates into simple hypocrisy and that is where the trouble starts.

POLITENESS VS. HYPOCRISY

There is and always has been a world of difference between politeness and hypocrisy and it baffles me that in our part of the world in particular, the two are so often interchanged. We seem to have decided that to be diplomatic, we must agree completely with what others, particularly those in power, think or say or do. In that scenario, we must not offer any constructive criticism, voice any unpopular (or even different) opinions, or in any way disagree (or even appear to disagree) with current thinking. Ironically, Islam teaches us to do exactly the opposite. In fact, Muslims are preconditioned to be "anti-hypocrites." The *Quran* includes many verses about hypocrites, referring to them as more dangerous to Muslims than the worst non-Muslim enemies. In fact, it includes a whole chapter entitled "*Al-Munafiqun*" ("Hypocrites"). It surprises me that devout Muslims continue to ignore this clear *Quran* instruction and refuse to recognize a key component of our religion. We seem to have taken the lofty concept of being politically correct to mean being a crass hypocrite, and the act of being diplomatic to mean being a bland conformist which, frankly, is demeaning. This type of hypocrisy, despite possible good intentions, is extremely destructive. It kills any chance to nurture leadership within our communities and leaves us facing a bleak future with no real prospects of meaningful improvement. It effectively robs us of attaining any traction in our efforts to move forward, leaving us spinning pointlessly in the same spot. If we cannot challenge current thinking, if we cannot propose alternative ideas, if we cannot point out weakness and address them, how can we possibly move forward? If we continue to blindly agree with everything just to be "diplomatic" or "politically correct," how can we possibly expect a better future? This issue has become such an integral part of our lives in the Middle East that we have developed our own Arabic term for it: *Khalak diplomasi,* literally "stay diplomatic." This is tragic advice thrown around in almost every social circle and community across the region. It will only make matters worse, as our youth, who account for the largest segment of our population, are robbed of critical thinking and instead taught to play along silently and accept their own hypocrisy. Conformity is not diplomacy, and hypocrisy is not political correctness. These are two fundamentally different things and the sooner we recognize that, the sooner we can work together with mutual respect to shape our collective futures.

OBSERVATION 13

WHY A WEALTH TAX?

The notion of a wealth tax is dangerously shortsighted and risks making a bad situation worse. We are already grappling with an outrageous distribution of wealth around the world. An Oxfam paper published in 2017, entitled "An Economy for the 99%," reports that eight men together owned as much wealth as the 3.6 billion people who made up the poorest half of humanity. In January 2020, Oxfam reported that the world's 2,153 billionaires had more wealth than the 4.6 billion people who made up 60% of the world's population. In 2022, the same annual report states that "Billionaire wealth has soared during the COVID-19 pandemic as companies in the food, pharma, energy, and tech sectors have cashed in [while] millions of people around the world are facing a cost-of-living crisis due to the continuing effects of the pandemic and the rapidly rising costs of essentials such as food and energy. Inequality, already extreme before COVID-19, has reached new levels." In short, global inequality kills one person every four seconds in today's world.

The report, which presumably considered only publicly disclosed wealth, shows that the gap between rich and poor is far greater than many had feared. It calls for a fundamental change in how our economies are managed so that they will work for all people, not just a fortunate few.

Oxfam had more to say:

> Our broken economies are funnelling wealth to a rich elite at the expense of the poorest in society, the majority of whom are women. The richest are accumulating wealth at such an astonishing rate that the world could see its first trillionaire in just 25 years. … … … … Public anger with inequality is already creating political shockwaves across the globe … … 7 out of 10 people live in a country that has seen a rise in inequality in the last 30 years. Between 1988 and 2011, the incomes of the poorest 10% increased by just $65 per person, while the incomes of the richest 1% grew by $11,800 per person, 182 times as much.

Oxfam also recognizes that, "Extreme inequality is not inevitable or accidental. It is the result of deliberate political and economic choices, and it can be reversed."

SHRINKING MIDDLE CLASS

It is a worldwide problem, and we in the GCC are part of this world. We are part of the problem, and we must work together to figure out how to be part of the solution. Our current thinking is not helping. For millions of people across the Middle East, the situation is exasperating and extremely frustrating, because they realize there is little they can do about it. In each of the past 25 years, we have watched our middle class shrink almost to the point of extinction.

The problem is serious because the middle class is the backbone of any economy and the only real path to sustainable development and, consequently, to stability. Eroding the middle class translates to eliminating sustainable development, which makes stability all but impossible. This is as true in the Middle East as it is anywhere else in the world.

In the GCC, our current approach further stresses the problems of the already stressed middle class, for whom individual purchasing power has been eroded in the immediate term by governments' lifting of subsidies. The rulers have explained that this action is part of their so-called reforms. They have also introduced taxation, while damaging long-term prospects due to reductions in infrastructure investments. All of this could lead to social disenchantment, which might in turn cause actual unrest.

VAT HURTS THE POOR

The Gulf countries are the Arab world's richest countries, yet tax increases there are hurting the general public. The tax is something we must all pay, with the exception of course of the rich. Rich people who wish to purchase expensive clothes and other luxury goods go wherever they like – to the US, the UK, maybe to France or Italy. When they purchase a car, they select it in another country and ship it to the Gulf. For someone who can spend a million dollars of income a month on luxury items, a tax of $20,000 is peanuts. For someone who can spend only $1,000 of their income a month on their version of extras – maybe a new dress and new makeup but, more likely, just food and fuel – an additional $20 to $25 is a lot of money.

I know a man who has been renting out his late father's house. One day, his renter informed him that he could no longer pay the monthly rent of $1,000, because his monthly electric bill alone had increased to that amount, to $1,000. This kind of additional household expense should comprise no more than 20% of the monthly rent but, today, it is often equal to 100% of the rent. This is crazy, but the government is not the only entity to blame. We should also blame the social contract between renters and rulers, between subjects and regimes. The social contract must be rewritten.

NEXT TAXES

The next tax the regimes will introduce will be an income tax. Or, governments might start with a corporate tax but, eventually, they will tax individuals. When people start paying individual income taxes, they might recall that they learned in history class that young Americans once shouted that, "taxation without representation is tyranny." When the government struggles to manage its losses while the people struggle to manage the basic cost of living, the social contract breaks down. The government once provided an adequate monthly income to the people in exchange for silence. The government managed everything so that the people would say nothing. It will not work this way for much longer.

As far as taxation in the Arab world is concerned, serious consideration should be given to introducing a wealth tax for all eligible individuals, whether citizens or residents. This is entirely different from *Zakat,* and we must never confuse the two. *Zakat* is one of the five pillars of Islam, a theological construct and sacred, deeply religious duty that is by definition a private matter between an individual and God.

The wealth tax is a financial instrument designed to force better use of wealth. Making everyone in the GCC with a net worth of more than $5 million pay tax would go a long way toward balancing our budgets without further stressing the masses.

WEALTH VIA RELATIONSHIP

A lot of the wealth of the Gulf's so-called new bourgeoisie was created two or three generations ago due almost exclusively to individuals' close associations with the ruling regimes of the time. In most cases, a first generation was granted exclusive privileges by the people in power that were then monopolized by their recipients to generate tremendous wealth. This was passed down, sometimes creating a convincing illusion of entrepreneurial spirit and competitive markets.

However, much of this was national wealth assigned to individuals for personal gain. It is now time to recoup some of it by introducing a wealth tax. This is not a particularly popular idea, but the fact is that a lot of wealth has been created over the past few decades, and many GCC citizens and residents have grown very wealthy. Some countries in the region have seen an explosion in the number of billionaires from South Asia in the last three decades.

If properly applied, a wealth tax could prove an ideal solution to our current challenges, both regionally and internationally. We might not want to step on rich toes, but we cannot afford to further stress the masses through additional reductions to their purchasing power. We must also invest in quality education, which we cannot afford to do without a wealth tax. Nor can we afford to wait for some other solution by hoping things will somehow revert to the way they were in some long-gone past.

We may think we have been here before. The 1985 oil price crash and the global financial crisis of 2008 do offer proof of other recent financial disasters. However, we must recognize that, this time, things are fundamentally different, not least because of COVID-19. In addition to the pandemic, the range of available energy resources has now expanded to include shale oil, which has finally allowed the United States to diminish some of its dependency on Middle Eastern oil as gas producers can now tap into shale formations across North America. This is a fast-developing alternative energy resource that could have dire implications for the future of oil production in the Middle East. A number of other new global energy resources can well be viewed as cause for alarm. Another source of concern is the dramatic increase in population in the GCC from about 14.5 million in 1985 to about 53.5 million in 2020.

This time, there is no going back.

OBSERVATION 14

TRYING TO AVOID A CRASH LANDING WITHOUT CRUSHING THE MIDDLE

Economically, it appears that the Middle East region might be able to avoid an all-out crash and face only a really rough landing. The immediate economic challenge is to mitigate risks and ensure that a landing is as smooth as possible.

A much bigger challenge is to ensure that the middle class is not entirely destroyed in an attempt to cushion this landing, although current indicators suggest that this is exactly what will happen. Direct and indirect taxation, coupled with subsidy reductions, promise to hit the middle class and further reduce its already deeply eroded spending power. This is a surefire recipe for disaster.

IMMEDIATE CHALLENGE

To address the immediate challenge, the region must first come to terms with some harsh realities, including the threat of a full-on crash. International bankers, analysts, economists, and even the financial media have spelled these out in a succession of damning reports. The region's elite ignore these at their peril, even if some of the reports make for painful and even embarrassing reading.

The uncertainty about oil prices cannot be overstated, but one thing already seems certain: the GCC can no longer afford to rely exclusively on oil revenues.

Shale oil alone, coupled with lowered costs, improved technology, and shifting supply-and-demand curves, has altered the global oil market since the 2022 start of the Russia–Ukraine War. Oil prices rose by almost 70% in 2021, and revenue in the energy-rich Gulf states of Saudi Arabia, Iraq, UAE, Iran, Kuwait, and Qatar increased dramatically. Nonetheless, these countries, like all countries in MENA, must find other ways to support their people and offer them real opportunity.

NEED FOR UNPOPULAR DECISIONS

Collectively and individually, economies must be prepared to make unpopular decisions. I am not being alarmist when I say that current realities have spurred Saudi Arabia, the largest economy in the region, to unveil previously unthinkable plans for economic reform. In late October 2022, HRH Crown Prince Mohammed bin Salman of Saudi Arabia launched an initiative to attract investments in supply chains to and from the kingdom, with an aim of raising an initial $10.64 billion. Last year, the Gulf state announced it would invest over $133 billion in infrastructure, including airports and sea ports, by the end of this decade in a bid to become a transport and logistics hub under an economic diversification plan.

The implementation of these reforms is already underway and the speed and scope of the transformation has caught many off guard. This is a powerful testament to the seriousness of our economic challenges and the equally serious manner in which decision-makers are addressing them. This approach could bode well for the region's future, promising great things over the next 10 years.

In the meantime, the foreign investment bankers, corporate lawyers, accountants, consultants, and public relations advisers traipsing in and out of Riyadh every week are reaping handsome financial rewards while the region's middle class receives nothing that compares with those rewards.

The money that is being spent on international advisers may

quite possibly be a sound investment, but none of it will trickle down to the middle class. Instead, people are facing increasingly challenging economic conditions in the immediate future; the introduction of direct taxes, including value added tax, increased indirect taxation, and reduced subsidies are all making a difficult situation significantly worse.

Only time will tell if Saudi Arabia, like many others in the region, will succeed in translating its ambitious Vision 2030 plan into reality. Meanwhile, it is important that such challenges be confronted head on. Chief among them is the region's ability to develop the private sector into a more prominent and productive segment of the economy. This is Economics 101 and an almost standard fixture in most of the region's strategic plans.

PRIVATE SECTOR

For example, Bahrain's Vision 2030 has long called for the private sector to serve as the key driver of economic growth going forward. This has been a recurring theme in Bahrain's economic narrative since at least 2008 and, yet, more than 14 years later, the International Monetary Fund must again point to increases in public-sector wages as a key component of the major fiscal adjustment so urgently needed.

Similarly, the current focus on lifting subsidies is remarkably shortsighted, even by Middle East standards, yet it seems to be the only solution currently under consideration. This is a necessary evil but, in addressing the issue, the emphasis should always be on subsidy reform rather than the generation of new funds to support subsidies and bridge a gap in the budget.

BALANCING BUDGETS

The current approach of trying to balance budgets by lifting subsidies and introducing taxes is not only ineffective, it is also dangerous. Increasing spending on big-ticket items only negates reductions in others, including subsidies. Necessity, real or perceived, ultimately dictates how money is spent, and decreasing some monetary components while increasing others will have a negligible overall effect on any budget.

The current approach is also dangerous, because it risks reducing the region's competitive advantage while further alienating the working middle class with disastrous consequences. History keeps reminding us of these disastrous consequences whenever such an approach is attempted. Instead, perhaps it is now time for the region's wealthy to start repaying their debt to society. The wealth created by citizens and residents of the region is largely the result of close alliances with the ruling regime and is often considered private wealth. However, it is in fact national wealth assigned to favored individuals for their personal gain, and we must recoup some of it and return it to the national economy. The introduction of a wealth tax is extremely unpopular, but it does eliminate the risks attached to any further stress on the region's poor and middle classes. Perhaps some Middle East countries can even use a portion of the surplus to invest in the youth, who represent our greatest opportunity.

FUTURE OF THE YOUTH

Youth have always been the largest, most powerful drivers of any economy. While Europe struggles with an aging population that might soon find itself unable to support its region, the Middle East is blessed with a young, strong, and rapidly growing population. According to data published by the United Nations, people between the ages of 15 and 29 account for nearly a third of the region's population, while another third of the population is represented by individuals below the age of 15.

The unemployment rate that Arab youth are contending with is the highest of any region in the world. The Middle East region needs to create more than 60 million new jobs to stabilize youth unemployment and accommodate the number of young workers struggling to enter the workforce. Over the past decade, a series of crises, including the 2008 financial crisis, the 2011

Arab Spring uprisings, armed conflict in the Syrian Arab Republic and Yemen and other countries, and the 2014 drop in oil prices that impacted remittances and Gulf migration, has increased youth unemployment in the MENA region.

The Middle East's youth, their needs, their energy, their potential, and their numbers, represent a massive opportunity of historic proportions. However, if this population and all that it has to offer is ignored or mishandled, the consequences may be devastating to all.

Crashing the economy would be painful for the Middle East, but crashing the middle class would be an absolute devastation. The middle class is the backbone of any economy and sacrificing it, or even just risking its continuing decline in an attempt to cushion an economic crash, would harm societies.

The economic importance of the middle class is distinct from that of the upper class. The middle class has excess human capital and a tremendous drive for higher incomes through increased employment, while the upper class is reluctant to relinquish any of the financial benefits it derives from the rentier economy. The upper class is actually the driver of transformation and innovation, both of which require financial and human capital, which are the key drivers of economic growth. It's true that the middle class has been responsible for a number of disruptive innovations but, in general, it lacks the financial innovation required.

What the middle class can effectively contribute is the promotion of the efficient and honest delivery of government services and forward-looking public investments. The political importance of the middle class is greater than the importance of the upper class. The middle class depends more on the public sector for quality education and healthcare than the upper class. While the middle class lacks the capacities of the rich to transfer their assets overseas, they can serve as a loud voice for investment in social issues like education and healthcare and other investments. The presence of a strong middle class is a very effective motivation for growth.

OBSERVATION 15

GREAT VISIONS AND WASTED OPPORTUNITIES

The 1971 commissioning of Aluminium Bahrain (Alba) marked the birth of industrial diversification in the oil-rich Gulf region. Bahrain launched the first aluminum operation in the region and, today, Alba ranks as the largest aluminum smelter in the world outside China.

Bahrain's success in the aluminum industry began in the mid 1960s when the government began exploring alternatives to revenue produced by the oil industry. The aim was to establish an industry that would provide valuable export earnings, develop the country's resources, and create training and job opportunities for the national workforce.

However, the Alba story is not unique in the annals of Bahraini innovation. Bahrain also has a progressive and highly valued educational system. Its public school system was founded in 1932; it is the oldest in the Arabian Peninsula. Bahrain was the first country in the region to establish a girls' school in the 1920s.

Bahrain has long been seen as a trailblazer. It has made a number of brave decisions concerning education and industry throughout its history. Today, the island nation is often hailed as one of the world's fastest growing financial centers. Its trailblazing ideas have driven momentum and helped create the modern-day GCC region, including Dubai, the internationally celebrated, razzle-dazzle center of the Middle East.

Bahrain has for all practical purposes pioneered the very concept of diversification away from oil dependency. The government of Bahrain had a clear vision, multiple visions in fact, which have led to the ultimate goal of creating a stable, sustainable economy through effective diversification.

Over the past few decades, however, we Bahrainis have struggled to implement many of our most cherished visions, instead allowing ourselves to get caught up in a vicious cycle of shortsighted, sometimes petty decisions. This is particularly sad because we have already demonstrated that we are capable of realizing these visions and translating them into tangible realities. We have done so before and have even taught our neighbors how to do it.

In my opinion, Bahrain's banking and finance story is the most painful example of this very phenomenon. When the Lebanese civil war broke out in 1975, the Bahrain government, as part of its master plan for diversifying the economy away from its dependence on oil, saw the opportunity to make the country the new banking capital of the Middle East. The vision was there, clearly spelled out, but the executives failed to implement it. It was there for the taking, but they let it go.

If Bahrain had efficiently and accurately implemented its vision for diversification in the 1970s and 1980s, the country might have been the only financial center in the Middle East, and we may never have even heard of the Gulf cities surpassing us today. Bahrain's vision was never actually implemented due to a lack of skill, a lack of operational efficiencies in the mechanisms, and a lack of leadership. Today, the competition between several Gulf cities vying to become the region's premier financial center is intense. Riyadh is in a privileged competitive position, with Doha also strongly placed. Abu Dhabi is also in the picture, while Dubai continues to dominate the region.

Bahrain must evaluate exactly what has changed and how the country can correct its bearings and return to the process of economic trailblazing. We have a plan and we know that it works. Now, we must implement that plan. Success will depend on whether we can designate competent leaders from business and government who can help realize our visions and translate them into concrete realities. The sooner we do so, the better.

OBSERVATION 16

LEADERSHIP THROUGH ETHICS

If even one individual decides he is above the law, a rule of law no longer exists. Leadership by example is the only model that can deliver meaningful, sustainable results. History has demonstrated as much many times in the past, across regions, religions, and ideologies. You can call for greater transparency, but if you are not yourself transparent, the call will go nowhere. You can demand ethical action, but if you are not yourself ethical, the demand will fail. You can initiate reform, but if you are not yourself prepared to reform, the reform will not succeed.

The lesson here is clear and obvious: you simply cannot succeed if you try to enforce two sets of moral standards, not in this age. The Arab world needs to practice the kind of thinking that challenges the status quo and envisions a future built on sustainable development and social inclusion. The creation of the world's largest sovereign wealth fund, the development of a non-oil-dependent economy, and the success of small and medium-sized enterprises require a legal system that inspires confidence and a system of corporate governance above reproach.

The Middle East continues to uphold Sharia law and practice Islamic finance while striving to encourage start-ups, entrepreneurial exploration, and corporate innovation. Can we evolve our current forms of government and religious practice to allow an upwardly mobile class to flourish? Can we examine Islamic absolute monarchy, parliamentary democracy, constitutional monarchy, and our Federal National Council and discover ways to improve opportunities for the younger generations searching for work and bursting with ideas? I believe we can and must implement reforms to start the evolutionary process. The Middle East must evolve in order to survive and thrive.

EVOLUTION VS. REVOLUTION

If a country believes in evolution without revolution but its current leaders are determined to retain control, then some version of a democratic process must be implemented. To sustain the rule of law, the governments must embrace freedom of expression and a freedom of the press devoid of threats of retaliation. In some countries, imprisonment and even death are weapons used by the government to ensure that media outlets report only what the rulers want them to. Rule of law is crucial to the well-being of the people. Laws are the vehicles through which basic rights are advanced and protected. They are meant to secure fairness as well as sustainable economic development.

As disappointing as this may sound, in order to analyze and motivate change, we may need to significantly intensify productivity and put aside the concept of political rule of law to focus on the rule of law in the economic dimension.

NO ONE ABOVE THE LAW

A strong rule of law in the realm of economics in the Middle East must include clear and fair business regulation, low levels of corruption and red tape, more support for business starters, and more autonomy for the court and judges presiding over commercial law. This would make the business environment friendlier and more secure while encouraging both domestic entrepreneurs and foreign investors.

This aligns with incumbent rulers' interests and is also pragmatic. The rule of law can boost a country's economy, strengthen its rulers' legitimacy, and improve people's lives. If the Middle East adheres to such practices, its economy will be less dependent on oil resources and more sustainable in the long run. Taking initiative to guide and monitor the rule of law early in the game is much better than waiting until social instability and unrest force the process on those who govern.

Although the rule of law will be rendered insufficient to the well-being of a country if it is enforced only with respect to the economy, the imposition of and adherence to effective and fair laws must be imposed on all economic concerns in order to attract serious investors. Without this, both businesspeople and investors will never be convinced of the security of their investments, their assets or money, in the hands of the Arab world.

In fact, the enforcement of a sound rule of law in the political realm is most salient when it incorporates the economic rule of law. When political reform occurs, the number and nature of social needs requiring financial resources increase and society's incentive to improve its business and finance sectors also increases. The economic rule of law can pave the way for a more conducive overall national environment characterized by peace and prosperity.

OBSERVATION 17

WHEN EXTORTION BECOMES LEGAL

Despite all the moral posturing and grandstanding that seem to define our region's elite, some elites have actually allowed extortion to become a part of our social fabric. A grown-up version of schoolyard bullying, extortion is shameful and embarrassing. Its most obvious example is the extortion engendered by powerful Western nations that enthusiastically prop up fragile regimes in a tragically shortsighted and painfully misguided attempt to create "world peace."

History has repeatedly demonstrated, often in extremely brutal and violent ways, that extortionate transactions do not work. Propping up repressive regimes to support immediate interests inevitably leads to the sacrifice of long-term needs, all the while creating a fertile breeding ground for radicals. It is the tragedy of our time.

Elites in the Arab world seem to be taking the liberty of implementing a literal, hands-on approach to extortion. Public-sector officials leverage the power they hold over public servants to extort obscene amounts of money from them. The fact that they claim to do so in the public interest makes the farce all the more tragic. It is a new and extremely dangerous low for everyone in the region. This is especially worrying because it destroys our credibility just when we need it most. It threatens to complicate our already formidable challenges and render them virtually insurmountable.

Although it is obvious that some of us in the region understand the significance of our future challenges better than others, we all seem to agree that failure is not an option. We also seem to agree that the status quo is no longer sustainable, and that Saudi Arabia's announcement of ambitious, revolutionary plans to wean itself away from its oil addiction perfectly captures the region's mood and outlook.

The plans, which quickly took root domestically, earned significant regional and international support. It was refreshing to see the official Saudi delegation so eloquently delivering their Vision 2030 report at a recent WEF Annual Meeting in Davos. As a result, the whole world took notice of Vision 2030 and the region's plans for its future. The world is now watching us, and we should be careful about what we say and do next.

We must take the next logical step while we still can. We must accept that to have any chance of realizing the region's aspirations, we need a solid legal system that cannot be manipulated or undermined by those in power. Otherwise, we cannot reasonably expect global investors to take us seriously.

This is not advanced economics, it is simply basic common sense that tells us we must not continue gagging our intellectuals and scaring away our innovators to instead support complacency and subservient compliance. Perhaps *that* is the problem.

LUCKY COMMON SENSE

In the mid 1990s, I had the privilege of lunching with the late Stephen Covey, international best-selling author of *The 7 Habits of Highly Effective People*. He had flown halfway around the world to deliver a presentation, but I had suggested that his list of important habits was actually nothing more than a list of common-sense actions. A tall man, Covey towered over me when he responded, "Son, who said sense is common?"

I remember that encounter vividly and, the more I think about it, the more I realize how insightful Covey was. Indeed, sense is not at all common. If it were, people capable of extortion would realize the practice is beneath them, and the problem would never have existed in the first place.

Had common sense actually prevailed throughout the history of the Middle East, we would long ago have focused on the creation of a level, merit-based environment in which equal opportunity for growth and prosperity was available to all and calculated risks were encouraged and innovations protected.

NONSTOP WALKING THE TALK

Growth and prosperity were some of the key elements of the Vision 2030 report and also a part of Bahrain's vision formulated years earlier. As always, the key lies in implementation. We cannot simply claim to be business-friendly; we must also demonstrate our friendliness over and over again.

This is the only way the world will take us seriously, no matter how many high-powered consultants we have on the payroll, or how many glossy advertisements or clever billboards we put up. The region's elite must find the strength of character to start laying the groundwork and implementing some of the important ideas we keep talking about.

OBSERVATION 18

THE CLEAR NEED FOR TRANSPARENCY IN THE GULF DRIVE FOR INVESTMENT

The single most effective way to attract investment, whether foreign, regional, or even domestic, is by embracing the system of legal redress.

LEGAL REDRESS

You can sing and shout all you want about how great you are, what great opportunities you offer, or even how great your support systems are, but until you can successfully demonstrate to potential investors that you have a solid legal system that will protect investors from theft, deceit, or mismanagement, it will be very difficult to attract and retain quality, high-net-worth investors. No one in your country can be seen as above the law. Otherwise, no one outside your country will take you seriously.

The Middle East has some of the best legal systems in the world but, as always, we seem to struggle with implementation. For a legal system to appear truly credible to potential investors, it must be seen to apply its laws in equal measure to everyone without exception.

The key here must be the emphasis on NO EXCEPTIONS. Even the best legal system in the world is of no use to potential investors if it appears to be manipulated by individuals in power. No one should be above the law, and that is the underlying premise of law in the first place.

Today, the world has evolved into one large village. Today, there is nowhere to hide, particularly when news travels at breakneck speed. More importantly, as interconnectivity increases by the minute, we can no longer expect any secrets to remain buried for long.

Today, people – and investors even more so – can immediately acquire all the information they believe they need to make the best, most effective decisions. As a result, we must work harder than ever to develop and maintain a superior reputation for upholding both transparency and the rule of law.

NEW DRIVER

To its credit, Saudi Arabia seems to have already recognized the importance of this fact and is taking key steps in the right direction. In 2016, Saudi Arabia announced it would wean itself away from what it called its "addiction to oil." The kingdom then unveiled a revolutionary plan aimed at transforming itself into a global investment power. The Saudi Vision 2030 plan is an extremely ambitious plan; critically speaking, it is also quite achievable.

The Saudi Vision 2030 is precisely the kind of revolutionary thinking Saudi Arabia and the rest of the region desperately need. It challenges the status quo and describes a future built on sustainable development and social inclusion.

Personally, I usually doubt strategies developed by international consultants. Over the years, and in many different countries, I have seen such strategies initially read with enthusiasm and then shelved out of frustration and disinterest. In this case, however, I really hope that Vision 2030 proves to be the exception to that course of events.

One key element of Vision 2030 is its support for the creation of the world's largest sovereign wealth fund and the development of Saudi Arabia's non-oil economy, particularly its small and medium-sized enterprises. These plans will bring unprecedented focus to our legal systems, our corporate governance, and our ability to protect investors. All of us, and our administrators in particular, must promise that our conduct will be purer than purity itself.

This is not a new challenge for the region, which had already pored over the very first UN *Arab Human Development Report* published in 2002. That report, which has since been widely referenced, highlighted poor governance as one of the three key areas by which Arab institutional structures hindered performance and crippled human development. Tragically, this seems to be as true today as it was in 2002.

Widespread admiration for Vision 2030 has increased the urgency with which change in the Arab world is being sought today. Recent, massive cultural shocks have transformed our collective mindset. In response, the Arab world must institutionalize a culture of accountability in which both action and inaction have consequences, people entrusted with any decision-making power must resign if they cannot or will not deliver, and officials must show tangible results for their efforts on a timely basis or be publicly held accountable for their failures.

This was an important part of the Vision 2030 narrative, whose many ideas were first presented in the 2002 *Arab Human Development Report* and discussed again in subsequent published reports. Perhaps if we had addressed certain issues identified 20 years ago, we would not be where we are today, and the latest report would not be so frustrating to read.

Change is long overdue. It must occur throughout the region if we expect investors – international, regional, or domestic – to take us seriously.

OBSERVATION 19

THE NEIGHBOR WHO FLEW TOO CLOSE TO THE SUN

I heard a modern mythical story about a man who fell from grace. Alas, his tale was no myth, but a true story of winning and losing in the Arab world.

The man completed his college education in a province east of his own small country. From that point on, he was part and parcel of the system.

After working in his own small country, he worked for an international investment bank for a year and a half and had several other stints at banks in the region. He soon became a co-founder of a bank and before long established a bank by himself with capital from the elites and from other banks in the region where he was from.

He made it big. He fit into the system and was rewarded

amply. Indeed, you can make it very big in that system. But to do so, you must pledge undying loyalty to the system's leaders as otherwise if you are not committed to them or fall from grace in any way, the system will fight you.

And that is what happened to the man when he got too big. In the Greek myth, Icarus uses waxen wings made by his father to escape imprisonment after fleeing from the Labyrinth but when he flies too close to the sun, the wings melt, and he falls into the sea and drowns. Like Icarus, the man fell from grace. Over time, the system he worshipped felt he had flown too close to the sun when they wanted him to simply stay within the confines of their labyrinth and make money that he shared with the top people in the system. The man began to prosper, he traveled outside of his small country, across borders and boundaries, to business meetings in other countries, including Libya, Egypt, Kazakhstan, Georgia, Jordan, Morocco, and Tunisia. He developed new and bigger ideas as his creative, independent mindset deepened, including a strategic plan for an offshore business empire that would exist out of reach of the powers that be.

He wanted to fly freely while enjoying the perks of life in his native country, but the system saw his daring new ideas as risky and believed he might no longer make the kind of money they were used to sharing. People running the system will treat you like you belong only as long as your efforts benefit them.

The man in the modern myth is an example of the fact that meritocracy does not work in this part of the world, not in the Gulf, and nowhere in the Middle East.

PAY TO PLAY

Within the framework of certain powerful people in the position of leadership, we must pay to play to survive. The man was rewarded generously when he closed profitable deals, generated wealth, and ensured the system benefited handsomely from his success.

He rubbed shoulders with billionaires, presidents, and aristocrats but, in the end, he paid a price. His relationships became difficult, and the backlash began. Whenever a deal failed, the system blamed him, because the only thing the people in power wanted was to continue receiving the easy flow of money they were accustomed to. When the global economic crisis of 2008 hit, the system made big trouble for the man. At first, one or two people blamed him, but soon things escalated, and the entire regime turned against him. The system does not respect meritocracy, nor does it understand innovation or risks that can lead to breakthrough discoveries and explosions of newfound wealth.

Alas, the man was never a yes-man, and his inability to fold his wings and stay in his place led to his inevitable downfall.

OBSERVATION 20

THE MIDDLE EAST NEEDS EVOLUTION, NOT REVOLUTION

As a child growing up in Bahrain, I remember thinking that the countries of the Middle East had much in common with countries in South America, Eastern Europe, Africa, and Asia. We were all part of the same experience, poised on the edge of evolution. I believed we would all soon evolve into liberal, modern, democratic nations full of free-thinking citizens rather than subjects, guided by leaders rather than rulers.

Since the 1980s, I have watched the world transform. My 30-year career in international business and finance has taken me from Argentina to Turkey to South Korea. During this time, I have witnessed incredible change in each place I have visited, except in the part of the world where I was born and raised, the Middle East.

DELIBERATE PROCESS OF EVOLUTION

Although we keep talking about it, the Middle East has yet to understand and undertake the slow but steady process of innovation that leads to evolution. It was not until right after the Arab Spring, during the WEF Special Meeting on Economic Growth and Job Creation in the Arab World in Jordan in October 2011, that King Abdullah of Jordan said, "We do not need revolution, we need evolution." This was a decade after the 2002 release of the *Arab Human Development Report (AHDR)* by the UNDP that outlined many of the Arab world's problems. Our failure to embrace any real evolution continues to worry me and many others. If we do not encourage evolution, the public's desire for change will build to the point of explosion, and evolution will no longer be an option. This is the scenario that triggered the Arab Spring.

The Middle East must begin by implementing specific reforms that can activate the process of evolution. We have already seen what the alternative looks like, and I dread thinking what the consequences of further delays may be. Reform, however painful, can wait no longer.

Evolution, not revolution, is an inspiring call to action and a principle upon which the people and rulers of our region seem to agree. However, in order to succeed, we must be ruthless in eliminating all possible barriers, including incompetence, corruption, and the other social ills holding us back.

CULTURAL SHOCK

We need a cultural shock strong enough to change our collective mindset. It is extremely important that we institutionalize a culture of accountability, in which people either deliver on key objectives or resign from their posts.

The continued failure to reform is a symptom of what is possibly our most dangerous weakness: a failure to think ahead and look past short-term objectives. Instead, we should begin in earnest to pursue concrete medium- and long-term goals. Our focus on instant gratification is robbing us of our shot at real development.

To allow for evolution, we must think and act strategically. We must have the vision to recognize that change is inevitable, concessions necessary, and compromise essential. Then we must find the courage to seize the moment and make these changes. If we continue to focus on our immediate interests, refusing to relinquish control over others and continuing to hoard absolutely everything, we will soon discover we have no treasures left to bury.

We must begin to address the core issues that plague the Middle East and feed our fertile breeding ground where dangerous, polarizing ideologies dominate the headlines, just as ISIS dominated the media not so long ago. ISIS is really just another iteration of an enduring problem. Yesterday it was al-Qaeda and, tomorrow, it will be something else, unless we acknowledge and fix the underlying problems.

Many in the West, particularly in the United States, are under the illusion that so-called moderate Arabs are the answer to all the region's problems. Although moderate Arabs, both politicians and intellectuals, have a role to play, so do moderates in the West. Like those of us in the Middle East, Western moderates must learn to look past immediate needs and embrace longer-term strategic goals.

History is sometimes a harsh teacher, but we cannot continue to forget the lessons of the past. We repeat the same expensive mistakes time and again. It is tragically shortsighted to support dictators because it is momentarily prudent. These kinds of choices ignore the price that must eventually be paid.

Change is inevitable but, unless we embrace evolution now, revolution may very well occur before too long.

OBSERVATION 21

BREAKING FREE FROM THE VICIOUS CIRCLE

The Middle East region is in a state of denial. Until we have the courage to face this reality, we will fail to break free from the vicious cycle that entraps us and prevents us from catching up with those countries that actually respect their citizens' rights.

This state of denial is reflected almost everywhere in our region. It is perhaps the single most challenging hurdle we must clear before we can embrace modernity. Ironically, denial is often the least apparent of attitudes, but putting a stop to the denial of the region's failure is the all-important first step forward. We must acknowledge our weaknesses before we can mend them.

This is simple and obvious. Developing the intellectual capacity to embrace modernity means evolving from subjects into citizens, from indentured subjects to individuals with personal rights and responsibilities.

This is where things get tricky. We continue to hide behind religion to justify maintaining the status quo, but this is dangerous and, to be honest, no longer sustainable. Religion has been used since time immemorial to control the masses, forcing them into quiet submission despite the fact that, by definition, religion should be viewed as a private, intimate relationship between individuals and their creator.

Islam is a defining component of our Arab culture and civilization; its significance is tremendous, but we cannot continue to use it as an excuse for inaction.

Ironically, Omar bin Khattab, one of the most powerful and influential Muslim caliphs in history, once famously said, "Since when did you enslave people born by their mothers in freedom?" This is a modern-day notion from the mind of a mid 7th-century holy man who would likely have found 21st-century Middle East constraints too much to bear.

Modernity, intellect, and citizenry are the prerequisites for breaking our vicious cycle. Unfortunately, they are often misrepresented simply to reinforce arguments against change.

TRUE MODERNITY

Modernity is not about how short skirts can be, or what architectural style we display, or which brands of consumer products we buy; it is about where we are as a civilization in relation to the rest of the world, how developed we are in thought and deed. Modernity is the ability to look critically at ourselves and self-reflect before we judge others.

TRUE INTELLECT

By the same token, intellect is not about how much we read, the academic degrees we have, or how much we have traveled. Rather, it is about how capable we are of processing experiences, behaviors, ideas, and attitudes, our own and others. It is about how carefully we consider ideas and information we receive from others, how willing we are to listen and consider opposing points of views and respond to them with empathy and respect. Such cognitive practices cannot be tolerated in an authoritarian state because autocrats cannot afford to entertain any sort of debate. Unfortunately, many rulers in the region, as well as their slavishly devoted subjects, choose to live in a state of denial.

STATE OF DENIAL

In recent times, the Middle East has experienced a considerable amount of migration away from the area. People of means are leaving our countries in search of opportunity, security, and freedom. This is creating modern-day ghost buildings. In some instances, it has even created ghost towns but, instead of acknowledging and examining this phenomenon, we choose to pretend it isn't happening. This is one more example of the impossible state of denial in which we choose to live, denial that leaves us treating anyone who doesn't agree with us or live like us as our enemy. As a result, we perpetuate our own problems while the rest of the world moves forward. We must stop hiding behind the interpretations of religious teachings and practices that confine us to despair, inaction, and boredom.

OBSERVATION 22

STABILITY THROUGH SUSTAINABILITY

The single most pressing and dangerous problem facing the Middle East today is unemployment. The total rate of unemployment in the Middle East is approximately 10%, the second highest rate in the world. But among young people under the age of 25, the rate of unemployment is almost three times as high. Soon, even more young people will need jobs because over 120 million youths in the MENA region today are under the age of 15.

This data means that the Middle East needs to create more than 33 million jobs by 2030. Unless the world's largest unemployment pool improves substantially, these people will probably resort to some kind of political violence or revolution. We must take a more determined and strategic approach to creating job opportunities and ensuring job readiness if we wish to survive.

POPULATION GROWTH AND UNEMPLOYMENT DILEMMA

The Middle East's population is growing almost twice as fast as the world's overall. The total population of the Middle East increased from approximately 100 million in 1950 to around 450 million in 2020, an addition of 350 million people in 70 years. However, it doesn't appear that the governments of the MENA countries are up to the task of creating jobs, and many MENA experts fear that a dangerous uprising is likely to occur when more than half of all youth are unemployed.

We must first fundamentally address our deplorably high levels of unemployment. International Labour Organization data from about 2018, just prior to the onslaught of the COVID-19 pandemic, revealed that 10.8% of people in the Middle East were unemployed, the second highest unemployment rate in the world. These facts should set off alarm bells and, taking into account population growth, our need for a serious, carefully conceived workforce development plan is painfully obvious. To accommodate all the jobless young people, we must dramatically increase our education curriculum to ensure that we are teaching the skills that are necessary for the *kind* of jobs we need to create. Strong and skilled adolescents and youth can drive positive change and can create a world in which they can thrive, one that promotes and protects their rights.

Establishing a sound plan for job growth can foster the stability we so desperately seek. Current approaches to reform rely on dangerous, short-term fixes that fail to deal with underlying issues, so they actually contribute to the problem rather than offer solutions.

INVEST IN INFRASTRUCTURE

Infrastructure development, including the building of roads, ports, railways, and other transportation networks, is a quick, easy way to create large numbers of new jobs. Well-developed infrastructure that can facilitate economic activity and subsequent growth is an added bonus and a welcome by-product of such development. These jobs can be made available very soon, and have the potential for accelerated growth in the near future. It sounds ideal. This infrastructure development, however, requires significant investment. By some accounts, the Middle East needs at least $1 trillion over the next 10 years alone.

Ironically, Arab nations have more than twice that amount invested abroad, but these investments bring a negligible amount of financial return and even less socioeconomic benefit. Instead of competing with one another over who owns more hotels abroad, maybe we should consider using at least some of that wealth to help develop our own region.

The MENA nations with surplus cash should reconsider their investment strategies and seriously think about infrastructure development in countries like Egypt, the Syrian Arab Republic, and other Arab Spring countries. Such investments will do far more to support long-term sustainability and stability than propping up old government systems by pumping cash and other financial aid into them.

To give credit where it's due, Saudi Arabia's leadership, via its Public Investment Fund, has stepped into the vacuum here, with the recent announcement of a $24 billion fund dedicated to expanding its portfolio of assets and boosting regional economies, including those of Egypt, Bahrain, Iraq, Jordan, Oman, and Sudan. Pragmatically speaking, this fund will support the expansion of Saudi business and financial returns and will also accrue benefits back to regional economies and livelihoods. This exceptional regional leadership could be further supported by other countries, like the United States.

One possible approach is to establish a MENA equivalent of the European Bank for Reconstruction and Development (EBRD), a multilateral development bank that uses investment as a tool to help build market economies. As in the EBRD example, the United States could become the largest shareholder, using some of the excess Arab cash it currently invests in its financial system, be it $20 billion a year or $50 billion a year, to invest in sustainable development across the MENA region.

If we in the Middle East fail to take action on the issue of workforce change, we will soon be looking at a prolonged state of chaos. In our struggle to come to terms with the new realities of a post-Arab-Spring Middle East, there is absolutely no time to waste.

OBSERVATION 23

SKEWED MIDDLE EAST EQUATION

The Egypt Economic Development Conference held in Sharm El Sheikh in March 2015 was a dramatic show of international investor support for Egypt's ambitious economic plans to restore security and stability to the Arab world's most populous country.

World leaders, industry captains, and investment heavyweights flew in from around the globe to deliver this very message and, by the end of the three-day conference, they had pledged $36.2 billion in investments. It was all very impressive but now, more than seven years later, it's clear that we must approach things more pragmatically, analyzing our missteps and achievements so that we can plan what to do next.

Sustainability was an important recurring topic throughout the conference and, while there is no arguing the importance of sustainable economic development to the security and stability we so desperately seek, we seem to remain entirely unable or unwilling to face a key fact: the fundamental equation regarding the Middle East has gone astray.

For the past post-colonial 70 years, most countries in the Middle East have operated under the assumption that security brings stability, and stability brings sustainable development. In reality, it is the other way around: sustainable development brings stability, and stability brings security. That is why we never quite managed to achieve the sustainable development part of the equation.

The Arab world needs hundreds of billions of dollars in the near future to create jobs and invest in hard and soft infrastructure that includes education and healthcare. In fact, I am uncertain how much of the money raised from the conference was truly earmarked for genuine sustainable development rather than for glamorous, big-ticket projects. Unfortunately, it appears that the majority of it was invested in the security end of the equation. Many of the investments were just thinly veiled attempts at purchasing security in the hopes this would somehow lead to those illusive concepts of stability and sustainability.

We already know this cannot work. That is why the entire effort was so tragic. What's even more tragic is that we already know what actually does work, because many developed economies have demonstrated that their strategies for growth have succeeded, but we failed to recognize these growth strategies.

LONG-TERM GOALS

We must consider our long-term goals and realize that all who participated in the Sharm conference were members of the establishment. Individually and as a group, all of us in the Middle East will pay a price if economic sustainability fails to become a reality. Defining economic inclusion is an important first step and a prerequisite to any meaningful attempt at ensuring economic inclusion. We have to begin by truly believing and then acknowledging that we are all born equal, and that all people are entitled to equal rights under the law and to equal opportunities in a merit-based society.

Unfortunately, even the concept of meritocracy is rarely discussed in the Arab world. For many of us in the Middle East, this is a hard pill to swallow but, until we do, we won't be able to fix the social ills that plague our communities.

OBSERVATION 24

YES-MEN TAKING OVER AS THE MIDDLE EAST ELITE

The middle class should account for any society's largest demographic. It should define the society. An eroding middle class erodes the entire fabric of a society. At the same time, the elites of a society are traditionally the ones who set the stage for the future, inspiring others and establishing direction. Eliminating the elite effectively eliminates a society's future.

TABALAS AND LAPPIES

Unfortunately, the elites have all but vanished from our part of the world. They have been replaced by a comical army of yes-men. This particular strain of parasite is, as far as I can tell, a relatively new one, and it seems to come in two versions. First, there are the "lappies," those who sit on the laps of the powerful and agree with everything they say when they know they shouldn't. The second version of this parasite has its own unique Arabic term: *tabala*. This parasite bangs on drums to ensure that the main act gets noticed. Today, the *tabala* is a key player in every industry I can think of in the Middle East.

The sage wisdom of the traditional elite is being replaced

across the Middle East with the submissive agreement of the lappies. In fact, the GCC might well possess the highest number per capita of lappies and *tabala* in the world, a dubious honor even if it were to earn us a mention in the *Guinness World Records* reference book.

Today, the vast majority of our elites no longer meet any of the traditional time-honored criteria that once defined them. Instead, most are yes-men clones. They are no longer the ones who offer unique solutions to contemporary challenges, nor are they the ones who offer constructive criticism and inventive approaches to problem-solving. The elites are no longer the ones who inspire and lead, and they certainly aren't the ones who question the status quo.

These nodding lappies and comic *tabala* yes-men have taken over as our modern-day elite, conforming rather than challenging, following rather than leading, all the while clapping comically and nodding blindly.

PARASITIC BEHAVIOR

The job of the *tabala* may be one of the world's oldest professions. Make no mistake, for some people, being a yes-man is a fine profession, but it is a catalyst for the degeneration of character witnessed in the region.

When I talk about parasitic behavior, I am not referring to harmless flattery or genuine admiration, which exists in all cultures and may serve a positive purpose. I am referring to the parasitic behavior of individuals who attach themselves to people in power, feed off their influence, and give nothing in return. In this regard, they are much like a mosquito that draws blood from someone's leg.

Such people exist merely to cement their place in the social hierarchy. They do so at the expense of everyone else, including their masters. Most shameful of all, these bloodsuckers often come from the upper echelons of society. They are either born to the upper echelon or they rise to it through some degree of genuine achievement.

There are exceptions but, overall, we seem to be taking a few steps back when we pat our lappies on the back and celebrate our *tabala* while punishing, persecuting, or otherwise driving away sincere and hard-working elites.

We should all be concerned about this situation, because it suggests a grim future for the region. A disappearing middle class is tragic, but a disappearing elite is truly terrifying.

OBSERVATION 25

NEPOTISM

Nepotism is a phenomenon that has existed since the beginning of history. It is more evident now than ever, particularly in view of the economic challenges and looming recession around the globe, including inside liberal democracies.

Unlike in the West, nepotism in the Arab world (and the developing world at large) is more the norm than the exception. It is rampant in both the public and private sectors.

In Western societies, nepotism to a larger extent is a door opener for a family member who has attained a high-level qualification from a top-notch institution. Conversely, in the Arab world, neither previous qualifications nor institutions matter, with favors handed out based more often on family lineage than on innate abilities.

When I am approached by youth from the region today seeking advice related to their careers, I always advise the same thing: they should work in a Western organization or, even better, move to the West. I offer this advice so they learn about meritocracy and being valued and judged for their abilities rather than for their family ties.

OBSERVATION 26

GOVERNANCE YES ... GOVERNANCE NO

Most Arab countries have excellent and exemplary corporate governance rules embedded in law. As regards implementation and practice, however, most often the governing authority "picks and chooses" when to apply the rules. One of the greatest problems of implementing effective corporate governance in the region involves human factors: the quality and interests of the people who are supposed to ensure adherence to the rules.

As an example, one of the region's central banks issued a directive to all banks in December 2019 on term limits for independent directors. It specified that, by 2020, all boards had to cap the number of consecutive terms an independent director could serve to three (a maximum of 9 years).

Then, in 2020, unsurprisingly, that same central bank made myriad exceptions. Individuals who had served for over 15 years and, in some cases, even more than 25 years, for example, received personal exemptions. In one bank, an independent chairman who had seen four chief executives serve during his 25-year tenure was able to remain. A question arises: who's more independent, the chairman or the chief executive?

"YOU DID NOT RAISE YOUR HAND."

Another example related to governance concerns executive-pay disclosure. Most countries, at least in the GCC, apply the latest best practice. However, in one of the Gulf states, the rules do not require top executives' salaries and bonuses to be disclosed. In a nuanced example, rules that only came into effect years later were used against one individual. This executive was singled out and penalized, forced to pay back his bonuses from years when no disclosure had been required. He was punished by the authorities and the system based on particular circumstances and unrelated disagreements. The stated claim at the time was that the executive had failed to stand up in the annual general meeting, raise his hand, and declare his bonuses. And yet, this requirement had never been stipulated or demanded before this incident, nor has it since. In this example, particularly when such facts come to light, it is difficult to understand how the responsible body can maintain a reputation of independence and credibility.

BOLLYWOOD SAGA

The region has had its share of corporate debacles. This includes two very high-profile entities: Abraaj Capital, the private equity firm that at its peak managed $14 billion, and NMC Healthcare PLC, a company listed on the London Stock Exchange that suspended trading in April 2020.

The alleged indictments against Abraaj are very technical in nature, including but not limited to the commingling of funds, window dressing, and misrepresentation to investors. In the NMC case, the accusation relates to $6.2 billion in banks loans to NMC and its sister company Finbar (also listed on the London Stock Exchange) that disappeared.

It is still too early for the truth to come out in these cases but, in the example of NMC, one might intuit the need to "follow the cash," but the media has yet to do that or to ask the right questions.

The story line in the Bollywood movies of the 1960s and 1970s was simple. The plot followed the dynamics between the typical hero–heroine–villain triangle. In most of the stories, the hero was thrown under the bus by the bad guy but he reemerged alive to, in turn, throw the villain under the bus, killing him and ending up with the heroine.

In this case, let's hope both gentlemen, the hero and the villain, reemerge from under the bus alive. In both instances, of course, the heroine was the same: money, ego, and prestige.

These examples show a failure to apply appropriate and often codified governance rules and a weakness in the regulatory enforcement of the rules in the region.

OBSERVATION 27

FREEDOM OF EXPRESSION

I am neither a scientist nor a philosopher, but pure logic tells me that I cannot be a critical thinker without freedom of expression. That freedom is a prerequisite for critical thinking and when the Saudis say they are starting to allow free and open critical thinking in their educational curriculum, I'm pleased, because it means that eventually they will have to allow real freedom of expression. Young people must get in the habit of thinking freely and thinking critically. Their voices must be part of the process of change and redefinition of the social contract.

For many young people in the Arab World, freedom of expression is limited to social media. The fashionistas are the Instagram influencers who indulge creative freedom through clothes, makeup, hair, and fashion accessories. Representing the younger generation, fashionistas are highly paid front people who introduce and endorse consumer products to their online followers. They are trapped in a culture that emphasizes material wealth and outward appearance over critical thinking. In fact, authoritarian countries are pleased when their people show interest in such frivolous pursuits, because they consider them harmless ways for people to release their frustrations and effective distractions from serious problems.

Many of these young women and men have no interest in attending university since they already have lucrative careers. No one deserves blame for this, not the consumer companies, the influencers, or their followers. The consumer brands use the fashionistas to show their products to young viewers. Some influencers have a million viewers. They encourage consumption in our part of the world, advising followers on what to wear, which perfume to use, and how to make up their eyes or style their hair. There is no intellectual or cultural value to what they do. It is just the way they express themselves, and the rulers are pleased that nothing is said about intellectual ideas or critical thinking.

The governments say it allows freedom of expression but it does so only when certain words appear on paper or social media. It is the same as flag-waving for your boss or praising the political system for the people in leadership positions. No voices offer constructive criticism during the fashionista shows. In fact, these shows serve as a kind of propaganda: the regimes point to them as proof of freedom of expression for the youth.

OBSERVATION 28

CREATING OPPORTUNITY

The first UN *Arab Human Development Report* published in 2002, entitled *Creating Opportunities for Future Generations,* identified three critical development deficits in the Arab world: the acquisition of knowledge, political freedoms, and women's empowerment. Arab thought leaders called for a new social contract between rulers and subjects, one in which innovation, critical thinking, and individual freedoms beyond the status quo were expected, even celebrated, rather than punished. No such social contract exists. In its absence, we will continue the current vicious cycle of digging ourselves in deep, and we must find a new means of climbing out or risk digging in deeper over time.

The rentier-state model prevalent in Arab countries is no longer sustainable. Unless Middle East nations implement material reforms, they will face severe economic collapse, followed by social and political upheaval. This is a ticking time bomb in today's

Arab region, where the unemployment rate among young people overall is 25% to 30%, and 42% to 47% among young women.

To put this in perspective, subsequent versions of the report note that the Arab region's military spending between 1988 and 2014 amounted to approximately $2 trillion, 65% higher than the global average and a per capita increase by a factor of 2.5 over the 26-year period. This focus on ensuring state security at the cost of developing our infrastructure has pushed the region into a rut. Still according to the report, the Arab region is home to 5% of the world's population while, in 2014, it accounted for 45% of the world's terrorist attacks, 57.7% of the world's refugees, and 68.5% of the world's conflict-related deaths.

OBSERVATION 29

EDUCATION AND EMPLOYMENT

In 2015, I was approached by a nongovernmental organization to be part of a working group to improve the output of education in the occupied Palestinian territory. In short, ensuring education would lead to greater employability and better skills for students. One of the people who was part of the working group was Samer Khoury, the chairman of Consolidated Contractors International Company. After fact-checking and surveying, in 2017, we developed and launched the Palestinian Education Trust. The end goal was to change the mindsets of teachers: our rationale was that if teachers thought differently, more critically, students would follow.

Unfortunately, soon before the launched, newly elected US President Donald Trump toured the Middle East. Supporters of the Palestinian Education Trust became less involved, as Arab regimes started warming to Israel.

Interestingly, to date, the biggest supporters of this Trust come from the Jewish community. As an Israeli friend said, "An enemy with a brain is not an enemy."

MISMATCH

The broader Middle East is currently experiencing a mismatch between labor supply and demand, which could have disastrous consequences. Entrepreneurs say it can be next to impossible to staff their workforce because so few job seekers possess the skills they require. Unemployment in the Arab world is actually highest among the most educated, which suggests that our educational systems must be significantly improved.

According to WEF data, people in the Middle East under the age of 25 are three times as likely as those over the age of 25 to be unemployed. To close this gap, youths must increase their technical and digital skills and prepare for the real world. As the production and distribution of goods and services will increasingly be automated over the coming years, Middle East workers must be taught to design and facilitate automated systems.

Schools must also prepare youths to successfully collaborate and conduct negotiations with their business associates. They must teach English language proficiency and such soft skills as basic business etiquette, empathy, emotional intelligence, and the ability to deal with conflict in a productive manner.

A multipronged approach from the public and private sectors is the only way to achieve this. An example of a private initiative contributing to this goal was recently launched by Crescent Petroleum that highlights the importance of collaboration between business leaders and the community. Crescent Petroleum announced a partnership with Edraak, the Arab world's leading platform for massive open online courses (MOOC), to develop a series of open and free online career readiness courses, with the aim of boosting the employability skills of young people across the Middle East region.

Egypt is implementing a new educational system that uses modern technology and emphasizes the importance of independent research and entrepreneurship. Saudi Arabia has also introduced several educational reforms under the National Transformation Program. These efforts seek to transform the country's educational institutions in an effort to produce graduates who can meet the demands of the job market.

The UAE is implementing a Hybrid Education Model of awarding professional certificates to students in addition to academic degrees, apprenticeships, and internship programs.

Government funds could be used to help youth gain work experience and then transition to full-time employment and regular paychecks. Using oil money to build beautiful campuses, recruit top professors, and attract talented foreign students should not be a top priority and is certainly not enough. We must educate local talent and accept international support to improve pedagogy and curriculum design.

Reforming school curricula to encourage critical thinking is crucial to achieve regional peace and political stability. We must also provide social and material incentives to enroll girls in schools.

I hope that a new paradigm can be designed to provide young men and women with a clear understanding of the relationship between the people and their government. Young people should be taught to believe they deserve to become citizens rather than remain subjects. I hope both men and women will find their own voices and will question, challenge, reflect on, and object to any resistance to the creation of better governance.

OBSERVATION 30

PROTECTION

In certain Arab countries (like most of the third world countries), controlling people through fear and dependency is the reason why some people in leadership positions conjure enemies. When people believe that some group or issue is on the brink of destroying their lives, they will gladly look to their people in leadership positions promise to protect them. But this kind of fearmongering is designed by people in leadership positions to protect their people from nonexistent harms. When danger is afoot, the government is correct in clamping down on their subjects' activities.

WASTED NATIONAL WEALTH

I recently asked a former top Arab League official, a man familiar with my playful, troublemaking questions at the WEF, "How much do you think Arab regimes have spent on arms and security in the past 50 years? Would it be a trillion dollars?" He replied, "Are you kidding me? It is trillions of dollars." I probed further, "And how much value or return on investment did that money provide?" Without hesitation, he said, "As good as zero."

Another form of protection deception exists in the form of military weapons and defense systems. Such sophisticated and outrageously expensive systems aren't actually designed to defend people from enemies outside their community. In reality, they are produced to protect the regime from their people's desire for self-control. This means the people are the enemies of the regime and the force against which regimes need protection.

Arms buildups represent a huge waste of resources that should be invested in sustainability efforts and job creation instead. The US, France, and the UK are the region's primary protectors. They receive tremendous benefits for their support of Arab governments and negotiate fat defense and security contracts that generate billions of dollars and numerous jobs for their own defense industries.

Another benefit to the Arab world of the perceived protection Western countries provide is their silence. The West is responsible for a substantial amount of inaction on issues such as the Israeli–Palestinian problem. They pay lip service to the cause for the sake of placating their own citizens and the Arab regimes. In reality, nothing is happening to advance this conflict toward a peaceful resolution, nothing that can offer the Palestinians anything positive.

Now imagine that even just a fraction of what was wasted in 50 years of defense and security spending had been spent on developing the indigenous human capital in the Arab world. That would have been a path to sustainable development and sustainability, which would have created effective stability and, ironically, increased security.

OBSERVATION 31

RED HERRINGS

PALESTINE

The important question concerning the Palestinians is the Right of Return for 3-4 million refugees. Will they become Gulf citizens? That is what many people fear, but it's a red herring, an excuse for the region's rulers to turn a blind eye to the issue. For the past 75 years, the rulers have played on this fear in order to avoid searching for a peaceful resolution.

The Abraham Accords, a joint declaration between Israel, the UAE, Bahrain, and the United States, were ratified on September 15, 2020 in an attempt to normalize relations between Arab countries and Israel for the first time since the peace agreements with Egypt and Jordan were signed: the Egypt–Israel peace treaty in 1979, and the Jordan–Israel peace treaty in 1994. The accords can be seen as a step to further peace negotiations in the region and to establish more opportunities for economic initiatives that benefit all the signatories, but they do not resolve the painful history of the Palestinians.

The Abraham Accords declare:

> *We, the undersigned, recognize the importance of maintaining and strengthening peace in the Middle East and around the world based on mutual understanding and coexistence, as well as respect for human dignity and freedom, including religious freedom.*
>
> *We encourage efforts to promote interfaith and intercultural dialogue to advance a culture of peace among the three Abrahamic religions and all humanity.*
>
> *We believe that the best way to address challenges is through cooperation and dialogue and that developing friendly relations among States advances the interests of lasting peace in the Middle East and around the world.*
>
> *We seek tolerance and respect for every person in order to make this world a place where all can enjoy a life of dignity and hope, no matter their race, faith or ethnicity.*

We support science, art, medicine, and commerce to inspire humankind, maximize human potential and bring nations closer together.

We seek to end radicalization and conflict to provide all children a better future.

We pursue a vision of peace, security, and prosperity in the Middle East and around the world.

In this spirit, we warmly welcome and are encouraged by the progress already made in establishing diplomatic relations between Israel and its neighbors in the region under the principles of the Abraham Accords. We are encouraged by the ongoing efforts to consolidate and expand such friendly relations based on shared interests and a shared commitment to a better future.

What is strikingly left out of the Accord is the question of annexation and occupation.

From a purely business perspective, I would have wanted it to be a win-win accord for all the parties involved, as I am sure many other people did too. The simple reality is that it doesn't actually resolve any issues and was probably signed for all the wrong reasons. Soon, many people will recognize that regimes cannot favor only those subjects who agree with them. For the accord to be sustainable, citizens must also be involved and encouraged to voice their own ideas and opinions. Transforming subjects into citizens must be part of this peace process.

SUNNI–SHIA DIVIDE

Those in power have always needed an enemy in order to survive. The Arabs needed an enemy and drew a straight line to the mullahs in Iran. The Sunni–Shia conflict only occurred after the revolution. At one point, the Shah of Iran was the enemy and, today, the enemy is the Iranian theocracy. But this, too, is a red herring, just like the Palestinian conflict. Hatred for the Iranian government is actually responsible for the shrinking power of the Arab world.

The Iranians themselves have willingly exacerbated these divides. The Iranian regime uses sectarianism as a cudgel whenever it suits, but it is also willing to overlook the Sunni–Shia divide when that narrative can be put to better use.

Through technological advancement, high-speed communications, and even the COVID-19 pandemic, many of us have grown less interested in using our differences to divide. The sooner the ruling powers realize they must implement reforms, provide freedoms to their people, and recognize them as citizens, the sooner they will secure a new form of power, and the safer their seats in their palaces will be. My worry is that we will have blood on the streets sooner rather than later, because people have become more and more desperate for survival. These accords will shed light on the disparity between the rights enjoyed by Israelis and the permissions doled out in dribs and drabs to the subjects of the Arab world. People will grow more demanding, more desperate, for the rights of citizens.

Islam has nothing to do with Sunni–Shia differences. I take exception to this business of Islam relying on Shia versus Sunni policies. This is not an ideological issue. It has been encouraged by the elites, but nothing is written in the *Quran* that divides one group from the other. Nowhere in the *Quran* do any statements regarding this difference appear. When one hears the scholarly interpretations of the issue, one understands that it is most certainly not about religion. It is about individuals and groups interpreting for themselves the words of the *Quran*. From time to time, the interpretations shift, depending on who is in power.

The *Quran* does not say anything whatsoever about Sunnis and Shiites. When looking at Islam, two elements come out of it: *Fiqh Al Ibadat* (jurisprudence of worship, between God and oneself) and *Fiqh Al Muamalat* (jurisprudence of transactions, which includes all other relationships). Never is the distinction between Sunnis and Shiites mentioned. The scholars, who interpret the elements, have adapted them to what the regimes want them to say, and this issue is a red herring to maintain power.

As Ibn Khaldun, an Arab historian, wisely noted in his writings in 1377, a dynasty can hardly survive beyond three generations unless it evolves.

Sectarianism
الطائفية

OBSERVATION 32

THE FOURTH ESTATE: WISHFUL THINKING IN THE ARAB WORLD?

I remember being glued to the radio during the Six-Day War in 1967. The negative impact of false information has left a lasting effect on my view of Arab media. During the 1973 October War in the Middle East, days passed before I could even make a judgment about what had happened, and I remember being in disbelief that the Arab armies were victorious until days later when I was able to draw conclusions from the global media that came trickling in.

Like most Arabs, for as long as I can remember, I have come to understand that the official media and the independent media are one and the same. Both are controlled directly or indirectly by the regimes.

NOTABLE EXCEPTIONS

The period between 2011 and mid 2013, the era of the Arab Spring, was an innovative time for freedom of expression in the Arab media. I recall the Egyptian equivalent of Jon Stewart, the host of *The Daily Show* in America, in the personality of Bassem Youssef. His satirical news program was a breath of fresh air. A few weeks after the army's takeover in Cairo in 2013, however, the show was cancelled. The situation reverted to what it had been before, with the media subjected to censorship and indirectly controlled by the regime.

THE SWORD OF DAMOCLES

Arab journalists, whether editors, writers, or TV presenters, give the impression that they have the sword of Damocles hanging over their heads in the way in which they deal with the news. Censorship exists in most of the countries, but the level of self-censorship that these journalists impose is equally profound.

DISSENT

The voice of opposition in the Arab world is as good as nonexistent except through social media. The official media often attacks such content and hurls accusations that it is fake or false. In most of the Arab world, the voice of opposition is presented as dissent. An increasing number of dissent translates to treason.

MERCENARY EDITORS

Over the past half century, some governments in the Arab world have imported excellent mercenary journalists (both Arab and foreign) to be editors-in-chief of newspapers or TV anchors to boost the professionalism of the regime's propaganda machine. In certain countries, the mercenary editors-in-chief are even given nationality to fulfill local legal requirements.

WESTERN MEDIA

Many negative issues and biases related to Western media are worth noting; my perspective is greatly informed by my early experience in the UK. I remember the frequent coverage of the Israeli–Palestinian conflict I observed when I moved from Lebanon to England in 1975. Every killing of an Israeli soldier or civilian made front-page news, while any reference to Israeli soldiers' aggressions on Palestinians was rare.

That said, from my experience in the UK in both the domestic and international news contexts, the UK has a well-functioning and independent media. Regardless of which party has had a majority of seats in government at any particular moment in time, politicians have had their media supporters in the British media while the opposition has also at the same time had their media supporters. Opposition is therefore not considered to be treason, as is the case in most Arab countries. In contrast, the media pushes the boundaries of the public debate and also presses the government to accept greater opposition.

The media is certainly at a loss in the current Russia–Ukraine War. Both parties claim to hold a monopoly on the truth, and it is indeed often difficult to discern the truth, because the intelligence services on both sides disseminate disinformation. Today, however, some news sources are making strides toward offering balanced and accurate reporting. An example is the BBC's good fact-checking regarding the recent protests in Iran and the evidence it produced about women burning their veils, a fact the regime denied but that was substantiated thanks to journalists using satellite images as evidence.

Unfortunately, the Arab masses, like their brethren in most developing economies, must rely on social media as a way to access independent reporting to learn about the issues in their own countries. The truth, like a reliable fourth estate in the Arab world, is as good as nonexistent.

OBSERVATION 33

GIVE PEACE A CHANCE

In the Middle East today, the main two scenarios for achieving peace involve the non-Arab actors of Israel and Iran. I believe peace is possible, and that the Abraham Accords offer a strong start in the direction of that goal, one that might easily gain momentum in the near future. But real people-to-people peace will only occur when the Palestinian issue is resolved, and those living as subjects become citizens. Where Iran is concerned, the West believes that change is essential; every year, the US Congress calls for regime change in Iran, which always makes me laugh. The American establishment is wasting time, money, and energy, because regime change will never be achieved by forces outside Iran. With the country controlled as it is by theological issues, regime change must evolve from the inside. Change in Iran will have to involve theology itself; the country must change from within.

It will take a bit longer, but it will happen. If we leave Iran to itself, in time we will see either a bloody revolution or a quiet evolution, one or the other. I can see nothing in between.

OBSERVATION 34

UNOFFICIALLY EXILED

In March 2018, I learnt from an acquaintance ("X") that he was invited by the promoters to attend and participate in a conference at the invitation of the government of a Middle Eastern country that X was a citizen of. However, subsequently X was informed by the promoters that an American adviser to a high-ranking official of the Middle Eastern country in question that stated that X had criticized the country in public forums and, as a result, X was "unofficially exiled". Upon contacting the high-ranking official in question, X was told not to worry about it as it must have involved a junior member of staff – to which X responded, "If your top American adviser is junior, that is embarrassing".

PART III

MOVIES

Since the first days I laid eyes on TV, watching silent or dubbed movies from the age of five onwards, I've had a passion for them. They are still an enormous part of my life. I am agnostic as to their type. I like Arabic, French, Indian, American, Italian and British movies.

The following is a selection of 100 movies that I have often watched, that have influenced who I have become, and that have fostered my wanderlust. They are ranked by year of release, not by order of preference.

THE KID (1921)

Written, produced, and directed by Charlie Chaplin

I saw this movie for the first time in 1965. By then, I had watched many short silent movies, but this was the first long movie I saw. It featured Jackie Coogan and Charlie Chaplin.

THE JAZZ SINGER (1927)

Directed by Alan Crosland, starring Al Jolson

This was the first "talkie" movie made in Hollywood that I saw, a musical. Although I was not a fan of the acting, I loved the music, especially the song "My Mammy."

MUTINY ON THE BOUNTY (1935)

Directed by Frank Lloyd, starring Charles Laughton and Clark Gable

I saw this movie for the first time on TV, dubbed in Arabic. This is the best version of the movie, which has since been remade several times. Marlon Brando and Mel Gibson reprised the role originally played by Clark Gable.

SALAMA FI KHAIR (1937)

Directed by Niazi Mostafa, starring Naguib el-Rihani

The title of the movie means “Salama Is Safe” in English. I first saw this film when I was six, and I’ve seen it countless times since. It’s still funny each time I watch it. Naguib el-Rihani was the Charlie Chaplin of Egyptian cinema; his movies were fun but also bore a strong and important message.

ANGELS WITH DIRTY FACES (1938)

Directed by Michael Curtiz for Warner Brothers, starring James Cagney

This film chronicles the friendship between gangster William “Rocky” Sullivan and his childhood friend, the future priest Father Jerry Connolly. I love James Cagney as an actor. He had such a presence, and I love the message of humanity that came through this movie.

ADVENTURES OF ROBIN HOOD (1938)

Directed by Michael Curtiz and William Keighley, starring Errol Flynn and Olivia de Havilland

I have watched the eight *Robin Hood* movies made since. This remains my favorite by far, due to the simplicity and flow of the story on screen, and the chemistry between Errol Flynn and Olivia de Havilland, the leading actors. This is the best of the nine movies Flynn and de Havilland collaborated on.

JESSE JAMES (1939)

Directed by Henry King, starring Tyrone Power, Henry Fonda, Nancy Kelly, and Randolph Scott

I first watched this movie dubbed in Arabic. This Western was based on a true story, in which the hero did bad things for the greater good. I loved the idea of placing the common good above all else.

GONE WITH THE WIND (1939)

Directed by Victor Fleming for MGM, starring Clark Gable and Vivien Leigh

I saw this film in 1970 at the cinema. At the time such movies were not featured on TVs in the region. I loved Vivien Leigh's acting in this American historical epic romance, and Clark Gable's famous closing sentence, "Frankly, my dear, I don't give a damn."

THE ROARING TWENTIES (1939)

Directed by Raoul Walsh, starring James Cagney, Priscilla Lane, and Humphrey Bogart

This movie is the one that made Humphrey Bogart a star. It featured corruption and criminal activities related to alcohol trafficking and prohibition, as well as the 1929 stock market crash.

THE PHILADELPHIA STORY (1940)

Directed by George Cukor, starring Cary Grant, Katharine Hepburn, and James Stewart

The story is simple and centered on the character played by Hepburn. I loved how smart the interactions were between the three lead characters. James Stewart deservingly received an Oscar for his performance.

CITIZEN KANE (1941)

Directed by and starring Orson Welles

This film is pure genius. Orson Welles was so ahead of his time.

CASABLANCA (1942)

Directed by Michael Curtiz, starring Humphrey Bogart and Ingrid Bergman

The first time I watched this movie was on Aramco TV, dubbed in Arabic. My mother was such a fan of Ingrid Bergman, one of the few actresses for whom she would indulge in watching movies.

HEAVEN CAN WAIT (1943)

Directed by Ernst Lubitsch, starring Gene Tierney, Don Ameche, and Charles Coburn

A story about Henry Van Cleve, who presents himself at the gates of hell to review his life with Satan, after which he would be allowed into the underworld. The story flowed much better than in Warren Beatty's 1978 remake.

GASLIGHT (1944)

Directed by George Cukor, starring Charles Boyer, Ingrid Bergman, and Joseph Cotten

I am a big fan of Ingrid Bergman, and this psychological thriller is captivating.

NOTORIOUS (1946)

Directed and produced by Alfred Hitchcock, starring Cary Grant, Ingrid Bergman, and Claude Rains

This was my first Alfred Hitchcock film, and my mother's favorite movie. We initially watched it dubbed in Arabic.

IT'S A WONDERFUL LIFE (1946)

Directed by Frank Capra, starring James Stewart, Donna Reed, and Lionel Barrymore

This is a positive and heartwarming movie, which I would watch during the holiday period every year in the United Kingdom.

THE THREE MUSKETEERS (1948)

Directed by George Sidney, starring Gene Kelly and Lana Turner

The motto of the musketeers is forever inspiring, and Lana Turner is the best Milady de Winter.

THE THIRD MAN (1949)

Directed by Carol Reed, starring Joseph Cotten, Alida Valli, Orson Welles, and Trevor Howard

A thriller about corruption after World War II. It is another great movie with Orson Welles, in which his short screen time makes such an important impact. I did not understand it fully when I saw it as a young teenager. It was one of the first videotapes I bought.

A STREETCAR NAMED DESIRE (1951)

Directed by Elia Kazan, starring Vivien Leigh, Marlon Brando, Kim Hunter, and Karl Malden

Inspired by the eponymous play, I saw this movie with the incredible chemistry between the actors when I was in Lebanon, in a cinema that was only playing “old” movies.

HIGH NOON (1952)

Directed by Fred Zinnemann, starring Gary Cooper, Grace Kelly, and Thomas Mitchell

This film is a Western with Gary Cooper that lasts for 1 hour and 45 minutes. It was almost entirely filmed in real time, starting just after 10:30 am until about 12:15 pm.

FROM HERE TO ETERNITY (1953)

Directed by Fred Zinnemann, starring Burt Lancaster, Montgomery Clift, Deborah Kerr, Donna Reed, and Frank Sinatra

At a young age, I loved Westerns and war movies. Montgomery Clift was a fabulous actor. He made the movie for me.

SHANE (1953)

Directed by George Stevens, starring Alan Ladd, Jean Arthur, and Van Heflin

The story is poignant, with an ending scene that still breaks my heart – Joey's desperate cries of "Shane, come back!"

ROMAN HOLIDAY (1953)

Directed by William Wyler, starring Gregory Peck and Audrey Hepburn

When I first saw this movie, I also saw its Arabic version, an Egyptian musical called *A Day in My Life*. I enjoyed watching them in parallel, one with great acting, the other with great tunes.

ON THE WATERFRONT (1954)

Directed by Elia Kazan, starring Marlon Brando, Karl Malden, Lee J. Cobb, Rod Steiger, Pat Henning, and Eva Marie Saint

I loved the acting and the actors in this movie, which has a great story line. The interaction between Marlon Brando and Lee J. Cobb is fantastic.

SEVEN SAMURAI (1955)

Directed by Akira Kurosawa, starring Toshiro Mifune, Takashi Shimura, Keiko Tsushima, Isao Kimura, Daisuke Katō, Seiji Miyaguchi, Yoshio Inaba, and Minoru Chiaki

This was the first Japanese movie I saw. I initially saw *The Magnificent Seven*, its US version. No wonder it was voted the greatest foreign-language film of all time in the BBC's 2018 international critics' poll.

MISTER ROBERTS (1955)

Directed by John Ford, Joshua Logan, and Mervyn LeRoy, starring Henry Fonda, James Cagney, William Powell (in his final film appearance), and Jack Lemmon

I first saw this movie on TV, dubbed in Arabic. It is a great story about patience.

EAST OF EDEN (1955)

Directed by Elia Kazan, starring James Dean, Julie Harris, and Raymond Massey

This was the first James Dean movie I saw, four years after *Rebel Without a Cause* in Lebanon. It is the story of two brothers, mimicking the story of Cain and Abel, with impeccable acting. James Dean truly was a legend!

REBEL WITHOUT A CAUSE (1955)

Directed by Nicholas Ray, starring James Dean, Sal Mineo, and Natalie Wood.

I loved the plot, about conflict between generations, in addition to the great acting.

DEVDAS (1955)

Directed by Bimal Roy, starring Dilip Kumar, Suchitra Sen, and Vyjayanthimala

This Bollywood movie is a real drama about a love story with a sad ending. Its remake in 2002 was the most expensive Bollywood movie made. An anecdote: Dilip Kumar's birth name was Mohammad Yusuf Khan. The new version starred Shah Rukh Khan.

THE KING AND I (1956)

Directed by Walter Lang, starring Deborah Kerr and Yul Brynner

I have seen many versions of this movie, as well as the musical on stage. It was incredible to see the macho actor, Yul Brynner, perform so well in a musical. He won an Oscar for his performance.

MOTHER INDIA (1957)

Directed by Mehboob Khan, starring Nargis Dutt, Raaj Kumar, Rajendra Kumar, and Sunil Dutt

This Oscar nominated movie for Best Foreign Language Film features Indian women, metaphorically representing India, who bear the burden of care and livelihood.

THE BRIDGE ON THE RIVER KWAI (1957)

Directed by David Lean, starring William Holden, Alec Guinness, Jack Hawkins, and Sessue Hayakawa

The whistling, after all these years, remains iconic. The acting and the story line immediately come back to one's mind upon hearing it.

ROD QALBY (1957)

Directed by Ezz El Dine Zulficar, starring Mariem Fakhr El Dine, Shukri Sarhan, Salah Zulfikar, and Zahrat El-Ula

The title means "Back Again". I saw this movie first in black and white on TV and then in color at the cinema. It is a class-based Egyptian movie with a love story, which ends well. The revolution brings the protagonists together and breaks social barriers.

LA ANAM (1957)

Directed by Salah Abu Seif, starring Faten Hamama, Yahya Shaheen, Omar Sharif, Emad Hamdy, Mariem Fakhr El Dine, and Hind Rostom

The movie title means "Sleepless". Faten Hamama was the queen of Arab films. This story was based on the Electra complex. Hamama was mesmerizing.

12 ANGRY MEN (1957)

Directed by Sidney Lumet, starring Henry Fonda, Lee J. Cobb, Ed Begley, E. G. Marshall, and Jack Warden

This American courtroom drama is about decision-making and the perception of truth. The movie keeps you on the edge of your seat until the very end, and the interaction between Fonda and Cobb is great!

BEN-HUR (1959)

Directed by William Wyler, starring Charlton Heston

This is a remake of the 1925 silent movie. The chariot race scene is captivating; it will be hard for remakes to capture it as well as Wyler did. I saw this movie for the first time in Shiraz, dubbed in Farsi. It was originally banned in many Arab countries.

NORTH BY NORTHWEST (1959)

Directed by Alfred Hitchcock, starring Cary Grant, Eva Marie Saint, and James Mason

This spy thriller stars Hitchcock's favorite actor, Cary Grant. The plane sequence is iconic.

MUGHAL-E-AZAM (1960)

Directed by K. Asif, starring Prithviraj Kapoor, Dilip Kumar, Madhubala, and Durga Khote

This epic Bollywood movie, whose title means "The Great Mughal", features an impossible love story. The two lead actors are extraordinary, outplaying each other.

THE APARTMENT (1960)

Directed by Billy Wilder, starring Jack Lemmon, Shirley MacLaine, and Fred MacMurray

This dramatic comedy is about Airbnbs before Airbnb; it's about the lead character who rents his apartment out as a garçonnière and the drama that ensues. Shirley MacLaine's and Jack Lemmon's acting make this movie unforgettable.

THE MAGNIFICENT SEVEN (1960)

Directed by John Sturges, starring Yul Brynner, Steve McQueen, and Charles Bronson

This film was based on the Japanese movie *Seven Samurai*. I liked the acting of the leads. The theme music, written by Elmer Bernstein, is essential to the movie.

BREAKFAST AT TIFFANY'S (1961)

Directed by Blake Edwards, starring Audrey Hepburn

Audrey Hepburn was at the top of her form in this film. Even today, the character she plays, Holly Golightly, has become an iconic pop culture reference.

THE HUSTLER (1961)

Directed by Robert Rossen, starring Paul Newman, Jackie Gleason, Piper Laurie, and George C. Scott

The chemistry between the two lead actors is unbelievable. Funnily enough, it is for the sequel, *The Color of Money*, in which Newman reprised his role, that he received an Oscar.

FI BAITINA RAJUL (1961)

Directed by Henry Barakat, starring Omar Sharif, Zubida Tharwat, and Rushdi Abazah

This movie brought Omar Sharif international stardom. The movie title was translated as *A Man in Our House*. It takes place during colonial times. Sharif plays the role of a rebel who must seek refuge.

EL-LIS WEL KELAB (1962)

Directed by Kamal El Shaikh, starring Shadia, Shukry Sarhan, and Kamal Al-Shennawi

The title translates in English to "The Thief and the Dogs." This movie is based on the eponymous novel by Naguib Mahfouz, who was awarded the Nobel Prize in Literature.

LAWRENCE OF ARABIA (1962)

Directed by David Lean, starring (among many others) Peter O'Toole, Alec Guinness, Anthony Quinn, and Omar Sharif.

This movie was censored for a time in Arab countries, so I saw it dubbed in Farsi, in Shiraz, for the first time. I subsequently watched the original version. Much of this version is fiction. But the drama flows nicely, and Omar Sharif added value to the production. His three-minute entrance into international stardom through the mirage at the beginning is exceptional.

AL NASSER SALAH AD-DIN (1963)

Directed by Youssef Chahine, starring Ahmed Mazhar

Translated as *Saladin the Victorious*, this movie preceded the decline of Egyptian cinema, when movies had much smaller budgets. This was a big production, retracing the story of the Third Crusade. It's a historical movie with current resonance.

ALIBABA (1963)

Directed by Harbans Singh, starring Dara Singh

This Bollywood production is the first movie I ever saw in a cinema, during a matinée. I saw it at Awal Cinema in Bahrain at the end of 1963.

A FISTFUL OF DOLLARS (1964)

Directed by Sergio Leone, starring Clint Eastwood

The first spaghetti western I saw in a cinema. It is part of the Leone trilogy. The movie made Clint Eastwood a global star. I saw it in 1965, at the Al Nasr Cinema.

DOSTI (1964)

Directed by Satyen Bose, starring Sudhir Kumar Sawant and Sushil Kumar Somaya

This is the first movie I saw during an evening session with my uncle, at the Zubara Cinema.

SANGAM (1964)

Directed by and starring Raj Kapoor

This is a classic love story with a love triangle: two men love the same woman. Beyond the plot, the acting and music make this movie outstanding.

BAYN EL KASRAIN (1964)

Directed by Hasan El-Emam and Said Tantawi, starring Yehia Chahine

Based on the first part of Naguib Mahfouz's trilogy, the film title is translated in English as *Palace Walk*. It depicts the life paths of Ahmed Abdul Jawad's family during the English occupation and before the outbreak of the 1919 revolution. I saw this movie on TV before I saw it in a cinema.

MATRIMONIO ALL'ITALIANA (1964)

Directed by Vittorio De Sica, starring Sophia Loren, Marcello Mastroianni, and Vito Moricone

Its title in English translates to *Marriage, Italian Style*. I saw this Italian movie for the first time in Beirut, in a cinema that played only old classics. It was subtitled in both English and Arabic, and it was the first time I heard Sophia Loren and Marcello Mastroianni speak in their mother tongue.

ZORBA THE GREEK (1964)

Directed by Michael Cacoyannis, starring Anthony Quinn

I first saw this movie in 1971, in the refurbished Awal Cinema. I had never been to Greece then but, because of this movie, I wanted to visit the country. The dancing scenes with Anthony Quinn are iconic, and the music is superb!

MY FAIR LADY (1964)

Directed by George Cukor, starring Rex Harrison and Audrey Hepburn

I've put this movie on my list because the acting was far superior to the performances in *The Sound of Music*. I was struck by the song "The Rain in Spain" and its lyrics, "The rain in Spain stays mainly in the plain." I saw this movie for the first time in the refurbished Awal Cinema.

DOCTOR ZHIVAGO (1965)

Directed by David Lean, starring Omar Sharif and Julie Christie

A classic for everyone, which I only saw in 1971. All these big classics were first played in Bahrain when the Awal Cinema was refurbished. I was unhappy that Omar Sharif, who had the lead role, was not featured prominently on the movie poster.

FOR A FEW DOLLARS MORE (1965)

Directed by Sergio Leone, starring Clint Eastwood

The second movie in the "Man with No Name" Western trilogy, I saw this film for the first time in Bahrain in 1965.

LA BATTAGLIA DI ALGERI (1966)

Directed by Gillo Pontecorvo, starring Jean Martin, Brahim Hadjadj, and Yacef Saâdi

This Italian-Algerian movie, titled *The Battle of Algiers*, was mostly in French and Algerian Arabic. It was the first time I heard a North African Arabic, and I needed to follow the subtitles. I liked how the liberation was depicted in a very realistic way.

THE GOOD, THE BAD AND THE UGLY (1966)

Directed by Sergio Leone, starring Clint Eastwood, Lee Van Cleef, and Eli Wallach

This is the third movie in the "Man with No Name" Western trilogy, which I saw in Bahrain in 1967 and have seen many times since. The best-known movie in the trilogy, it benefited from a larger budget, and the production was great. Eli Wallach was a great addition to the cast. I preferred the plot of the second movie though.

QASR EL SHOUQ (1967)

Directed by Hasan El-Emam and Said Tantawi, starring Yehia Chahine

Based on the second part of Naguib Mahfouz's trilogy, the movie's title translates to "The Palace of Desire".

THE DIRTY DOZEN (1967)

Directed by Robert Aldrich, starring Lee Marvin with a supporting cast that includes Ernest Borgnine, Charles Bronson, Jim Brown, John Cassavetes, Richard Jaeckel, George Kennedy, Ralph Meeker, Robert Ryan, Telly Savalas, Donald Sutherland, and Clint Walker

I saw this war movie for the first time in Shiraz, and then saw it again in 1970 in Bahrain. It felt like every big actor was in this movie. It's one of the best war movies I've seen. I've used *Dirty Dozen* to refer to Bahraini oil apprentices at the company

BAPCO who were sent to the UK to the Institute of Cost and Management Accountants. When they came back, near the time of independence or shortly thereafter, they occupied government or banking positions. Most of these people stayed glued to their seats – what I call a catholic marriage to their seat.

GUESS WHO'S COMING TO DINNER (1967)

Directed by Stanley Kramer, starring Spencer Tracy (in his final role), Sidney Poitier, and Katharine Hepburn

This movie was ahead of its time, placing emphasis on racism issues, which unfortunately still prevail today.

THE GRADUATE (1967)

Directed by Mike Nichols, starring Dustin Hoffman and Anne Bancroft

I saw this movie when I was quite young. It made an impact on me, because of the story line and, initially, because of the dynamics between the characters and, later on, when I saw it again, because of what it meant in terms of responsibility. Simon and Garfunkel's music is also unforgettable.

BONNIE AND CLYDE (1967)

Directed by Arthur Penn, starring Warren Beatty and Faye Dunaway

Based on a true story about two criminals, the plot is put together so well that you cannot help but feel sympathy for the two protagonists.

THE ODD COUPLE (1968)

Directed by Gene Saks, starring Jack Lemmon and Walter Matthau

This duo playing two divorced men who decide to live together, who featured in a total of 11 films together, made the movie. It was so successful that it was followed by a dedicated TV series, with different actors.

THE PARTY (1968)

Directed by Blake Edwards, starring Peter Sellers

This movie featuring cultural differences and *quid pro quos* is highly entertaining. I wonder how people view it nowadays, as the cultural context has changed significantly.

BUTCH CASSIDY AND THE SUNDANCE KID (1969)

Directed by George Roy Hill, starring Robert Redford and Paul Newman

Inspired by a true story about the Wild West outlaw Robert LeRoy Parker, this movie is high on my list because of the chemistry between the two lead actors.

MIDNIGHT COWBOY (1969)

Directed by John Schlesinger, starring Dustin Hoffman and Jon Voight

I saw this movie in 1969 at the Awal Cinema for the first time. Dustin Hoffman's walk throughout the movie is iconic. I still wonder how was able to walk the way he did throughout the movie. I have often tried to mimic it.

AL ARD (1969)

Directed by Youssef Chahine, starring Mahmoud Al Meleji, Nagwa Ibrahim, Ezzat El Alaili, and Hamdy Ahmed

The title of this movie in English is *The Land*. It is a heavy drama, about the value of attachment to the land, with many subtle messages in the script. This movie has always reminded me of my grandfather's words, advising me to buy land whenever possible.

ABI FOQ AL-SHAGARA (1969)

Directed by Hussein Kamal, starring Abdel Halim Hafez and Nadia Lutfi

This is the first movie I saw many times in a row in a cinema. The Al Hamra Cinema, which was the first air-conditioned cinema in Bahrain, featured this film for eight weeks upon its opening. I loved the music of this coming-of-age movie, which takes place in Alexandria and Beirut, and still know all the songs. In English, the title of the movie means "My Father Up on the Tree."

CARRY ON AGAIN DOCTOR (1969)

Directed by Gerald Thomas, starring Sid James, Kenneth Williams, Charles Hawtrey, Joan Sims, Barbara Windsor, and Hattie Jacques

This is another movie I saw for the first time at the Al Hamra Cinema. This movie is a typical British comedy, the 18th release in a series of 31 *Carry On* films. It was the first of the series that I saw. All *Carry On* movies contributed to shaping my sense of humor.

M*A*S*H (1970)

Directed by Robert Altman, starring Donald Sutherland, Tom Skerritt, and Elliott Gould

A dark comedy about the Korean War and three medics pursuing their path. The movie is excellent, but the series was the true hit, running for 11 seasons from 1972 to 1983. Despite the humor, the reality and tragedy of war come through. The theme song, *Suicide Is Painless*, is iconic.

THARTHARAH FAWQ AL-NIL (1971)

Directed by Hussein Kamal, starring Emad Hamdy, Ahmed Ramzy, Adel Adham, Mervat Amin, and Suhair Ramzi

With its title translated in English as *Chitchat on the Nile*, this move is based on the 1966 novel, *Adrift on the Nile*, by Egyptian Nobel Laureate Naguib Mahfouz. The film addresses the decadence of Egyptian society during the Gamal Abdel Nasser era. Mahfouz's plot was subtle; he was excellent at offering a message about the system without being personal. In the 1970s, when we could not simply google movies, we read about them in magazines. A few Arabic magazines existed, notably *Al Mawad* magazine, published in Lebanon, and *El Kawakeb*, in Egypt. The latter gave rise to a celebrity culture in Egypt. My cousin and I would purchase these magazines and read all about the movies and TV celebrities.

THE GODFATHER (1972)

Directed by Francis Ford Coppola, starring Marlon Brando, Al Pacino, James Caan, Richard Castellano, Robert Duvall, Sterling Hayden, John Marley, Richard Conte, and Diane Keaton

Everyone has seen *The Godfather*! In Bahrain, when it was released, a person had to be 18 to see it. I could not watch the movie at the Awal Cinema, where I was known. I was only 14 but looked older than my age. I saw the movie with a 20-year-old cousin in a cinema on the outskirts of town to bypass the age limit. This movie was a real comeback for Marlon Brando, who famously did not collect the Oscar he received for his performance, deciding to feature the plight of Native Americans instead.

THE STING (1973)

Directed by George Roy Hill, starring Paul Newman, Robert Redford, and Robert Shaw

The second and, unfortunately, the last collaboration between Robert Redford and Paul Newman. This movie keeps you on the edge of your seat throughout, until everything is revealed at the end. I saw it for the first time in Beirut.

THE GODFATHER – PART II (1974)

Directed by Francis Ford Coppola, starring Robert De Niro, Al Pacino, James Caan, Richard Castellano, Robert Duvall, and Diane Keaton

This move is the best of the trilogy. It really made the series.

CHINATOWN (1974)

Directed by Roman Polanski, starring Jack Nicholson and Faye Dunaway

This film is a fantastic American neo-noir mystery drama, in which Jack Nicholson excels. I saw it in Beirut for the first time, where movies were uncensored.

YOUNG FRANKENSTEIN (1974)

Directed by Mel Brooks, starring Gene Wilder, Peter Boyle, and Marty Feldman

This black and white movie (a great idea) featuring the life of a descendant of Dr. Frankenstein is a parody of the classic horror film genre. Marty Feldman in the role of Igor is phenomenal.

SHOLAY (1975)

Directed by Ramesh Sippy, starring Dharmendra, Sanjeev Kumar, Hema Malini, Amitabh Bachchan, Jaya Bhaduri, and Amjad Khan

I saw this movie in Bahrain after leaving Beirut and before I moved to Manchester. It is a mix between *Seven Samurai* and a spaghetti western in a Bollywood context, with heroes and villains, where everything is exaggerated: only two heroes do the job of seven! It's a true masala, making it a grand Bollywood movie. It was rereleased in 3D in 2014.

ONE FLEW OVER THE CUCKOO'S NEST (1975)

Directed by Miloš Forman, starring Jack Nicholson and Louise Fletcher

The first movie I saw in Manchester. A sad, dark comedy drama and by far Jack Nicholson's best acting.

CLOSE ENCOUNTERS OF THE THIRD KIND (1977)

Directed by Steven Spielberg, starring Richard Dreyfuss, Melinda Dillon, Teri Garr, Bob Balaban, Cary Guffey, and François Truffaut

It was not my first Spielberg movie, but it's the one in which his genius as a director is most apparent. It is one of the best science fiction movies ever made. It was great to see the collaboration between Spielberg and the great French actor/director François Truffaut.

THE GOODBYE GIRL (1977)

Directed by Herbert Ross, starring Richard Dreyfuss, Marsha Mason, Quinn Cummings, and Paul Benedict

Neil Simon, who wrote the movie, did a wonderful job. The story line makes the movie.

SATURDAY NIGHT FEVER (1977)

Directed by John Badham, starring John Travolta

A movie that, when it first came out, I saw many times in a row in Manchester. I loved the music – a real rebirth for the Bee Gees – and how it featured the disco decade. The plot also makes some good points, showing the struggle of a young man and the harsh treatment of young women.

STAR WARS (1977)

Directed by George Lucas, starring Mark Hamill, Harrison Ford, Carrie Fisher, Peter Cushing, and Alec Guinness

This movie ushers in the birth of the George Lucas franchise!

THE DEER HUNTER (1978)

Directed by Michael Cimino, starring Robert De Niro, Christopher Walken, and John Savage, with John Cazale (in his final role), and Meryl Streep

A drama about war and post-war trauma after the Vietnam War.

APOCALYPSE NOW (1979)

Directed by Francis Ford Coppola, starring Marlon Brando, Robert Duvall, and Martin Sheen

Another movie about the Vietnam War and corruption in the army. Marlon Brando does not have a big role in the movie, but he makes it!

ORDINARY PEOPLE (1980)

Directed by Robert Redford, starring Donald Sutherland, Mary Tyler Moore, Judd Hirsch, and Timothy Hutton

This is a drama about the interaction between family members after a tragic loss. It was interesting to see Mary Tyler Moore, a comedian, performing so well in a drama. It was the first movie directed by Robert Redford.

TERMS OF ENDEARMENT (1983)

Directed by James Brooks, starring Debra Winger, Shirley MacLaine, and Jack Nicholson

This film is another family drama, examining the relationship between a mother and daughter. MacLaine, whose best movie, in my view, was *The Apartment*, got the recognition she deserved here by receiving an Oscar.

CHILDREN OF A LESSER GOD (1986)

Directed by Randa Haines, starring William Hurt, Marlee Matlin (in her film debut), Piper Laurie, and Philip Bosco

I saw this movie in the Empire Cinema at Leicester Square, right after I saw the person who would become my wife.

WHEN HARRY MET SALLY ... ... (1989)

Directed by Rob Reiner, starring Billy Crystal and Meg Ryan

It's a romantic comedy, but so realistic! I enjoyed the happy ending.

DANCES WITH WOLVES (1990)

Directed by and starring Kevin Costner

This movie is a nice change from the Western movies. It depicts the plights of Native Americans, in the line of *Soldier Blue* (1970), which featured Candice Bergen. Kevin Costner took a risk in making this movie, but he deserved all the success he received as a result.

PULP FICTION (1994)

Directed by Quentin Tarantino, starring John Travolta, Samuel L. Jackson, Bruce Willis, Tim Roth, Ving Rhames, and Uma Thurman

I love all of Quentin Tarantino's movies. *Pulp Fiction* tops my list. It's a crime thriller with an iconic dance between Travolta and Thurman.

THE SHAWSHANK REDEMPTION (1994)

Directed by Frank Darabont, starring Tim Robbins and Morgan Freeman

It's a story about solidarity between inmates, and injustice, inspired by a Stephen King novel.

THE USUAL SUSPECTS (1995)

Directed by Bryan Singer, starring Stephen Baldwin, Gabriel Byrne, Benicio del Toro, Kevin Pollak, Chazz Palminteri, Pete Postlethwaite, and Kevin Spacey

This move is a thriller with a superb script and great dialogue. It's hard to know who the bad guy is until the very end.

LA VITA È BELLA (1997)

Directed by and starring Roberto Benigni

Better known in English as *Life Is Beautiful*, this Italian comedy drama film is fascinating for the tone adopted and the depth of the story. The actor was the first man to win an Oscar for a non-English speaking role.

AS GOOD AS IT GETS (1997)

Directed by James L. Brooks, starring Jack Nicholson and Helen Hunt

A romantic comedy drama in which Jack Nicholson's role keeps you glued to the movie. Both actors received an Oscar for their performances.

WEST BEIRUT (1998)

Directed by Ziad Doueiri, starring Rami Doueiri, Mohamad Chamas, and Leila Karam

I saw this movie at the Scala Cinema in Geneva, where they used to play author movies. The movie brought back many beautiful and sad memories about Beirut. After all these years, Beirut has not regained its splendor.

CROUCHING TIGER, HIDDEN DRAGON (2000)

Directed by Ang Lee, starring Chow Yun-fat, Michelle Yeoh, Zhang Ziyi, and Chang Chen

Because I grew up in the 1960s and 70s, Bruce Lee made my generation fall in love with martial arts. This Chinese movie took it to the next level, with a beautiful plot in addition.

THERE WILL BE BLOOD (2007)

Directed by Paul Thomas Anderson, starring Daniel Day-Lewis

Although the story is beautifully written, Daniel Day-Lewis' acting makes this movie. For me, this is by far his best performance.

AVATAR (2009)

Directed by James Cameron, starring Sam Worthington, Zoe Saldana, Stephen Lang, Michelle Rodriguez, and Sigourney Weaver

This movie stemmed from the imagination of James Cameron. It exemplifies how technology can enhance creativity. I am impatiently waiting for the sequel, to be released soon, *Avatar: The Way of Water.*

THE GRAND BUDAPEST HOTEL (2014)

Directed by Wes Anderson, starring Ralph Fiennes

I like all Wes Anderson's movies. This one epitomizes his style.

CONCLUSION

JACK OF ALL BRANDS

Just as the title of this book proclaims, I am a nonconformist. For years, I have embraced this label with great pride. At the same time, I have rejected the labels that inspired baseless rumors and allegations about my ideas and observations. Of course, a nonconformist is by definition someone who opposes the status quo. By calling myself a nonconformist, I have sought to draw attention to the problems of the Arab world and ignite meaningful dialogue and positive change in response. However, my critics have employed the word "nonconformist" to ridicule me in the way many labels are designed to mock or demonize individuals and their beliefs. Indeed, sometimes incendiary labels are the only ones that attract and unite people in groups.

Since 1974, when I left Bahrain for the first time, I have collected many labels. I have been branded a "liberal," a "Shia sympathizer," a "socialist," and an "anti-Zionist." In 1977, my UK critics called me "Bloody Paki" and "Bloody Indian" although, in recent years, they've called me a "Bloody Arab."

In 1995, I was characterized as completely antiestablishment, a claim to which I do not subscribe, because my antiestablishment views apply only to specific circumstances. In 1996, I was said to be a Freemason while, in 1998, I was accused of being a fundamentalist and, in 2000, an Iran sympathizer. My image underwent a big makeover in 2002 when I was identified as "pro-Zionist" and a "Jew lover." In 2008, when I introduced myself as *Holi*, I was told I was a Persian Sunni (*Farsi Sunni*, in Arabic) and, in 2010, I was accused of being both a Muslim Brotherhood sympathizer and a Salafist.

I am none of the above, yet I collect these brands like badges of honor, the way others collect medals. They are proof of my willingness to speak my mind and exercise critical thinking. All individuals committed to pursuing truth should agree to speak their minds and acknowledge reasonable ideas, regardless of who or what group introduces them. Life is not all black and white; it is important to maintain an honest, critical mindset rather than wasting time and energy adhering to propaganda or false ideology.

DISRUPTIVE

I believe we can be disruptive without being destructive. I am disruptive and, even as I advance in age, I will continue attempting to disrupt harmful policies and practices. I will continue to tell it like it is, because we must lay down solid tracks for future generations. I see things differently than others, probably because of the way I was trained. My experiences are unique to me. The things I have been through, the roads I have traveled, were never easy. I worked in environments where competition was encouraged, and people enjoyed the freedom to grow and help others advance. When competition is prohibited, people are pushed down. Disrupting a system that is outdated and ineffective is the only way to instigate positive change and elevate people.

CONTEMPORARY PERSPECTIVES

As I began writing this book in February 2022, Russia invaded Ukraine, causing death and destruction everywhere. This devastating global crisis continues to unfold, and it is impossible to predict when or how it will end. Sadly, the war and the enormous suffering it is causing could have been avoided through better diplomacy and dialogue.

During a speech in Munich in 2007, Vladimir Putin warned NATO not to get too close to Russia's borders. The following year, at a meeting in Bucharest, NATO promised Ukraine and Georgia that they would be invited to join NATO in the future but not at the present time, despite the fact that the US was calling for them to immediately be offered NATO membership. In 2009, during a private session of the WEF, a European head of state disclosed that they had specifically warned the US against inviting Ukraine and Georgia into NATO. The head of state then expressed disappointment that the warning had fallen on deaf ears. What we are witnessing today was entirely predictable, and the horrors of the war need never have occurred. No one will win this conflict, but two of its players will refuse to lose. Vladimir Putin and the US will sustain the struggle while Ukrainians, Europeans, and Russians will continue to suffer. I hope I am wrong and the world finds a way to embrace peace and harmony but, given the prevailing interest-based conceptions of leadership, that seems unlikely.

In the fall of 2022, Iranian women made headlines as they protested the harsh policies of their country's morality police. One can only admire their incredible courage and their determination to fight for the right to choose how they wear their headscarves. The protests will not overthrow the current regime as it has successfully snuffed out all social unrest since 1980. Nonetheless, I hope the regime will begin to reform a few of its policies at a minimum, and provide its people with at least a taste of freedom.

ARAB WORLD TODAY

Today, my biggest worries are for the youth of the Arab world. Our region has one of the youngest populations in the world, with the majority under the age of 25. The future of these youth will be compromised and their opportunities limited, and these realities appear unavoidable given the lack of action on unemployment from the region's regimes. Conflict, climate change, unemployment, corruption, nepotism, and a lack of unity are depriving the region of all its young people have to offer. I hope young Arabs will challenge the people in leadership positions and demand the reforms they deserve, but I fear change will not come soon enough.

I also worry about the victims of the other conflicts in our region, the Yemeni, Syrian, and Palestinian people that the world is ignoring. How can these people, so beaten and brutalized, ever forgive their neighbors for the complete lack of compassion and solidarity they demonstrate?

Like the war in Ukraine, the outcomes of these other wars are impossible to predict. Until countries are governed by leaders rather than rulers, many people will lose their lives, and their survivors will lose hope for a brighter future.

LOVE THY NEIGHBOR

As I was writing this book, Saudi Arabia announced the creation of investment companies in six neighboring Arab countries, funded to the tune of $24 billion. This news was music to my ears, as I'm sure it was to most people in the region. It is the sort of initiative that we've been prescribing for years without any action being taken. Before and after the Arab Spring, we called upon the oil rich Gulf states to invest in infrastructure and strategies for other Arab countries to create sustainable development and jobs for the future. This is informed by rather simple intuition: when your neighbor is stable and secure, you will be too. The road to a secure future is paved with sustainable solutions and investment in lasting infrastructure, soft and hard, to create long-term jobs for the young people in the region. I only wish more of this were done, and an extra zero were added after the four.

BORN FREE

Ultimately, each of us must take ownership of our own souls. We are born free and should treasure that freedom, however limited, as the gift that it is. We can consciously choose to perpetuate a master–slave relationship, or we can seek a different destiny free from repression. Some of our people blame history for our fate. Some say that the British are responsible for our pain, others that the Americans did this to us, but we cannot continue to blame others. Instead, we must find the agency within ourselves to evolve, educate ourselves, build homes and families, and develop businesses, institutions, and governments that encourage us to live as citizens rather than as subjects. We must see to it that the rule of law is upheld as a basic human right.

We can affirm both our faith and our intellect by embracing God within ourselves. We can evolve from subject to citizen and still preserve the role of Islam in a new social order as a respecter of personal devotion to God and individual choice of direction and destiny. Rulers must become leaders and invite and respond to questions from their people. In turn, the people must hold their leaders accountable and, if their leaders fail them, the people must be willing to fight to determine their own destinies. They cannot wait forever for recognition.

Ihsan (Arabic: إحسان *ʾiḥsān*, also romanized *ehsan*) is an Arabic term meaning “beautification,” “perfection,” or “excellence” (Arabic: *husn* meaning “beauty”). It means taking one’s faith – *iman* – and incorporating it into all our deeds and actions in the most socially responsible way possible, with the most sincere of religious convictions to guide us.

We must demand that the people in leadership positions in the Arab world learn, listen to, practice, and celebrate the many magnificent attributes of leadership. Every man and woman, young and old, should aim to manifest attributes of strong leadership in their own lives. We will not find freedom, prosperity, and sustainability until we all become citizens and find our own voices. Only then will we practice critical thinking and innovative exploration. Only then will we believe that a sustainable, ever-evolving society can be realized by future generations of Middle East citizens.

If we are to have any chance of success, we must practice what we preach. This is true for those in political, business, religious, and intellectual leadership positions. From kindergarten to the corner office, each person must strive to think for themselves and recognize that moral responsibility cannot be passed on to others through instruction alone. Every man and woman must *act* like a leader, nurturing critical thinking, self-determination, and compassion.

We must all be prepared to accept full moral responsibility for our actions, regardless of the circumstances. This will require unflinching integrity and strength of character. Exhibiting such qualities will transform our attitudes and behaviors, and provide a fresh understanding of the ethics of everyday, real-life challenges. This is how we will build a future of peace and prosperity in the Middle East.

EPILOGUE

Ever since that whisper in 2005, I have been thinking about what could be done about leadership. It's a topic I have addressed in different fora and about which I have written op-eds, but I feel it's not enough.

In 2011, I started working with Dr. Erik Berglöf, at that time the chief economist of the EBRD, to support Arab countries in transition during and after the Arab Spring. We shared an understanding about the deficit in leadership throughout the MENA countries. This lack of leadership was also reflected in the region's virtual absence from global debates.

As our collaboration developed, we realized that leadership deficit was widespread, beyond the Arab world. With our eyes on the future, we started discussing creating a platform, grounded in evidence-based research, to help young people develop leadership attributes and become better leaders themselves. We soon realized that young people also had a great deal to contribute in terms of fresh perspectives and innovative ideas.

Perhaps most importantly, they asked difficult questions and challenged established ways of doing things.

This is how the idea of the Maryam Forum was born. We launched its inaugural conversations and research projects at the beginning of 2020, just as the pandemic broke out. We worked with researchers and students at the London School of Economics. In a virtual launch on July 4th that year, we organized some 30 events on six global challenges, which gathered more than 25,000 participants overall. In spite of two years of COVID-19, we developed co-labs with researchers, students, policymakers and business representatives to tackle these issues and build dedicated tracks dealing with:

1. Global emergencies and responses
2. The rethinking of global finance and global financial infrastructure
3. Innovation and inclusive growth
4. Climate and the oceans
5. Populism and sustainable governance
6. Human mobility

In the coming years, I will dedicate my time to the platform. I believe better leadership is more critical than ever in a world that is changing fast and that faces many crises and emerging challenges. New generations have proven their appetite for positive change and their ability to lead.

If they can be further empowered with tools to serve their aspirations, I have no doubt they will create a better tomorrow, for us all.

ACKNOWLEDGMENTS

This book is the result of insights and reflections based on my life experience over the course of more than half a century in the part of the world that I come from. Along this journey, I have benefited from the opportunity to exchange and deepen these observations through encounters and discussions with similarly curious and analytical thinkers from a range of origins, backgrounds, and world views. The synthesis of my ideas owes a debt of appreciation and gratitude to those who supported the inspiration, conception, planning, and execution of this body of work. I would therefore like to acknowledge the following individuals.

I would like to start by commending Julie Mandoyan for bringing rigor, process, structure, and an outside-in perspective to the writing process. While an observer from the beginning, she dove in at the right moment to help me sharpen my pen, and I am immeasurably grateful. Matthew Miller was present when I decided to launch the process. He brought direction, resources, and solutions to ensure that the job was done, even when the fog of COVID-19 delayed the original publication.

Others who played an important role in producing this memoir include:

Fabienne Stassen, who deserves commendation for making the book publishable and accessible for the intended audience.

Tania Willis, who brought a great deal of talent to create the illustrated maps chronicling the key venues of my misspent youth.

Teymour Raouf, who spread messages around the region about what I aimed to achieve in terms of impact.

Khalid Al Hashimi, cartoonist extraordinaire, with whom I have collaborated for over two decades and whose cartoons, without exception, have always stood out and been on point. I am pleased to include his contributions in this book. Instagram: Khalid.alhashimi.cartoon

I would also like to recognize two departed individuals for the role they played in shaping my outlook and with whom I shared profound mutual respect:

First, HRH Prince Khalifa bin Salman Al-Khalifa, the first prime minister of Bahrain, who offered me both his direct and indirect support from within the system, and who from the very beginning understood me to be a nonconformist. He gave me room to raise issues in my own country even though they were not always pleasant subjects for those in the system at large.

Second, HRH Prince Mohammed Al Faisal Al Saud, someone whom I worked for and advised, someone who knew I was always ready to bring up issues and address them in their full complexity, and who, in my experience, was known for his open-mindedness and critical thinking.

Special thanks also go to long-term thought partners who provided critical input for the book.

They include the co-founder of the Maryam Forum Foundation, Erik Berglöf, a valuable collaborator who even as a development economist understands the MENA region as well as anyone and is a testament to the mantra that good economics make good politics.

The students at the London School of Economics who participated in various co-labs with the Maryam Forum Foundation, who all deserve recognition along with Jintao Zhu, Dr. Hassan Gali, and Karina Rodriguez, to whom I offer special thanks.

Nik Gowing, a fellow traveler for over 20 years, whose *Thinking the Unthinkable* has brought insights and the spirit of a common mission and purpose to the Maryam Forum Foundation and many other initiatives in Davos and beyond.

Oliver McTernan, founder and director of Forward Thinking, who has been a great inspiration and help on a personal level and throughout our mutual efforts in the Nyon Process, Bahrain, Egypt, Tunisia, and the Helsinki Policy Forum, as well as in addressing regional economic and health challenges, and dispute resolution.

Sean Cleary, who provided invaluable feedback and who has offered amazing insights since our days together working on the Arab Business Council based on his myriad experiences ending apartheid in his native land and working across emerging and frontier economies.

Amr Moussa, who was one of the few pan-Arabists I encountered in all my years participating in various international forums. He consistently spoke on behalf of all Arabs, superseding geographic borders, before and after his time as Secretary-General of the League of Arab States. His approach was very non-pharaonic, unlike that of most of the Egyptian elites of yesterday and today.

Arab Business Council Chairperson Shafik Gabr, who is always present even when he is absent, and who is directly and indirectly a part of this book because of all we co-authored together or wrote separately.

Appreciation is due to Faisal Abbas, Ricardo Karam and

Khaled Abou Zahr, who lent ears and media platforms, and special thanks to Richard Gere, for the inspiration and for the whispered phrase many years ago in Davos.

I would also like to acknowledge Dr. Abdulla Al Hawaj, my one long-lasting, true Arab friend, besides my family, for his continuous advice and support, and my Compost Corner and associates for their friendships spanning over 40 years.

Extra special thanks go to my wife for her patience, understanding, and support throughout the process of developing this memoir during the extended 2020 lockdown and as we looked to reprioritize our time together, with family, and with our individual pursuits throughout the course of the past three years. Without probing or questioning my intent, she always trusted that I was undertaking an important process of reflection and reconciliation, for which I am eternally grateful.

Finally, a nod to all those individuals who consider me to be, at most, their nemesis and, at the very least, a troublemaker and agitator, simply because they are uncomfortable with the truth being told.

All other names are intentionally omitted.

APPENDIX

EXTRACT 1

Extract 1 is an e-book compilation of policy papers from the inaugural Maryam Forum Annual Conference which took place in December 2020 at the London School of Economics.

PREFACE

The COVID pandemic may well be remembered as the biggest challenge humanity has faced since the Second World War. Indeed, in many respects it has felt like a *war* with unprecedented simultaneous health and economic shocks hitting every country and many lives lost. The pandemic has also exposed the horrendous risks humanity faces if it ignores addressing issues related to 'global public goods': goods or assets whose benefits and/or costs transcend national borders and jurisdictions and on which, however critical, uncoordinated national action will ultimately fail.

Yet the pandemic will also be remembered as *transformational*. An extraordinary global scientific cooperation has produced several vaccines in less than a year from when the COVID-19 genome was posted on the Internet in January 2020. Under lockdowns, digital technologies, while already extensively in use, have allowed an accelerated shift in the way we work, study, shop, interact and enjoy leisure. While policy responses have varied by government, by and large, the global economic meltdown has been averted. This has come at a considerable economic and societal price, whose full extent will be recognised only in the years to come. The ultimate cost will very much depend on the type of policies governments employ now and the extent of their cooperation.

Designing policies for the post COVID world requires both cooperation and a healthy competition of ideas. This debate of ideas must occur now.

We can draw inspiration from the remarkable endeavour of the vaccine creation. The speed with which several vaccines have been created – squeezing what would normally be years of research into a few short months – has reminded us of the creative nature of the human spirit as well as the power of competitive-yet-highly-cooperative research across countries and continents.

At the London School of Economics and Political Science (LSE), we are keenly aware of the urgency of the policy challenge. As a novel way of proposing policy options, under our Maryam Forum Initiative we have assembled expert groups of leading academics, policymakers, representatives of the private sector and our LSE students to contribute to and accelerate this global debate. In this unique public-private policy research platform, our expert groups work directly together on the biggest challenges of our time, organised into six work streams.

This eBook contains policy assessments and recommendations that the expert groups presented at the virtual Maryam Annual Forum Conference in December 2020 and first published in the LSE School of Public Policy COVID blog series, along with a short video of the conference's high level policy panel on a new policy paradigm for the post-COVID world. It also includes a Manifesto by our student leaders to world leaders, respectfully demanding a meaningful role in designing policies that directly determine much of their future.

A key lesson we draw is that *leadership* matters more than ever, and not only in government but in business and civil society as well. Another is that *science* and *evidence* matter but we need to find new and more inclusive ways to draw on evidence and inform our policy makers and citizens. We are also learning that the *young generation,* whose economic and labour market prospects have been particularly hit by the pandemic, is eager to have its voice heard more clearly, particularly in areas where policy decisions today irreversibly impact their future. Science-informed inclusive leadership is what we need to tackle the big challenges ahead of us.

Our expert groups, led by renowned academics and LSE students, have produced a set of recommendations for the coming period:

- **Reforming the way we deal with global emergencies.** Existing systems for dealing with global emergencies have struggled to rise to the challenge of the pandemic. Preparing for and dealing with global emergencies requires a multi-disciplinary approach, combining expertise in global health, epidemiology and economics. COVID-19 has shown the need for an integrated approach weighing in health, financial stability and development outcomes without sacrificing one for the other. *Erik Berglof, Adnan Khan and Hassan Gali* sets out what needs to change, including adaptation of locally optimal smart containment strategies; creating pre-existing integrated data infrastructure to support preparedness at national levels along with protocols for data sharing and coordination; and standardising debt restructuring and pre-emptive debt relief for the poorest countries.

- **New rules for finance and the global financial architecture.** The pandemic has triggered radical changes in both national policies and the global financial architecture. At the national level, the policy mix has fundamentally altered with fiscal policy providing extraordinary stimuli, in unprecedented coordination with, and direct support from, monetary policy. The changing global financial architecture reflects both the rising importance of central banks and the gradual encroaching of key institutions on each other's traditional roles. Altogether, a new international architecture is in the making. *Franklin Allen, Piroska Nagy-Mohácsi, Ricardo Reis and John Gordon* propose measures to enhance the credibility of the rapidly changing national institutional arrangements for fiscal and monetary policy, including transparently defining the rules of the game for monetary and fiscal authority cooperation and introducing a periodic review of their policy mix. They also call for identifying and managing the risks from the emerging new global financial system.

- **Transforming global linkages and industrial policy.** COVID-19 and related policy responses have led to an acceleration of some key pre-existing trends, namely geo-political fragmentation, the reorganisation of global value chains and the adoption of new technologies. Access to the Internet is no longer a luxury – jobs and livelihoods now depend on it. Many pro-recovery policy tools – focusing, for example, on innovation, health and 'green' – are intrinsically 'exclusive' in terms of their beneficiaries due to their managerial and other complexities. Industrial policy is unfit for the new era. *Riccardo Crescenzi and Jintao Zhu* call for a new generation of evidence-based public policies to promote innovation and inclusive growth. Education and skills should be at the centre of policy focus to simultaneously achieve innovation and inclusion; internet access should be expanded by subsidising fix investment costs; and digitalisation, artificial intelligence and automation should be directly integrated into public policies for innovation and inclusive growth.

- **New path on climate change, oceans and financial risk.** Climate change and the oceans are primary global commons and risks to them are rapidly increasing. The urgency to act in these two areas has never been greater and the global context in which to do so has recently improved. Focussing on climate and ocean resilience and related financial risks, *Swenja Surminski, Elod Takats, Torsten Thiele and Karina Rodriguez-Villafuerte* argue that decision-makers undervalue investment in climate resilience, even though evidence shows that strengthening resilience is highly cost effective and can generate multiple benefits. This has caused a major imbalance in funding, with significantly more spent on recovery and repair than on risk reduction and increasing resilience. They note that the case for incorporation of financial stability risks is now well established and stress that these assessments need to be made more comprehensive to include risks to oceans and natural capital.

- **Disinformation is a systemic risk to democracy.** Digital technology has fundamentally undermined previous definitions of a democratic information environment. In earlier periods, non democracies were defined by censorship and control over media, while democracies guaranteed freedom of expression and pluralism. Today dictators and political actors in democracies and 'hybrid' regimes use freedom of speech as an excuse to spread massive amounts of disinformation. *Peter Pomerantsev and Benjamin Grazda* posit that as a result, pluralism is tipping into polarisation and fracture so extreme that they risk making a common debate based on evidence and trust impossible. They argue that disinformation should be recognised as a new systemic risk to society and propose a holistic policy response that combines regulation innovation within the media industry and political consensus-building.

- **Human mobility, enhanced integration and social cohesion.** Migration is a politically sensitive topic, and the narrative surrounding it is often not rooted in solid evidence. Yet integrating refugees into labour markets not only benefits refugees, but also host communities and refugee-citizen relationships. The COVID crisis has further highlighted the central contributions that refugees and migrants make to their host countries. *Dominik Hangartner, Angelo Martelli, Bilal Malaeb and Doménica Avila* offer practical policy recommendations ranging from using technology to match labour market supply and demand for refugees to adopting holistic active labour market programs for refugees and redesigning the asylum process with a focus on integration with frontline cities playing a key role to promote better reception processes and faster asylum-decision processing.

1. REFORMING THE WAY WE DEAL WITH GLOBAL EMERGENCIES

Erik Berglof, Adnan Khan, Hassan Gali

COVID-19 is the first true global emergency in modern human history outside wartime. While the national policy response has varied by leadership and state capacity, the pandemic has highlighted how the systems we have in place for dealing with global emergencies are either not fit for purpose or have been hamstrung by those upon whose leadership they depend. Global emergencies demand coordinated responses and global public goods – they cannot be prepared for, or overcome, without creating the necessary global public goods and without the effective use of global institutions by exceptional leaders. Preparing for and dealing with global emergencies requires a multi-disciplinary approach, combining expertise in global health, epidemiology and economics. COVID-19 has shown the need for an integrated approach weighing in health, financial stability and development outcomes without sacrificing one for the other.

What needs to change?

Recommendation 1: A paradigm shift in crisis policymaking, which learns and adapts quickly to local circumstances.

When we design policy responses for global emergencies, we need to recognise that they are "black swan" events: unpredictable, with a potentially massive global impact. Humanity needs a change in mindset: we need to prepare as much as possible, but also factor into planned responses the extreme uncertainty around the impacts when the shock actually hits. Planning for policy responses must incorporate the need for experimentation, and the mechanisms to learn from it in real time.

The same shock can have very different impacts depending on local conditions. Africa has seen a muted health crisis thanks to a combination of demographic factors and infectious disease awareness, but it has suffered a major economic crisis as recessions in the rest of the world hit its economies. This means policy responses have to capture all relevant dimensions – both health and economic – and the intended and unintended consequences of policy.

Smart containment is key. Policymakers need to learn and act on real-time evidence. The approach will vary by space, time and phase of the crisis.

An integrated multi-disciplinary response is vital. The approach needs to manage financial stability, health and development outcomes without one jeopardising another.

Recommendation 2: Create integrated data infrastructure to support national preparedness, with protocols for data sharing and coordination.

This digitised, geo-coded data infrastructure will incorporate layers of demographic and public sector data and new digital sources. These systems can be activated quickly and built on in real time to support planning and coordination. Traditional "early warning systems" may not be helpful in an unexpected shock, but a data infrastructure can be flexed and enable governments to take prompt action.

Digitalised data collection in real time can help with immediate responses to shocks such as natural disasters. Governments should invest in it. In emerging and more digitalised economies, private sector data can also be harvested to this effect (although this may miss specific groups, including the most vulnerable).

National data collection and analysis has been reasonably effective during the COVID crisis, yet data sharing and coordination between authorities (agencies, states, nations) has been poor. Fighting a catastrophe that does not recognise borders requires effective protocols for coordination and data sharing among different authorities.

Recommendation 3: A common set of principles for debt restructuring and debt relief, with possible pre-emptive debt relief for the poorest countries.

For the poorest countries in Africa, COVID has primarily been an economic crisis. Under guidance from the IMF and the

World Bank, the G20 has adopted limited debt relief. But those measures are unlikely to be enough to avert a debt overhang, or to create fiscal room for supporting a green and inclusive recovery. Moreover, China, a major creditor country, is not a member of some traditional debt restructuring processes such as the Paris Club.

Recommendation 4: Build resilient institutions at home and globally.

The COVID-19 response had mixed results, but it was considerably better at the national than at the global level. Global institutions have made significant efforts, but have not been able to scale up their firepower. The shock has sometimes been beyond the institution's mandate and toolkit.

Global institutions such as the WHO need to be reformed – or even replaced. They should learn from the competitive yet highly co-operative research efforts. An alignment of national and global interest, data/information and research sharing, and active national government support have all contributed to the fast development of effective vaccines.

We urgently need to improve knowledge sharing. One way could be to develop a network of regional bodies to assess and disseminate best practice.

2. NEW RULES FOR FINANCE AND THE GLOBAL FINANCIAL ARCHITECTURE

Franklin Allen, Piroska Nagy-Mohácsi, Ricardo Reis and John Gordon

As governments and central banks have worked to prop up the economy through fiscal stimuli, the relationship between the two has become blurred. Financial markets are being impacted by scaled-up quantitative easing. And a new international financial architecture is in the making. Central banks are revising their mandates; fiscal authorities are adjusting to constraints and upgrading cooperation with central banks; and the changing global financial architecture reflects both the rising importance of central banks and the gradual encroaching of key institutions on each other's traditional roles. We propose measures to enhance the credibility of the rapidly changing national institutional arrangements for fiscal and monetary policy and call for identifying and managing the risks from the emerging new global financial system.

The pandemic has triggered radical changes in both national policies and the global financial architecture. Fiscal policy has provided large stimuli to prevent major economic depressions, reduce inequalities, and deal with large and rising private debt. Monetary policy has scaled up its support for fiscal policy, with quantitative easing (QE) increasing in size, and purchases that target new market segments. The lines between government and central bank policies have become even more blurred. Central banks like the Federal Reserve, the European Central

Bank (ECB) and the People's Bank of China have expanded their swap and repo lines. Emerging market policies have also changed in radical ways. Due to positive spillovers from advanced country monetary policies and their own improved credibility, emerging market central banks also have been able to conduct QE for the first time, without immediate impact on inflation and the exchange rate.

Meanwhile, financial markets have also been reacting to changes in monetary policy, with implications for the monetary transmission mechanism, market structures and ultimately financial stability. Less understood, but critically important, is the interaction between monetary policy and financial market structure, and ultimately financial sector resilience. Central bank swap lines complemented the role of international financial institutions (IFIs), but also blurred the lines between these types of institution – notably with the IMF's mandate on reserve and exchange rate policies.

A new international financial architecture is in the making. Central banks are revising their mandates; fiscal authorities are adjusting to constraints and upgrading cooperation with central banks; and international institutions are caught by the retrenchment of multilateralism. But all this has risks. A lot can go wrong when central banks are monetising debt without apparent limits, when sovereign and corporate debt levels reach historic highs with rising default probabilities, and when superpowers increasingly ignore international organisations.

Recommendation 1: Don't stop stimulus now, but watch out for QE tipping points.

QE has played a much-needed role in financing fiscal expansions, and it should be continued to help economies bridge to the post-COVID world. However, monetary and fiscal authorities should watch out for potential QE tipping points – in particular, the risk of inflation, and the capacity of the central bank and the fiscal authority to each service the interest payments on their debts.

Continued low interest rates create additional debt service capacity for governments which borrow in their own currency. But risks are higher for corporates and in emerging markets, where governments borrow significantly in foreign exchange. Given the exceptional times, debt (in local currency and held by the local central bank) could be issued at very long maturities to eliminate rollover risks.

The lower interest rates induced by QE create risks. As returns on 'safe' assets are low, banks and other asset holders may seek higher risks to compensate. Low spreads could make banks unprofitable and hence more fragile as they seek out higher risks. And although rates are low now, they may not be in future, and governments may struggle to service their debts and put pressure on central banks to keep rate low.

Many emerging markets have been able to perform larger-scale QE, but in the developing world, this has not been an option, and countries need scaled-up IMF. Central bank swap lines have proven helpful on a temporary basis but may not be the appropriate mechanism to help with foreign exchange finance on a permanent basis, except for the liquidity needs of cross-border entities operating in multiple currencies across various jurisdictions.

Recommendation 2: Central bank mandates should be periodically reviewed.

Central banks and governments should conduct periodic, pre-announced reviews of central bank mandates. Some already are: in 2020, the Federal Reserve has published its first-ever comprehensive and public review of the monetary policy framework and concluded that it would do the same roughly every five years. The ECB will complete the second review in its history in mid-2021.

Transparent reviews help realign society's preferences for what central banks should do and reduce the perceived democracy deficit. They can help central banks adapt to emerging challenges and assess the impact of their policies, especially those that go beyond the monetary domain (e.g. sectoral allocations resulting from corporate asset purchases). Pre-announced periodic reviews are preferable as they can help reduce the expectations about their outcomes. Ad hoc reviews could feed expectations that important changes to interest rates would be announced, leading to volatility.

For reviews to be an integral part of accountability mechanisms, they need to be open and involve representation from both government and the legislative branch. However, reviews may be risky for countries where central bank independence is fragile, particularly if there is political involvement.

Recommendation 3: Conduct cost-benefit analysis of any proposed new area for central banks.

When central banks are asked to move into new areas, or decide to do so, they should carry out a cost-benefit analysis of the change and communicate it to the public. This would help identify the skills required, support the delivery of the bank's mandate and better align its aims with those of government. On the other hand, there is a risk of putting central bank independence at risk, diverting resources away from other priorities, and intervening in the market excessively. Crisis-induced activity must be clearly distinguished from the rest, and time limits may be appropriate.

The QE policies and other instruments launched since the global financial crisis have often had knock-on impacts on financial and economic issues. Sometimes these have had little impact on inflation and may not be worth pursuing if the side effects are too great. Cost- benefit analysis would help to formalise these deliberations.

Many central banks have moved beyond the role of "lender of last resort" to "market-maker of last resort." This raises questions about potential crowding out and the balance between government (broadly defined) and markets. In some countries the corporate bond market is growing, thanks to central bank purchases. Proportionality is an important principle, and should be a central consideration.

Several central banks actively consider the climate emergency as part of their mandate, and others are considering doing so. Greening financial sectors and lending is a very important societal objective, but may be best handled by central banks within their financial stability mandate (where it exists) or by other institutions concerned with financial risks in the economy. More broadly, the benefits and downsides of the climate policies deployed by central banks would benefit from proper assessment. It may well be that the priority of governments in coming years is not climate change or inequality, but rather keeping the high levels of debt affordable.

Recommendation 4: Define the rules of the game for monetary and fiscal authority cooperation and introduce a periodic review of their policy mix.

Catastrophic events like the pandemic have highlighted the crucial importance of cooperation between monetary and fiscal authorities. During these crises, central banks necessarily become less independent to help enlarge the country's policy space by directly or indirectly financing governments. Often, they also help with the design of fiscal packages. Calls for monetary policy to align with government objectives are becoming increasingly loud, particularly given the climate emergency.

We need to lay down the rules of monetary and fiscal cooperation. This might jeopardise cherished central bank independence. But should we not accept that central banks can be less independent in the face of catastrophic events? The issue is what the right accountability mechanism for today's era would be.

Greater monetary and fiscal cooperation raises two broad issues. It should not compromise the primary objective of price stability, and the independence of central banks that enables it. And if central banks are to venture into the fiscal or political domain, they need to have the appropriate legitimacy and accountability mechanisms to do so.

Moreover, we need to differentiate between developed and developing countries. For the latter, what matters is not only how developed the financial markets are, but how strong their institutions are. Countries with fragile institutions may not want to risk independence, and could opt for less intrusive cooperation mechanisms.

There is increasing attention to the interactive impact of monetary and fiscal policies – the so-called "policy mix". In our view, there should be periodic reviews of the policy mix that a country pursues.

Recommendation 5: QE necessitates better regulation of non-bank entities.

Although monetary policy has not raised inflation, QE has sustained increasing asset prices. This has led asset management firms and other non-bank financial institutions to become increasingly large, concentrated and overall systemic, even if they do not take household deposits. What systemic risk do non-bank entities pose and how should they be regulated? Central banks may be reluctant to do it as it is may not be their area of expertise, but this large hole in regulation needs to be addressed.

Recommendation 6: The global financial safety net needs a reality check.

So far, the global economy has reacted reasonably well in the face of the COVID shock. But this is in spite of the current global financial architecture, rather than because of it.

The role of the IMF and IFIs in the crisis has been limited, despite many proactive efforts. Instead, emerging markets have been able to conduct QE without inflation and exchange rate risks, thanks in part to positive spillovers from developed countries – QE and expanded currency swap lines. The role and impact of these swap lines and repo operations deserve further research.

Additionally, the role of the US dollar as the international currency may be set to decline, but no other major currency is in a position to take over. This also carries risks and needs heightened policy attention.

3. TRANSFORMING GLOBAL LINKAGES AND INDUSTRIAL POLICY

Riccardo Crescenzi and Jintao Zhu

COVID-19 and related policy responses have led to an acceleration of some key pre-existing trends, namely geo-political fragmentation, the reorganisation of global value chains and the adoption of new technologies. By accelerating digitalisation, the pandemic has placed a huge premium on digital literacy and access. Sectors are being rapidly digitalised and remote working will be integrated into business models. Access to the Internet is no longer a luxury – jobs and livelihoods now depend on it. Governments should support internet access with subsidies for fixed investment costs. Digitalisation, artificial intelligence and automation should be directly integrated into public policies, recognising their potential but also putting in place mitigating measures, particularly for dislocated workers. Evidence also suggests that many pro-recovery policy tools – focusing on innovation, health and 'green' – are intrinsically 'exclusive' in terms of their beneficiaries due to their managerial and other complexities. Policy makers thus must focus more than ever on inclusion in the design of public policies, highlighting gender, age and sub-national regions as key lenses, including to measure success. Inclusiveness should be assessed at both the international and domestic level.

Recommendation 1: Build supportive ecosystems and sound institutions to deal with crises and respond to global challenges.

Both domestic and foreign investors can operate better in supportive ecosystems that can link global opportunities with local economic development. Building these ecosystems calls for a gradual approach, based on a careful diagnosis of existing bottlenecks, as well as potential solutions. It also demands a strategic understanding of the areas that will attract potential investors, and investment in the skills and incentives they want. This is especially important for developing countries that are experiencing structural transformation or have not yet discovered their comparative advantage. Investment Promotion Agencies (IPAs) can play a pivotal role if they have a focused mandate and can work in close contact with investors.

Strong institutions are not easy to build, and demand active capacity-building at the local and national levels.

Pure export-led growth strategies, based on the premise of hyper-globalisation, appear to have had their day. We need to figure out how to unlock new economic potential in countries that have traditionally been export-oriented.

Recommendation 2: Education and skills are key.

Education generates skills and talent, and is the foundation of more inclusive societies. Rapid technological change will make it even more important, and governments need to support lifelong learning, especially in the post-pandemic world.

Continued training and professional skills development also needs to be provided to civil servants who are dealing with increasingly complex problems in rapidly-changing environments. Such continued professional development should better facilitate the design and implementation of sound evidence-based public policies, including for well-functioning 'eco-systems.'

Recommendation 3: Digitalisation, artificial intelligence and automation should be directly integrated into public policies.

Trade in goods, and the global value chains (GVCs) supporting it, was already weakening before the pandemic. A combination of the rising costs of GVCs and declining costs of automisation led to some re-shoring. COVID has reinforced these trends, but also exposed the enormous potential in cross-border trade in services with remote working. Whether this will lead to a return to globalisation – albeit modified – or to more regionalisation remains to be seen. Either way, the critical challenge is to move to a new, sustainable growth pattern that provides good jobs both in advanced and emerging countries.

In advanced countries, this may require *active labour market policies* and possibly employer tax incentives to avoid a net loss of jobs resulting from automisation. In emerging countries, international financial institutions should support *investment in automisation* to keep these countries attractive for off-shoring possibilities, even if pure export-led development strategies need to be abandoned.

Less advanced sub-national regions within all countries suffer the most from the economic contraction, and they may also struggle the most to recover and adjust to new challenges and opportunities. Dedicated regional and local policies are needed to deal with the asymmetric job impacts of digitalisation and allow less developed regions to exploit new opportunities.

Education and training systems need to be modernised so that they better complement investment in automation. Elementary education should develop creative, social and emotional skills as well as basic literacy and numeracy. Adults should be able to access training and further education to allow them to adjust to new labour market realities. Digitalisation and fintech (e.g. blockchain) could be used to develop sustainable finance.

Recommendation 4: Expand internet access. COVID-19 has exposed the enormous premium on digital access for both households and businesses.

Internet access should become a right: without it, access to basic services such as education and health are hampered and ability to work diminished. Policy should not only focus on building infrastructure, but also pay attention to individual accessibility especially for vulnerable groups and for specific categories of firms. One proposal is to subsidise the fixed investment costs of new infrastructure.

Recommendation 5: Global taxation of capital can help expand the fiscal space and create jobs.

The burden of taxation falls disproportionately on labour relative to capital. This penalises employment and undermines fiscal capacity. However, increasing capital taxes at the national level is challenging. Global agreement, coordination and information sharing are urgently needed.

Changing work patterns that include remote working from abroad also suggest a need for a harmonisation of tax regimes.

Fiscal space is also needed to accommodate increased debt service (possibly even after some debt relief to the poorest countries).

Recommendation 6: Connect global savings to SMEs with innovative financial products and link them up to GVCs.

Global savings have grown during the pandemic, even in an era of historically low interest rates. At the same time small and medium-sized enterprises (SMEs) are hugely constrained in their financial capacity. Matching savings and investment is a major challenge that calls for both innovative fintech solutions and supportive institutional arrangements to manage risk. Fintech solutions leverage big data on credit risk to reduce information asymmetry problems. Private equity funds whose stocks can be pooled to trade on stock markets can help address the SME equity shortage.

4. A NEW PATH ON CLIMATE CHANGE, OCEANS AND FINANCIAL RISKS

Swenja Surminski, Elo˝d Takáts, Torsten Thiele, and Karina Rodriguez

Decision-makers undervalue investment in climate resilience, even though evidence shows that strengthening resilience is highly cost effective and can generate multiple benefits. This has caused a major imbalance in funding, with significantly more spent on recovery and repair than on risk reduction and increasing resilience. This is unsustainable, and there is an urgent need to redirect financial flows towards investments that help reduce climate risks. Policymakers tasked to ensure financial stability, including central banks and regulators, need to assess and manage better the financial stability risks from climate change and also include risks to natural capital and to oceans. We also call for governments to ensure that post-COVID recovery packages explicitly invest in resilience and in the protection of the world's natural assets.

Humanity faces horrendous risks if it ignores "global

commons" – that is, goods or assets whose benefits and/or costs transcend national borders. COVID-19 is one of these. Climate change and the oceans are primary global commons, and the urgency to act on them has never been greater. Fortunately, the global context in which to do so has recently improved. The G7 UK Presidency and the G20 Italian Presidency in 2021 are expected to bring these issues back to the global emergency list, with the COP26 conference being hosted in Glasgow next November.

An important focus should be climate and ocean resilience, and related financial risks. Decision-makers undervalue investment in climate resilience, even though evidence shows that strengthening it is highly cost-effective and can generate multiple benefits. This has caused a major imbalance in funding, with significantly more spent on recovery and repair than on risk reduction and increasing resilience. This is unsustainable, and so there is an urgent need to redirect financial flows towards investments that help reduce climate risks. Policymakers tasked with ensuring financial stability, including central banks and regulators, need to assess and manage the financial stability risks of climate change. Indeed, their effective management is already a key consideration for investors and regulatory authorities.

Recommendation 1: COVID recovery finance packages should explicitly support green, nature-friendly solutions and reduce risks to nature, including ocean ecosystems.

A nature-based stimulus investment scenario outperforms a business-as-usual stimulus investment scenario globally, and significant social, economic and environmental benefits could be realised if we channelled more of the stimulus packages towards nature-based solutions like the restoration of the world's forests, wetlands and ocean ecosystems. COVID-19 recovery packages can be used to bring about a material shift toward climate and green activities. Multilateral Development Banks are already working in this area, and in co- operation with governments can help to mobilise additional private capital and engagement. More broadly, it is imperative to shift the policy and business focus from "post-event response" to "pre-event resilience". Ultimately this will depend on how well resilience can be made a bankable investment proposition – a major challenge today. Partnerships between public and private sector and civil society, such as the Zurich Flood Resilience Alliance, can help facilitate much needed progress.

Recommendation 2: Restoring our "natural capital" should be a key policy goal.

The UK Natural Capital Committee is a good example of this approach. Prioritizing adaptation and resilience projects in climate portfolios is a cost-effective strategy to implement this approach.

Recommendation 3: Central banks and regulators need to incorporate the climate emergency as a risk to financial stability.

The case for incorporation of financial stability risks is now well established, but these assessments need to be made comprehensive to include risks to oceans and natural capital. Climate change poses risks to financial stability through two main channels. Firstly, the physical risks resulting from the ongoing manifestation of climate change (floods, droughts, etc.) can impact financial assets and liabilities. Secondly, transition risks can materialise when the economy adjusts towards a low-carbon economy (stranded assets, revaluation risk of brown industries). Even though the full impacts of climate change would not be felt until further into the future, both risks can affect financial stability in the short term.

The case for "greening" monetary policy would need to be made through a public cost- benefit analysis, as also highlighted in the Rethinking Finance and the Global Financial Architecture working group's policy recommendations.

Recommendation 4: Governments should encourage "natural capital" solutions for business investments.

While the role of natural capital is gaining recognition in the private sector, it tends not to be seen as an investment opportunity. Making this work at a commercial level, under commercial financing terms, is still a key challenge. To make it happen, we need to move away from a classical cost- benefit analysis that is rooted solely in physical infrastructure.

5. DISINFORMATION IS A SYSTEMIC RISK TO DEMOCRACY

Peter Pomerantsev and Benjamin Grazda

Disinformation has polarised democratic societies and threatens to make common, evidence-based debate impossible. There is a systemic crisis going to the roots of democracy. The principles for a democratic information environment need to be reimagined for the digital age.

In the past, non-democracies were defined by censorship and control over media, while democracies guaranteed freedom of expression, pluralism, and promoted the free flow of information across borders. Although there has always been space for disinformation in a democracy, there was also an underlying belief that good information would eventually win out in the 'marketplace for ideas.'

Today all these assumptions have been turned upside down. Dictators, as well as political actors in democracies and 'hybrid' regimes, use freedom of speech as an excuse to spread massive amounts of disinformation at the click of a button, while employing online mobs and troll farms to drown out and intimidate critical voices and obscure truth. This constitutes a sort of censorship through noise, but one which does not contravene freedom of expression legislation. The ease with which this digital disinformation can be created, scaled and targeted also questions the validity of the concept of the idea marketplace.

As a result, we are seeing pluralism tip into polarisation and fracture so extreme that they risk making a common debate based on evidence and trust impossible. Societies where people live in separate realities are also more vulnerable to subversive campaigns from hostile states and extremist groups, who take advantage of the borderless information environment for malign ends.

Authoritarian powers like China and Russia are also rapidly defining their own versions of the online space. They have doctrines of 'sovereignty' founded on censorship, and are making technological advances and restricting the rights of their populations, even as they deliver effective online services for them.

In short, there is a systemic crisis going to the roots of democracy. The principles for a democratic information environment need to be reimagined for the digital age.

We propose a *holistic approach* to combat disinformation that combines new regulation, innovations within the media and political consensus building.

Recommendation 1: The public should be given the ability to evaluate the algorithms governing online platforms through government oversight, academic analysis and public interest reporting.

A true democracy has public accountability for how our public sphere is shaped, and a say in its governance. The public should have the ability to evaluate the algorithms governing online platforms through government oversight, academic analysis and public interest reporting. The human right to information and unhindered communication should serve as the benchmark by which to judge these platforms. Greater transparency would also allow the public to understand whether online platforms are designed to uphold rights, whether they truly promote freedom of choice, and what they are doing to slow the spread of disinformation and malign campaigns.

The Forum on Information and Democracy proposes 250 specific recommendations for states and platforms to radically change the way the internet is governed and bring it more in line with democratic norms. At the core of their philosophy is greater transparency: transparency over the algorithms and content moderation practices that shape online spaces; and transparency in how human rights are considered in the way online spaces are designed.

Specific tools from the practice of economic regulation with "carrots and sticks" (incentives and regulation/prohibition) can be also explored.

Recommendation 2: Democratic governments, tech companies and other stakeholders need to invest in public-interest funds to support media that counters disinformation.

The 'infodemic' of disinformation and misinformation around the COVID crisis has again highlighted the vital importance of quality, trusted content – but such public-interest journalism is financially unsustainable in the digital era. Existing institutions and arrangements are not well suited to addressing this economic challenge. An unprecedented, ambitious and differently-organised response is needed. Democracies, technology companies and other stakeholders globally need to invest in public-interest funding that supports media that counters disinformation, while making societies more resilient to extremist propaganda and hostile state subversion.

To this end BBC Media Action, the charity arm of the BBC, is building a major new global fund to strengthen public interest reporting throughout the world, especially in low income countries. Business models were already failing before the COVID-19 pandemic but revenue losses, as well as increasing political pressures, have made independent media increasingly unsustainable despite increased public demand for trustworthy information in what the WHO calls an 'infodemic'. International development agencies currently allocate just 0.3% to independent media support – a pittance, given the severity of the crisis. According to its leaders:

"The Fund would solve five problems: increasing resources to meet the financial needs of independent media; ensuring legitimacy by putting in place an independent, expert and credible governance structure to take decisions on how funding is allocated; reducing transaction costs to make funding media more straightforward for donors; understanding what works and does not work in supporting media by investing in learning; and formulating effective exit strategies by deploying financial, political and knowledge capital to bring different stakeholders together to shape long term system wide solutions to the business model challenge."

Meanwhile the Arena Initiative, based at the LSE and Johns Hopkins University, has been piloting projects in Ukraine, Italy and Hungary that combine sociology and journalism to design and pilot evidence-based approaches to overcome polarisation.

Recommendation 3: Democratic governments and other stakeholders in democracy should urgently build an alliance for information security.

Tackling the crisis of disinformation will require democracies to unite behind common principles and a shared, positive vision for a democratic and secure information environment online.

To this end The Institute for Strategic Dialogue, DEMOS, the German Marshall Fund and Arena are combining to create a new initiative – 'The Good Web.' The Good Web will engage policy and opinion makers in democracies to articulate a shared vision defining the rights of the empowered citizen online, and, perhaps most urgently, what a democratic philosophy for 'information security' looks like. The arrival of a new US administration intent on rebuilding alliances means there is an opportunity to build consensus among democracies on how to design an online space aligned with democratic values. This vision has to encompass new regulation, innovations in media and a common definition of security. Information and its connection to democracy needs to become as central to the agenda of discussions for international meetings among democracies as topics like the environment or corruption.

6. HUMAN MOBILITY, INTEGRATION AND SOCIAL COHESION

Dominik Hangartner, Angelo Martelli, Bilal Malaeb, Doménica Avila

Migration and forced displacement take central attention in national, regional, and global policies, yet the debate is often confounded by a political and populist narrative that is not founded in evidence. While recognising the political sensitivities around migration-related policies, we provide recent evidence supporting feasible policy solutions to improve integration of refugees in labour markets and promoting healthy attitudes towards them to bolster and preserve social cohesion. We also note that the COVID crisis has further highlighted the central contributions that refugees and migrants make to their host countries.

Our set of proposed interventions range from using technology to match labour market supply and demand for refugees to adopting holistic active labour market programs for refugees and redesigning the asylum process with a focus on integration with frontline cities playing a key role to promote better reception processes and faster asylum-decision processing. Through a number of tools governments, business and civil society should actively leverage research and evidence to counter disinformation about refugees.

Recommendation 1: Use technology to match labour market supply and demand for refugees.

For resettled refugees, labour market integration starts by placing people in the location where they are more likely to find a job. Too often this fails to happen, either because of a lack of information about refugee preferences and labour market characteristics, or dispersal policies that do not take this information into account. Recent academic research has developed data-driven matching mechanisms to overcome these barriers and to connect refugees to places. These matching algorithms are an extremely cost-efficient policy intervention that can be adapted to country-specific contexts, dynamically updated over time, and implemented at scale.

Recommendation 2: Holistic, active labour market programmes to help refugees.

Refugees face three main barriers when accessing the labour market: proficiency in the host country language, knowledge of the local labour market, and lack of qualifications. They also face institutional barriers that stop them working legally, such as restricted occupations or difficulty in obtaining work permits. In addition, refugees may face discrimination in hiring decisions, forcing them to accept lower-paid and informal jobs. The earlier refugees have access to the labour market and active labour market programmes, the faster they integrate.

Language training is imperative to break basic cultural barriers. While training in schools is effective, the evidence suggests a multiplier effect when learning language in the workplace. Short-term work placements with language training and cultural orientation modules can help.

Due to labour market frictions and a lack of transferable qualifications, refugees are often overqualified for the jobs they do. Host countries could consider more flexible screening processes, incorporating translation services, and standardising cross-country educational frameworks.

However, some refugees lack the necessary education and skills to join the labour market. In this case, entrepreneurship programmes and volunteering opportunities are powerful options.

They help to create social networks and prevent exclusion, while enhancing skills that increase future job opportunities.

In many countries, refugees have problems obtaining legal work permits, pushing them into the informal sector and precarious work – especially in fragile states and emerging economies. Denying refugees the legal right to work places them at a serious disadvantage and exposes them to exploitation and trafficking. It forces them to take perilous decisions, perpetuates dependency on aid, and increases their vulnerability to health issues and workplace hazards. Governments in host countries should facilitate new regulatory frameworks to overcome this obstacle.

Labour market programmes should give particular attention to women, making sure they have equal access to job opportunities, work permits, and financial services.

Recommendation 3: Redesign the asylum process with a focus on integration.

Besides the violence they fled from, refugees can also be at risk of deprivation, gender- based exploitation, and threats to their lives when housed in camps. Cumulative exposure to violence and traumatic events has long-term impacts on refugees' physical and mental health, complicating social and economic integration.

Recent evidence suggests that lengthy asylum decisions are particularly detrimental to refugees' chances of finding work. Ensuring fast and adequate asylum processes, perhaps with the help of technology, can improve this.

For resettled refugees, who do not have to take perilous journeys to their destinations, pre- departure programmes may facilitate integration by smoothing cultural and labor transitions. Effective programmes do not just provide general information about the host country. They also embrace cultural orientation, with bicultural trainers, language courses, job market information, an early qualifications assessment, job search orientation and support for job applications where possible.

Frontline cities are key to promoting better reception processes and faster processing of asylum decisions. They need to build capacity to respond effectively to refugees' needs while easing the path for their future integration. Multilateral and international cooperation can enable this by providing technical assistance and funding. Refugees should receive user-friendly roadmaps to access public services, to receive guidance from cross-cultural, trained locals, and to provide information to facilitate labour integration.

Recommendation 4: Governments, business and civil society should actively leverage research and evidence to counter disinformation about refugees.

Tackling hostility towards refugees–often expressed in the form of xenophobia and discrimination–should be at the top of the migration agenda. The cost of these tensions for the host community is poorer social cohesion and a lack of shared prosperity. The role of media and public figures such as politicians is key in encouraging positive attitudes– explaining the public effort to receive and resettle refugees, emphasising the humanitarian element of helping people in trouble, and providing an accurate description of both the costs and benefits of successful integration.

Governments that invest in inclusive education actively promote cross-cultural relations and prevent segregation within schools. They provide an opportunity for language skills training, social cohesion, and pro-social behaviour, as well as exposure to other ethnic communities. Programmes can also train school staff to create multicultural curricula and enhance cultural diversity narratives in teaching. They can also include parental engagement, with the help of interpreters.

The pandemic has highlighted the central contribution that refugees and migrants make to their host countries. They often make up an essential component of the workforce, working in key sectors of the economy like the health and care sector, public transport, schools and universities. During the crisis they helped save lives, provided essential services, and developed new treatments, despite the undervaluing of their skills and legal barriers that the face. Given their vulnerability, they may have been disproportionately affected by the economic fallout. Promoting these positive contributions can contribute to improving attitudes towards them.

MESSAGE TO WORLD LEADERS FROM LSE MARYAM FORUM STUDENT LEADERS

We divide history into two parts, the one we like to remember, and the one we seek to actively forget. With an effective distribution of a vaccine still far off, it is important to think about how we will remember COVID-19. The pandemic has been a watershed for all of us. It has shaken us to the core, challenged our innate sense of invulnerability, and forced us to question everything, from our healthcare system to the legitimacy of our governments.

We, the next generation of leaders, have expected a lot from our current leaders. The COVID challenge is enormous. It can be overcome only if the world is able to unite, drawing on our diversity and power of collective wisdom. Yet what we have seen too often is distrust and division. Many leaders have failed us by not acting quickly and disregarding/abandoning global cooperation; others have even profited from corruption in the face of a global emergency. We have suffered enormously from this unspoken collective trauma. We now suggest radical changes to ensure that lessons are learnt from this crisis. As the young citizens of nations, we respectfully demand a shift in perspective to find a new momentum:

- We demand that our leaders ensure transparency, trust and national unity along with robust economic measures. Leaders that stand in solidarity are especially valuable now that we have come to terms with how fragile we are as a human race.

- We need our leaders to build resilient governments that can effectively manage crises, with the wellbeing and protection of their citizens at the forefront of policy decision.

- We demand the leaders of developed countries that have a comparative advantage in the production and distribution of vaccines to join hands and build partnerships across the world, by combining their capacities in making testing mechanisms, vaccines and treatments accessible to everyone, regardless their age, gender or socioeconomic status. In our global world we are protected only if all of humanity is protected.

- We request that countries which have been more resilient support developing countries to deal with the economic impact of COVID-19 and to tackle job losses and economic and financial instability.

- We ask leaders of the developing world to adapt "smart" targeted policies in which lockdowns do not disproportionately affect the most vulnerable.

- We ask leaders to design policies for recovery and post-COVID growth that help reduce poverty and inequality. We suggest inclusive recovery strategies that do not leave anybody behind and ensure communities such as migrants and refugees also get access to medical services.

- We strongly support "build back better" policies from the pandemic to confront the climate crisis and change global attitudes and intentions. Climate change is a looming emergency where we expect our leaders to take action and preserve what is truly important: the planet. Our leaders must ensure governments and industries are active defenders of the planet. Therefore, we expect strong green and blue recovery packages.

- We demand more representation by young citizens in tax reforms and social benefits policy. As our economic systems are under tremendous stress, much of the burden will be intergenerational. We seek to actively participate and shape economies to build back better, with green-minded investments and decent jobs.

- We demand leaders and governments devise strategies that effectively tackle disinformation. In an era of massive disinformation with devastating real-world impacts, we want healthy democracies with competing ideas instead of struggling democracies flooded by strategic misinformation and fake news/propaganda. We reject information that seeks to divide our societies and dismantle vital institutions.

- We ask our leaders to look beyond winning elections and redirect their focus and politics towards good governance. The leaders of today need to ask what kind of legacy they want to leave behind, and what kind of world their children and grandchildren will inherit.

- Finally, we ask our leaders to hear the fresh perspectives, the digital nativism, and the activism from young people in every corner of the world, in every debate and every policy design. We need policy-making to be inclusive, with representation of the young generation from around the world. We need you to please trust us and listen to us. We are eager to contribute with ideas and creativity to frame recovery strategies and shape the future of the next generation.

This is why, as young citizens from around the globe, we are joining platforms where our voices can be heard. This is why we have joined the Maryam Forum, where we work with policy-makers, business leaders and academics to seize the moment and rise beyond the COVID crisis.

Source: The Maryam Forum. A New Policy Paradigm for the Post-Covid World: Proposals for Changes from the Maryam Forum Platforms, 2021.

EXTRACT 2

Extract 2 contains extracts of the overview of the first UNDP *Arab Human Development report*, published in 2002, referenced several times in this book.

From the Atlantic to the Gulf, people-- women, men and children--are the real wealth and hope of Arab countries. Policies for development and growth in the Arab region must focus on freeing people from deprivation, in all its forms, and expanding their choices. Over the last five decades, remarkable progress has been achieved in advancing human development and reducing poverty. However, much still needs to be done to address the backlog of deprivation and imbalance. Looking forward, much also needs to be done in order to empower the people of the Arab region to participate fully in the world of the twenty-first century. Globalization and accelerating technological advances have opened doors to unprecedented opportunities, but they have also posed a new risk: that of being left behind as the rate of change accelerates, often outpacing state capacity.

Development is being reinvented by new markets (e.g., foreign exchange and capital markets), new tools (e.g., the Internet and cellular phones), new actors (e.g., non-governmental organizations, the European Union and World Trade Organization) and new rules (e.g., multilateral agreements on trade, services and intellectual property).

CHALLENGES

Entering the new millennium, people in Arab countries face two intertwined sets of challenges to peace and to development. The first set has been made ever more conspicuous and pressing after the tragic events of 11 September 2001. These are the challenges to the pursuit of freedom from fear. Regional and external factors intersect in this realm of peace and security. The second set of challenges is equally important if not more critical. It encompasses challenges to the achievement of freedom from want. These are the challenges faced by people and governments states and societies as they attempt to advance human development. These challenges are fundamental, not only for their instrumental significance to development and growth but also for their intrinsic value. Equity, knowledge and the freedom and human rights integral to good governance matter for their own sake as well as for their critical role as enablers of development. They are both means and ends. They are central to both the process and the state of human development. Some key aspects of both sets of challenges are highlighted below.

OCCUPATION STIFLES PROGRESS

Israel's illegal occupation of Arab lands is one of the most pervasive obstacles to security and progress in the region geographically (since it affects the entire region), temporally (extending over decades) and developmentally (impacting nearly all aspects of human development and human security, directly for millions and indirectly for others). The human cost extends beyond the considerable loss of lives and livelihoods of direct victims. If human development is the process of enlarging choices, if it implies that people must influence the processes that shape their lives, and if it means the full enjoyment of human rights, then nothing stifles that noble vision of development more than subjecting a people to foreign occupation.

Firstly, for Palestinians, occupation and the policies that support it, stunt their ability to grow in every conceivable way. The confiscation of Palestinian land, constraining their access to their water and other natural resources, the imposition of obstacles to the free movement of people and goods, and structural impediments to employment and economic self-management all combine to thwart the emergence of a viable economy and a secure independent state. Moreover, the expansion of illegal settlements, the frequent use of excessive force against Palestinians and the denial of their most basic human rights further circumscribe their potential to build human development. The plight of Palestinian refugees living in other countries is a further manifestation of development disfigured by occupation.

Secondly, occupation casts a pall across the political and economic life of the entire region. Among neighbouring countries, some continue to suffer themselves from Israeli occupation of parts of their lands, subjecting those people directly affected to tremendous suffering, and imposing development challenges on the rest. In most Arab states, occupation dominates national policy priorities, creates large humanitarian challenges for those receiving refugees and motivates the diversion of public investment in human development towards military spending. By symbolizing a felt and constant external threat, occupation has damaging side effects: it provides both a cause and an excuse for distorting the development agenda, disrupting national priorities and retarding political development. At certain junctures it can serve to solidify the public against an outside aggressor and justify curbing dissent at a time when democratic transition requires greater pluralism in society and more public debate on national development policies. In all these ways, occupation freezes growth, prosperity and freedom in the Arab world.

CONFLICTS, SANCTIONS AND INSTABILITY PREVENT DEVELOPMENT

Political upheavals, military conflicts, sanctions and embargoes have affected many economies of the region, causing declines in productivity and disrupting markets. Some countries struggling to recover from the ravages of war have emerged with substantial debts, limiting options for public expenditure. All affected countries have emerged with compounded socio-political problems that have retarded progressive moves towards liberalization and democratization.

The direct impact of wars is registered in slowed growth, damaged infrastructure, social fragmentation and public-sector stagnation. Some countries have experienced hyperinflation, severe currency devaluations and curtailed foreign-currency earnings. Others have seen their standing in the international community collapse. Most affected countries have lost important human and capital resources critical for the renewal of stability and competitiveness.

ASPIRATIONS FOR FREEDOM AND DEMOCRACY REMAIN UNFULFILLED

There is a substantial lag between Arab countries and other regions in terms of participatory governance. The wave of democracy that transformed governance in most of Latin America and East Asia in the 1980s and Eastern Europe and much of Central Asia in the late 1980s and early 1990s has barely reached the Arab States. This freedom deficit undermines human development and is one of the most painful manifestations of lagging political development. While de jure acceptance of democracy and human rights is enshrined in constitutions, legal codes and government pronouncements, de facto implementation is often neglected and, in some cases, deliberately disregarded.

In most cases, the governance pattern is characterized by a powerful executive branch that exerts significant control over all other branches of the state, being in some cases free from institutional checks and balances. Representative democracy is not always genuine and sometimes absent. Freedoms of expression and association are frequently curtailed. Obsolete norms of legitimacy prevail.

DEVELOPMENT NOT ENGENDERED IS ENDANGERED

Gender inequality is the most pervasive manifestation of inequity of all kinds in any society because it typically affects half the population. There have been important quantitative im- when other dimensions of poverty remain substantial.

Source: United Nations Development Programme. Arab Human Development Report: Creating Opportunities for Future Generations, 2002.

EXTRACT 3

Extract 3 is a chapter presenting the Arab Business Council written by Shafik Gabr and Khalid Abdulla-Janahi as part of the 2005 *Arab Competitiveness Report*.

Introduction

All recent studies, by the United Nations Development Programme, the World Economic Forum, and others suggest that weak governance, inadequate education, inadequate skills development and research and development, and poor growth are hindering economic and social advancement in the Arab region.

The 2002 *Arab Human Development Report* pointed to three critical deficits in the Arab region:

1. a knowledge deficit
2. a freedom deficit
3. a deficit in the empowerment of women

The Report proposes that Arab countries " ... ... embark on rebuilding their societies on the basis of

- full respect for human rights and freedoms, as the cornerstone of good governance, leading to human development;
- the complete empowerment of Arab women, taking advantage of all opportunities to build their capabilities, and to enable them to exercise those capabilities to the full;
- the consolidation of knowledge acquisition and its effective utilization; as a key driver of progress, knowledge must be brought to bear efficiently and productively in all aspects of society, with the goal of enhancing human wellbeing across the region."

In considering the knowledge deficit, the 2003 Arab Human Development Report noted that

- higher education in the Arab countries was characterized by falling quality and enrolment, and lower public spending;
- scientific research was hampered not only by weak basic research and the absence of advanced research in information technology and molecular biology, but also by very low R&D spending (averaging only 0.2 percent of GNP), and too few research scientists and engineers (only 371 per million of population, when the global average is almost three times that, at 979 per million);
- the regional ICT infrastructure is very weak; the Arab region has only 20 percent of the telephone density of the OECD countries; there are only 18 computers per 1000 persons, while the global average is 78.3 per thousand; only 1.6 percent of Arabs had Internet access, as compared to 68 percent in the United Kingdom or 79 percent in the USA.

In the first Arab World Competitiveness Report, the authors assembled by the World Economic Forum offered a tentative assessment of the competitive position of the Arab region, defining competitiveness as " ... ... the set of institutions and economic policies supportive of high rates of economic growth in the medium term." A distinction was properly drawn between the preconditions ("necessary conditions") for growth and development, such as peace and security, quality of infrastructure (including ICT), macroeconomic stability, competent institutions, and "engines of development," such as startups and entrepreneurship, capital accumulation, low taxes, innovation, transfer of technology, and exports other than natural resources. The authors argued that too much policy discussion was focused on meeting the preconditions for growth, and not enough on deploying and synchronising the engines of development. The Arab region, it was argued, had pursued a one-dimensional growth strategy, premised exclusively on capital accumulation.

The summary conclusion of the report was that, due, in part, to high population growth and heavy dependency of most economies on oil revenues, *per capita* incomes in the Arab world had stagnated in the last quarter of the 20th century, underperforming all regions other than sub- Saharan Africa. Fifteen percent of the labour force— perhaps 30 percent of persons between 16 and 24 years of age—were unemployed. Levels of knowledge, innovation and technological advancement were poor, as were the macro-economic environment, the quality of governance and public institutions, the functioning of goods and factor markets, and the extent of regional integration into the global economy—all of which did not conduce to entrepreneurial risk-taking.

The results are apparent:

- As a result of the dependence on oil exports, the contribution of non-oil merchandise exports in the Arab region is only 6 percent of GDP, as against approximately 20 percent in South-east Asia.

- The current ratio of FDI to GDP is only 0.5 percent in aggregate. Central Europe and Chile have seen their FDI/GDP ratios rise to between 5 and 6 percent.

- Growth in real output of 5 percent and more will be needed to prevent a worsening of current levels of unemployment.

FOREIGN DIRECT INVESTMENT (FDI)

The Arab world's share of global FDI flows fell from 1.2 percent over the period 1985–1995, to 0.4 percent in 2000. Its share of the flows to developing countries fell from 4.3 percent in that same ten-year period to 1.9 percent in 2000. Moreover, this investment is disproportionately concentrated in the petroleum sector, although Bahrain, Egypt, Morocco, Tunisia and Lebanon have also seen investment in tourism, banking, telecoms, construction and manufacturing. Eighty percent of total FDI stock is concentrated in Saudi Arabia, Egypt, Tunisia, Bahrain and Morocco, with the first three having 70 percent of the total. Intra-Arab investment flows, though poorly documented, appear to account for a high percentage of total FDI flows, perhaps over half of those recorded in 2000.

The average return on new investments is exceptionally high. Some see this as suggesting that there are many untapped investment opportunities, but this overlooks three factors:

1. High returns correlate with high risk and many other factors, including political turbulence, poor macro-economic management, weak capital (and often current)

account positions, small local and sub- regional markets, debilitated infrastructures, and skills shortages, which increase the risk and cost of investing; only projects offering high returns compensate for the assumption of such risks.

2. High intra-regional and inter-regional transportation costs, and restricted access to developed markets, constrain the returns on production for export; this is particularly true in agriculture and agri-business, where farm subsidies leading to excess production in the EU and the United States depress world prices; only if these distortions are addressed can the Arab world escape from negative terms of trade, and vulnerability to the vagaries of commodity cycles.

3. Investment projects in the Arab world compete for allocation of investment capital in a global marketplace; standard risk assessment methodologies, which encourage the aggregation of risk factors, rather than sophisticated discrimination between them, has encouraged regional contagion.

This low level of private domestic, intra-regional and foreign direct investment translates into low growth, high unemployment and poor economic development.

But this is not a necessary circumstance!

The Arab Business Council has four major objectives:

1. Identify and define emerging issues of regional and global importance to create an issue-based agenda for its members;

2. Elaborate practical solutions to these issues and partner with other business, political, academic and civil society decision-makers in addressing them;

3. Work with Arab governments and institutions to strengthen the competitiveness of the Arab region and

4. Facilitate its integration into the global economy;

The region and its peoples have a rich cultural and scientific heritage. For centuries they competed with, and occasionally surpassed, the best that European civilization had to offer. Between the 9th and 13th centuries CE, the Islamic world sustained and advanced the learning of the Greeks, the Jews, and the Romans, and laid the foundations for the Age of Maritime Discovery, the birth of the great European universities and the Italian Renaissance.

ADDRESSING THE STRUCTURAL IMPEDIMENTS

Reversing the decline experienced by the region requires Arab governments and societies urgently to address the structural impediments to sustained growth, including macro-economic stability, appreciable improvement of infrastructure and public institutions, and the development of efficient markets, as well as the deficits identified in the 2002 Arab Human Development

Report: human freedom, women's empowerment, and knowledge acquisition and use.

These are all necessary, but, as the first Arab World Competitiveness Report indicated, not sufficient, conditions for sustained growth and development.

THE ARAB BUSINESS COUNCIL

The publication of the first *Arab World Competitiveness Report* caused shockwaves among leading members of the Arab business community, and led to the establishment of an Arab Business Council (ABC) in June 2003, with the mission *of facilitating cooperation between the leading Arab private sector actors, to help equip their societies to compete more effectively in the global economy, and contribute to the development of an equitable regional and global society.*

- Advise and guide the World Economic Forum in the Forum's activities in the Middle East and North Africa.

The ABC has 77 members at present, from 16 Arab countries. It has set a goal of recruiting 100 members, with the best possible gender and country representation. Membership is limited to the leaders of the foremost Arab enterprises, characterized by a leading position in relevant markets, a top industry ranking, solid projected growth potential, an active role in promoting regional competitiveness, and commitment to the ABC Charter.

Since they share a common commitment to get their own

houses in order, if they are convincingly to advocate wider regional change, ABC members have adopted two Covenants on *Corporate Governance* and the *Elimination of Corruption and Bribery*, and two Declarations on *Accounting and Audit Standards* and *Corporate Social Responsibility*, to promote global best practice standards in the business community.

Preliminary working papers were prepared on pan-Arab trade, finance and investment, corporate governance, legal and judicial reform, communications and media, research and development, intellectual property rights and education.

The ABC has been received by several political leaders in the region and several Heads of State have appointed Ministers as national government coordinators between their respective governments and the Council.

At a meeting in Aqaba in October 2003, supported by the Jordanian government, the ABC produced a Blueprint for Economic Reform in the Arab region, based on three focal areas: *economic liberalization, superior governance* and *human resource development*, and established a channel of communication between Arab governments, business, and civil society. After extended further consultation, this was published at the Annual Meeting of the World Economic Forum in Davos in January 2004.

Economic liberalization was divided into focal categories:

- **Diversification of exports:** developing non- traditional export markets, incorporation of technology, simplifying trade-related procedures, building institutional capacity, and upgrading trade- related infrastructure;

- **Competitiveness and FDI:** reducing exchange rate misalignment and overvaluation, improving access to trade financing, encouraging high levels of FDI; removing restrictions on sector and ownership levels, and developing human resources for FDI;

- **Structural reforms:** engaging the private sector as a partner, accelerating privatization processes, promoting financial and administrative reforms, increasing market openness and global integration, and developing an environment conducive to business investment.

The focal areas for *governance* are

- respect for the rule of law and property rights;
- enhancing transparency and accountability;
- addressing corruption and favouritism;
- improving the quality of public sector institutions;
- improving the legal mechanisms for dispute settlement;
- developing an independent and efficient judiciary.

Within *human resource development*, the areas of emphasis are

- improving the efficiency and quality of education;
- strengthening vocational and technical training;
- investing in scientific, R&D, and IT infrastructure;

- developing links between academia and economic production;
- empowering women and youth in society.

The ABC then joined the Alexandria Library and other non-governmental organizations in organizing a Conference on Reform in the Arab region, 12–14 March 2004, to develop the Alexandria Declaration, which was adopted by 180 leading participants from 18 Arab countries.

In January 2004, in Davos, the ABC Executive Committee decided to promote the establishment of National Competitiveness Councils in Arab countries, to assist in improving the quality of data and promoting national competitiveness. The ABC supported the launch of the Egyptian National Competitiveness Council on 15 February 2004, to assess the current state of Egypt's competitiveness, and to prepare recommendations on means to improve it, within the overall framework of economic, political, social and educational reform in Egypt. The Council is also working to ensure that economic and socio-economic data is available at global best practice levels. Jordan has agreed to establish a Jordanian National Competitiveness Council, and discussions to the same end are underway with Bahrain, Morocco and the UAE.

At a meeting in Cairo on 14 September 2004, the ABC established five Task Forces on:

1. education and vocational training
2. national Competitiveness Councils
3. integrating and deepening capital markets

4. improving the quality of governance
5. information and communications technology.

Each task force comprises members of the ABC, with specialized knowledge in each area, who are developing policies to support regional and national competitiveness.

These ABC initiatives have been recognised outside the region as well. At the initiative of the King of Jordan, ABC representatives joined 36 Asian business leaders from Malaysia, Korea, Singapore, Thailand, India, Japan, Hong Kong, China, Philippines, Vietnam and Cambodia at a retreat of "New Asian Leaders" in Malaysia, from 23–25 February, 2004. Following discussions about cooperation between Arab and Asian business leaders, a *Langkawi Declaration* was issued on exchange programs in trade, investment, employment, education and training.

Each task force comprises members of the ABC, with specialized knowledge in each area, who are developing policies to support regional and national competitiveness.

These ABC initiatives have been recognised outside the region as well. At the initiative of the King of Jordan, ABC representatives joined 36 Asian business leaders from Malaysia, Korea, Singapore, Thailand, India, Japan, Hong Kong, China, Philippines, Vietnam and Cambodia at a retreat of "New Asian Leaders" in Malaysia, from 23–25 February, 2004. Following discussions about cooperation between Arab and Asian business leaders, a *Langkawi Declaration* was issued on exchange programs in trade, investment, employment, education and training.

Even more significantly, the Heads of State at the 2004 G-8 Summit in Sea Island announced that the G-8 would: *"establish with partners in the (Broader Middle East) region a Task Force on Investment, comprised of business leaders from the G-8 and the region, including from the Arab Business Council, to assist the region's efforts to improve the investment climate."*

The G-8 Summit undertook to work with governments, business, and civil society in the Broader Middle East to expand reform initiatives, given especially that *"these activities respond to reform priorities identified by the region, including by the Arab League Summit Tunis Declaration, the Alexandria Library Statement, the Sana'a Declaration, and the Arab Business Council Declaration".*

Members of the ABC Executive Committee were invited to join in a *Business Dialogue,* organized by the G-8 in New York, as part of the *Forum for the Future,* to discuss the role of the business sector in supporting reform. At this meeting, an ABC Agenda for Development was presented to the Ministers of Foreign Affairs of the G-8 and the BMEA.

At a meeting with an OECD delegation in Paris on 19 November 2004, the Chairman and Vice Chairman of the ABC presented a preliminary proposal for the establishment of a private sector Investment Task Force (ITF). The OECD delegation agreed to work with the ABC in establishing this task force, which will comprise leading business persons from the BMEA, the G-8 countries, and other leading economies. The ITF will collect regional investment data and identify impediments to investment, develop policy recommendations to improve the investment environment, monitor and report on progress achieved, and attend meetings of the Forum for the Future and the MENA-OECD Investment Programme to foster private sector development. The ABC Annual Meeting in Marrakech on 25–26 November 2004, which addressed Investment, Trade and Competitiveness in the Arab World, endorsed this initiative, and discussions are now underway with G-8 governments and private sector institutions regarding the establishment of the ITF.

NECESSARY POLICY CHANGES: THE CONTEXTUAL FRAMEWORK FOR INVESTMENT

Only significant improvements in the quality and efficiency of investment, and related non-oil trade, will enable growth in the Arab region sufficient to meet the demands of the high levels of population growth. Achieving this requires significant policy changes.

Recent research suggests that the 20–30 year stagnation in growth in the Arab world can be explained by two factors in particular:

1. poor levels of private, and inefficient public investment, due to the crowding out of investment opportunities by governments, ineffective capital markets and protected, politically-connected banking sectors;

2. decline in total factor productivity, due to socio- political disturbances, over-regulation of markets, and low human capital productivity.

Poor *human capital productivity* is obviously closely related to the three factors mentioned earlier in the *Arab Human Development Report, 2002*: knowledge deficit, freedom deficit, and deficit in the empowerment of women. These comprise a vicious circle, ensuring poor performance.

Therefore, the ABC decided to focus its efforts on promoting national and regional competitiveness, on these two factors. Mindful of the political obstacles to much-needed reforms, in an era characterized by pressures from some quarters for religious fundamentalism, it drew inspiration from the golden age of Arab/ Islamic civilization, and called for an Arab *Renaissance*.

A rebirth of Arab culture and society is long overdue, in the context of the challenges of globalization in the 21st century. The ABC has taken up the challenge of working with political, religious and social leaders throughout the region, to promote investment in human capital, the improvement of political, economic and corporate governance, and channelling entrepreneurial talent and investment into productive areas. The aim is to spark an Arab *Renaissance,* to enable the region to take its rightful place in a fast evolving, tightly integrated global environment.

Given the broad canvas of reform needed to improve competitiveness, it is easy to fall victim to *paralysis through analysis*. While there is much we do not know about the workings of complex human systems, it is clear that delivering superior, business-relevant education is central to a revival of economic activity in the Arab world. This must, however, be supported by four key policies, designed to:

1. Celebrate Arab heritage and civilization, rebuild a sense of cultural integrity and pride throughout the region, and ensure that religious zealots do not dominate the field of education, and constrain progress in finance and commerce;

   If we are to reduce bureaucratic constraints, and enable entrepreneurship and sustained growth, there must be established a solid foundation of:

2. deeper and better integrated capital (and bond) markets, to enable transparency; transactional efficiency, and more effective access to capital for established companies, Arab individuals and institutions with large capital sums invested abroad, and entrepreneurs alike;

3. integrate the Arab region into global ICT networks, in order to widen access to global best practices and other

standards of excellence, and spark a growth industry in Arabization and the development of local content;

4. Facilitate effective international banking access, to lower the cost of capital and enable access to finance for emerging entrepreneurs;

Dismantle trade barriers to expand the size of markets, permit economies of scale to reduce delivered unit costs, and facilitate entrepreneurship and domestic, intra-regional and foreign investment.

Better political, macroeconomic and corporate governance, and more effective institutions, focused on facilitating, not controlling, legitimate activity.

COMPETITIVENESS AND RENAISSANCE

The experiences of Scandinavia, Japan, the United States, South-East Asia, and, more recently, China and India, make it clear that, while certain core fundamentals are common to all, there is no one-size-fits-all model of development that ensures global competitive success.

Each of the countries in the Arab region will, therefore, have to develop indigenous development models for success. The configuration of the optimal development path for Egypt, Saudi Arabia and the UAE is obviously not identical. Nonetheless, certain core elements are common.

There are three key components of a revival of the social, economic and political fortunes of the Arab region:

1. Building intellectual capital, to enable a rebirth of learning and science, by
2. building human capacity through education, research and development
3. celebrating Arab culture and heritage

Progress in this realm can be measured in three areas: *education, research and development*, and *local content*. The *education* component would reflect participation in, and the quality of, education, with attention to levels of attainment measured against best global standards, and gender variables. Participation in the labour market and opportunities for lifelong learning should also be considered.

The *research and development* component should address numbers of scientists and engineers graduated, research articles published, citations recorded, and patents and other forms of intellectual property registered.

The *local content* component will measure the number of translations of leading foreign books, research articles and educational material published in Arabic, and the extent to which Arab print, electronic and digital media focus attention on current and historical scientific and educational attainments in the Arab world.

Creating an enabling policy environment, to allow learning, innovation and entrepreneurship to flourish by

- crafting an appropriate policy environment
- nurturing entrepreneurship
- stimulating innovation

This index focuses on the environment conducive to fostering innovative ideas and successful businesses. Transparent, effective and accountable governance, and minimal economic distortions are needed, if those businesses which are already established, as well as those new ones which are promising are to flourish. The Innovation and Entrepreneurship sub-index will thus assess the quality of the business environment, including the operating conditions for businesses, especially startups, as well as the support provided for innovation.

Integrating the region into the leading global networks, so as to leverage these linkages, by

- expanding intra-regional and global trade
- increasing domestic and foreign investment
- diffusing ICT
- exchanging insights, ideas and best practices

No region can flourish in isolation. Arab institutions and businesses must have access to the best ideas and technologies offered internationally. This requires strategic trade growth, capturing desired investment flows, opening channels for exchanges of ideas, and facilitating diffusion of information and communication technologies. This sub-index will thus cover selected trade, investment and ICT variables, as well as indicators providing benchmarks of openness to, and exchange of, ideas.

All these components are closely inter-related, and either mutually-reinforcing or—if they fail—mutually- debilitating.

Recognizing the richness of the Arab region's historical contributions to science, mathematics, medicine, and the arts, it is clear that with an appropriate set of institutions, policies and programmes, the region can once again enable scientific, cultural and technological excellence to flourish. Such a *renaissance* will position and integrate the Arab region successfully in the global economy.

Thus, the ABC's Arab *Renaissance* project aims to spur a systemic, structured and collective effort to enrich and build upon the unique legacy of the Arab world. It is not merely a response to the challenge of globalization, by challenging the region to move to the vanguard of a multi-cultural advance to global betterment. External cultural influences pose no threats to Arab or Islamic identities in this context; however, they do provide opportunities to affirm, strengthen, and disseminate an Arab identity, even as the cultural heritages of the Indian, Chinese, Greek, Roman and Byzantine cultures enabled and formed the foundations of the Golden Age.

The Arab region has the potential to launch its *renaissance,* and the ABC has assumed the task of unleashing this capacity.

As a means of benchmarking, an *Arab Renaissance Index* can supplement the Arab World Competitiveness Report as a means of engaging policymakers, business leaders and other stakeholders in a constructive process of policy discussion and reform. The analysis can be conducted at both the country and regional levels: the former will be a catalyst for national policy changes, while the latter will allow for regional cooperation and cross-border initiatives.

An *Arab Renaissance Index* will be framed in the global context, to provide a comparative assessment of the region's performance, and a useful perspective on its progressive integration in the world economy.

FOCUS ON INVESTMENT

The ABC's focus on improving the investment environment in the Arab region is evident in its engagement with the G-8 and OECD, in incubating the BMEA-OECD Investment Task Force.

There are two reasons for this emphasis:

1. Competitiveness—the set of "national institutions and policies that support high rates of economic growth in the medium term"—can be defined by the quality of technology (and technological advances) in a society, plus the capital stock, both physical and human, available, and the extent to which strengthening of that capital is occurring. Given the poor quality of the technology and capital stock available in the Arab region, inward investment and associated skills and technology transfer are essential to overcome these deficits.

2. The policies, practices and institutions that comprise an enabling environment for investment, are identical to those that that will serve to make the region more competitive, and indeed, underpin an Arab *Renaissance.* From this perspective, focusing on creating an enabling environment for investment is an effective proxy for the range of targeted reforms needed to render the region globally competitive.

This can easily be illustrated by a simple example.

The purpose of investment is to earn an attractive return on capital put at risk. The required return correlates with the risk; the higher the risk, the greater the expected return. Prudence dictates that the risk must be quantified to enable calculation of the return required to justify it.

All surveys of the criteria employed in deciding on new investments produce similar results: safety, legal and macroeconomic policy stability and predictability, and a market orientation in economic policy are the most important requirements cited by potential investors.

These allow investors to calculate prudently, and assume or decline, the risk associated with the expected return.

In principle, investors need adequate physical infrastructure—water, power, transport and ICT—and access to educated and skilled human resources.

Weaknesses in some of these can be overcome, if high

returns and long dividend flows are probable, but additional costs incurred in providing infrastructure or importing skills are capitalized and the expected return, premised on the risk assessed, is calculated on the total investment needed to bring the project to profitable production.

It is thus not surprising that few significant foreign investments outside the petroleum sector been attracted to the Arab region in the past two decades. Moreover, Arab investment *outside* the region has risen far faster than that within it. Estimates within the Arab banking sector suggest that over US$1,000 billion of Arab money is invested *outside* the Arab region. Recent high oil prices have, moreover, increased the capital sums available for this purpose.

However, the impediments to domestic and foreign investment are many and varied, and most, though not all, are the result of government policies. The cost of establishing a business is high in most countries.

Investment procedures and regulations are often opaque and dependent on political or bureaucratic interpretation, or, worse, whim. The stock of state-owned enterprises is too high, and their management usually inefficient, adding to the cost of doing business. The quality of macroeconomic management has been weak in many countries, increasing the risk to investors. Trade barriers, both within the Arab region, and in many developed countries, limit the size of export markets. Correction of these weaknesses, and development of effective, transparent banking and capital market instruments are needed to enable higher levels of investment.

The ABC believes that leading private sector bodies must work with Arab governments and civil society institutions to manage the risk of instability in this period of profound change, and ensure that the opportunities to add social and economic value are properly exploited. There are several key priorities in the context of the extensive policy and institutional reforms discussed earlier:

- Removal of impediments to intra-regional and global trade and investment, recognising that macro- economic stabilization and exchange rate alignment are prerequisites for capital account liberalization;

- An immediate focus on education-for-employment-and-entrepreneurship, to mitigate the social pressure occasioned by exceptionally high and rising rates of joblessness among the young;

- Tax reform, budgetary transparency, and application of the rule of law to enable the private sector to play its proper role of wealth-creation for the benefit of society.

In its engagement with the G-8 and OECD, the ABC will continue to stress the need for these governments and their business sectors, where applicable, to

- work with their regional counterparts in the BMEA- OECD Investment Task Force to identify, and, where possible, eliminate investment and trade impediments in the BMEA;

- support BMEA governments, business enterprises, and NGOs, which are pursuing sensible reforms;

- recognising the severe weaknesses in institutional capacity in many parts of the region;

- eliminate domestic and export subsidies for OECD agricultural sectors and allow effective access to their markets for agricultural exports from the BMEA and other less-developed countries;

- facilitate access to their markets for manufactured products from the BMEA, through investment, technology-transfer and local development;

- engage more consistently in helping to facilitate the just and sustainable resolution of the remaining conflicts in the BMEA.

CONCLUSIONS

The Arab world must take responsibility for determining its own future. This demands appreciation of the challenge of competing in a global economy, and development of the skills, policies and institutions needed to do this effectively. Only Arab leaders can ensure comity and security in the region, and effect proper standards of political and macro-economic governance, respect for the rule of law, and social harmony.

The Arab business community and other important

segments of Arab civil society must work in partnership with their governments to effect change in the social and institutional fabric, and build both trust and broader social capital. This has already begun, as the Arab Human Development Reports, the Alexandria Declaration, and the emergence of the Arab Business Council make clear.

The governments of the G-8 and the broader OECD must recognize that they, too, bear responsibility for the condition of the Arab region and the Broader Middle East, and that they have an obligation, in partnership with the Arab region—and other communities of the MENA—to work collaboratively to create the conditions that will make the region peaceful, competitive, and prosperous. Fortunately, once again, there are signs that this is appreciated in G-8 capitals.

An effective partnership between these component groups will enable collective success. We are obliged to realize this partnership in the interest of the region, and of the world.

Source: Gabr S. and Abdulla-Janahi K. Partnership for Global Integration and an Arab Renaissance: the Arab Business Council in World Economic Forum. Arab Competitiveness Report.2005.

ABOUT THE AUTHOR

Khalid Abdulla-Janahi is a leading financier, global strategy pundit, world traveler, and philanthropist. He is co-founder of the Maryam Forum Foundation (UK), an initiative aimed at accelerating the development of transformative leadership grounded in evidence-based research, and exercised by accountable, global leaders. Khalid chairs a family office, whose investment strategy focuses on venture and infrastructure, based in Dubai, United Arab Emirates.

Khalid advises numerous policy institutes and public institutions in Europe on initiatives related to governance reform in the greater Middle East and North Africa region. He previously served as co-chair of the World Economic Forum Global Agenda Council on the Middle East and North Africa and vice chair of the Arab Business Council.

Khalid is a frequent contributor to the opinion page in Arab newspapers, such as Arab News, and he participates in numerous televised debates in global and pan-Arab media.

Khalid was born in Bahrain in 1958. His university studies at the American University of Beirut were interrupted by the Civil War in Lebanon, after which he completed his studies in Computer Science and Accounting at the University of Manchester. He launched an eighteen-year-long career at PriceWaterhouse (now PwC) as a Chartered Accountant in the UK and Bahrain, prior to becoming the CEO of Dar Al-Maal Al-Islami Trust, based in Geneva, Switzerland, and assuming the leadership and board membership of financial institutions in Europe the Middle East and Asia.

Printed in Great Britain
by Amazon